Also by John H. Bunzel

The American Small Businessman (1962)

Issues of American Public Policy (ed., 1964)

ANTI-POLITICS
IN
AMERICA

ANTI-POLITICS
IN
AMERICA

*Reflections on
the Anti-Political Temper
and Its Distortions
of the Democratic Process*

BY

JOHN H. BUNZEL

GREENWOOD PRESS, PUBLISHERS
WESTPORT, CONNECTICUT

Library of Congress Cataloging in Publication Data

Bunzel, John H   1924-
   Anti-politics in America.

     Reprint of the 1st ed. published by Knopf, New
York.
     Includes index.
     1. Political science--United States--History.
2. Democracy. 3. Power (Social sciences)
I. Title.
[JA84.U5B8 1979]   320.9'73   78-27675
ISBN 0-313-20834-4

First published in 1967 by Alfred A. Knopf, New York

Reprinted with the permission of Alfred A. Knopf, Inc.

Reprinted in 1979 by Greenwood Press, Inc.
51 Riverside Avenue, Westport, CT 06880

Printed in the United States of America

10 9 8 7 6 5 4 3 2 1

To

two who have mattered:

H. H. Wilson

and

Norman Jacobson

Preface

"Anti-politics" is one of those imprecise terms whose meaning does not emerge from a definition but from the way it is used. Stated another way, the concept of anti-politics has a number of different meanings, each of which depends on the purpose to which it is put. In the first chapter I have tried to show the meaning and intent of anti-politics as I have used it here. Since a book ultimately must speak for itself, it is my hope that the special construction I have given to anti-politics and its particular application in each of the differently oriented chapters will be clearly understood. Inasmuch as I do not claim to have exhausted all the sources of anti-politicism in the United States, it seems prudent to use this prefatory note to indicate what I do not mean by anti-politics and how it will not be used—in a word, what this book is *not* about.

Anti-politics here will not refer to what is usually understood to be its common-sense meaning, namely, the so-called revulsion of the ordinary American against politics and politicians. Together with the range of apathy that has characterized much of our political behavior in the last century or so, this basic theme of disenchantment with politics has increasingly become the focus of many books and articles. In fact, there are many social

scientists today who devote their research almost exclusively to
the many dimensions of political indifference in American society, with special emphasis on its implications for voting behavior and other forms of political activity. This, clearly, is a legitimate area of concern, but it is not ours.

There are many sub-themes to this general notion of anti-
politics, the most familiar of which is that politics is dishonest
and politicians corrupt. Another charge often heard is that
American politics is simply a contest between good-looking or
odious personalities (one hears it both ways), or that our two
major political parties are merely choices between Tweedledum
and Tweedledee. Along with other variations, the idea of a
"retreat from politics" is frequently expressed and explored, although there is as yet no unanimous opinion on whether or not
there is, in fact, such a retreat, or, if there is, why it exists and
what it means. In any event, it is not the principal subject of this
book.

There are other major themes embracing social and psychological as well as political overtones which some people might
insist should be included in any discussion of anti-politics. These
themes are likely to span a broad spectrum of social criticism of
American society, from Justice William O. Douglas's contention
that we are in danger of slipping into a kind of coercive conformity, centralized in the hands of the Pentagon, to Herbert
Marcuse's belief that a highly industrial and rationalized society
like our own is characterized by "a calm, mostly nonviolent,
democratic loss of freedom." In spite of the great temptation, this
book makes no attempt to deal with these or any number of
other equally provocative observations on the nature and condition of American life today.

It should also be made clear that this is not a "conservative"
or "liberal" book as these terms are normally used. It does not
justify the status quo or the present political organization of the

status quo. By the same token, it does not propose some new approach to bring about social change in the United States.

There is a feeling in many quarters that anyone who writes a book should make his own values explicit. How this is done or should be done is not always clear. I am not persuaded that the requirement is fully met simply by indicating one's political opinions, party affiliation, or voting habits. This is relatively easy and superficial. A serious statement about one's values, it seems to me, should have a deeper meaning.

A number of years ago a colleague of mine in political science said to me, "You should not waste your time writing books that will be read by people outside the academic community. When I write a book," he declared, "I write it only for my professional colleagues." This person also announced, not surprisingly, that after spending nine years in a small midwestern college where teaching was given the first priority of consideration, he had finally "gotten over all that stuff." As he put it even more succinctly, "I have gotten students out of my system. Maybe each year one or two graduate students will turn up who can be turned into specialists. Otherwise I want to be left alone to do my research. I don't want anything to do with undergraduates. In fact," he concluded, "this whole university would be a lot better off if there were no students around at all."

These comments are significant and revealing for a number of reasons, but I call attention to them here because they reflect a point of view that is in sharp contrast to my own and to my whole approach to this book. Unlike my colleague in the preceding paragraph, I start from the assumption that all men are capable of using knowledge to gain a better understanding of human affairs, not just scholars or scientists or some other selected few. In a democracy all men should consider the **true ends** of knowledge which, in the final analysis, is the quest for the good society. Max Weber spoke of "intellectual clarity" as one of the most important goals of social science, and he meant intellectual clarity for the many, not just for the future specialists who would be inducted and indoctrinated into a particular discipline. My colleague assumes that such clarity can only be attained through the scientific method, but more than this, that this method can only be taught to and understood by a limited few. This is not a minor opinion but a major underlying assumption having to do with the relation of knowledge and power and the role of the intellectual in a democratic community. Its elitist implications cannot be glossed over. Quite apart from the problem it examines, this book rests on the belief that part of the responsibility of an educator who is also a democrat is to share his thoughts, his enthusiasms, and his doubts with all those who, in their own way, are seeking clarity on the significant social and political problems of our time. This fundamental belief has an important bearing on my feelings about the commitment to democratic politics and the problem of anti-politics as I have treated it here.

Not only have I not "gotten students out of my system," but I am in their debt—constantly. Over the years I have learned much from them and their work—in seminars, in independent research projects, and as research assistants. Several of them, graduates of Stanford University, deserve specific mention here. Ilene H. Strelitz, one of the most talented and rewarding students I have ever known, pulled together a large amount of historical material that was useful to me in the chapters on the Quakers and the right wing. Amoretta Matthews, who took a seminar from me in her senior year, wrote an excellent Honors Thesis on utopian societies, and some of her findings and sources are included here in Chapter Six. Gordon M. Adams wrote an Honors

Thesis under my supervision, parts of which dealing with the Socialist and Communist parties in the United States I have used as a reference guide in one section of Chapter Three.

I owe a special word of deep appreciation to the members of the Advisory Committee in Constitutional Democracy of the Rockefeller Foundation for their generous award of a research grant for the academic year 1965–6, thereby making it possible for me to sit down and write this book.

For their careful work in typing the manuscript I want to thank Barrie Thorne and Elizabeth Rafferty.

Finally, to my wife, Barbara, for her light and warm touch, I owe more than I could put in words here. I will have to find some other way.

J. H. B.

Contents

ANTI-POLITICS
IN
AMERICA

CHAPTER ONE

Politics—and Anti-Politics

*The spirit of politics is the spirit which is
not too sure that it is right.*

JUDGE LEARNED HAND

*When we lack commitment to a thing we
are capable not only of standing by pas-
sively while it is chopped to pieces, but
even of reaching for the nearest axe ourselves.*

NORMAN JACOBSON

1

This is a book that deals with several variations on a central
theme. The theme is anti-politics, and has to do with those
who, for one reason or another, look upon politics in a democratic society with hostility or contempt, or both. The variations on this theme, each of which is reductionist in nature,
reflect different forms, styles, and purposes of this anti-political
temper. The common bond that is shared is the rejection of
politics in the name of some nonpolitical "truth." Unable to
appreciate that politics is not the pursuit of perfection, those who
would wash their hands of it are insensitive to its historic development as a democratic institution and its unique role in attend-
ing to public concerns. In short, they are moved by something
other than a political commitment.

It is important to point out that the temper of anti-politics and
the impulse to reductionism are two sides of the same coin.
Reducing something to absurdity is a phenomenon familiar to

everyone. But this is not the meaning of reductionism intended or used here. I am talking of the tendency to treat a subject or idea or argument not on its own terms but by reducing it to something else. Example: two persons are having a friendly argument about baseball, one claiming that Willie Mays is the greatest player of our generation, the other holding out for Mickey Mantle. A third person, overhearing the discussion, turns to the Willie Mays fan and, with undisguised irritation in his voice, says, "If Mays is that great, why hasn't he gone to Mississippi and marched with the Negroes in their struggle for civil rights?" Suddenly the whole conversation is altered and the particular point at issue, in this case Mays vs. Mantle, is lost. Some casual banter about baseball has been reduced to an issue of civil rights because the third person, lacking any interest in baseball, believes that everything of any real importance should be viewed in politcial and social terms. Thus in this form of reductionism Willie Mays is to be judged not as a baseball player but as a Negro who may or may not be living up to someone's predetermined standard of approved behavior in the struggle for civil rights. The point is not that baseball is equally as important as civil rights. The important point is that there are times when baseball (or any other subject) ought to be discussed for its own sake.

Other examples of reductionism readily come to mind. A Socialist makes a speech deploring the economic and social inequality of American life. The most likely reaction is that he will be immediately applauded by those who agree with him and attacked by those who do not. Neither side has really listened to what he said because each is more interested in who said it. The substance of his ideas is less important than knowing that they come from a Socialist. In other words, a man's ideas are reduced to his political affiliations, thereby relieving all concerned of the burden of examining the ideas *as ideas* and judging them on their own merit.[1] I once distributed to the students in one of my classes a statement criticizing the role of the United States in Southeast Asia, with special emphasis on the war in Vietnam. I then asked them, after they had read it carefully, to indicate whether they agreed with the statement or not. More than half the class had no opinion. When I told them the writer was a journalist from Communist China, more than two-thirds of the class said they disagreed with it. By now the students were aware of what I was trying to get across. In point of fact, I told them, the statement came from a recent column by Walter Lippmann. The number in disagreement fell off sharply.

One of the serious consequences of reductionism is that whatever is being discussed or analyzed becomes grossly distorted in the course of being reduced to something else. When the Italian Communist party attacks the comic strip "Peanuts" by calling Lucy Van Pelt a social fascist, two things happen: (1) the creative talent of Charles Schulz is wildly distorted by a corrosive and coercive political doctrine that has absolutely no place or relevance in the magnificent world of Lucy, Linus, Charlie Brown, and all the others; (2) the art form of a comic strip is reduced to the determinist doctrine of Marxism-Leninism which insists that all art necessarily involves political and social comment. In other words, the whole idea of "Peanuts" is distorted when it is wrenched out of its own ingenious context and reduced to the angle of communism.

---

[1] Alistair Cooke made a similar point in his review of Theodore Sorensen's book *Kennedy* (New York: Harper; 1965). "A big thing has been made of Mr. Sorensen's having deleted from the later galleys the names of the members of the so-called Excom who proposed different solutions in the Bay of Pigs and the missile crisis. Mr. Sorensen has been accused of sacrificing to discretion his 'duty' to tell all. . . . But Mr. Sorensen has had the good second thought that what matters, in a crucial debate over policy, *inside the circle of the men who must carry it out,* is the range of suggested cures—not the identity of the doctors." The emphasis provided is Mr. Cooke's.

The major proposition of this book is that democratic politics is similarly distorted by those who have no understanding of its functions, lack any appreciation of its role in a free society, and have no real commitment to its basic purposes. Our concern is with the particular form of reductionism and distortion common to those whose hostility to politics impels them to vulgarize its meaning and deny its importance. This is the temper of those whose impatience with the democratic process I have described as anti-political. They cannot see nor do they really care that politics is what it is largely because society is what it is: because men and women, in their social and political situation, find themselves divided in terms of their condition of life and their views of what ought to be done to improve or change their lot. They do not understand that politics is a natural reflex of the differences between the members of society. Insensitive to the reason for politics, they seek to reduce it to something other than what it is, as each of the succeeding chapters will attempt to show.

It is surprising how many people are motivated by an animus against politics. For this reason our first task is to give some attention to the nature of politics and to consider the reasons why politics is indispensable to a democracy.

꧁꧂꧁꧂꧁꧂꧁꧂   2

"But what is government itself," James Madison once asked, "but the greatest of all reflections on human nature?" If men were angels, there would be no need for government. The world of angels would be the paradise of heaven, and in heaven there would be no government because there would be no problems. The angels would have reached their goals, and with nothing more to strive for they could live in eternal peace and harmony.

But men are not angels, and there is no heaven on earth. Men have problems, and usually issues emerge out of problems. The more important point is that problems are obstacles between men in their present condition and the goals which they are trying to achieve. In this sense problems are the raw material of politics.[2] The essence of a political (in contrast to a heavenly) situation is that someone is trying to do something about which there is no agreement. He is trying to use some form of government as a means to advance and protect his interest. In other words, politics arises out of disagreement. For politics to exist there must be disagreement over what to do about the particular problem. Where there is perfect agreement, there is no politics.

What must be re-emphasized is that conflict lies at the heart of politics. There is no politics in a totalitarian society because conflict is looked upon as a form of illness. There are no strikes in the Soviet Union not only because they are not permitted but because Soviet doctrine proclaims that there is no conflict of interest between those who run the factories and those who work in them. In the communist scheme of things conflict is a symptom of an unhealthy society and, like any disease, it must be eliminated. In their promise to create the "good society" the Soviet Politburo has employed a science of rulership much like that of the Platonic Philosopher King who, knowing the "right" ends to pursue, needed only to use the "best" means available to achieve them. Not only have they rid the community of the evil of politics, but in their disallowance of any value disagreements at all the Soviet rulers have substituted the science of manipulation for the art of leadership. Only in a closed society, where the

[2] Herbert J. Spiro, speaking for more political scientists than himself alone, has pointed out that "The function of a political system is to deal with or to 'process' its problems. Problems are the 'input' of the political 'machine' or 'organism.' Its 'output' consists of policies. Policies are made up of series of decisions." Herbert J. Spiro, *Government by Constitution* (New York: Random House; 1959), p. 17.

people are accustomed to accept what the rulers are convinced is "good" for them, can the distinctive context of politics be totally removed in favor of the art of imposition.

Some of the wisest words I have seen on this subject are those of Professor Sheldon Wolin. Those who equate the "art of politics" with the "art of medicine," he points out, are arguing by analogy and a misleading one at that. Political society does not experience "disease," but conflict. It is not overrun with harmful bacteria but "individuals with hopes, ambitions, and fears that are often at odds with the plans of other individuals; its end is not 'health,' but the endless search for a foundation that will support the mass of contradictions present in society." Unless the framework for politics is preserved, "political theory tends to vanish into larger questions, such as the nature of the Good, the ultimate destiny of man, or the problem of right conduct, thereby losing contact with the essentially political questions that are its proper concern: the nature of political ethics, that is, right conduct in a political situation, or the question of the nature of the goods that are possible in a political community and attainable by political action." The neglect of the political context, Professor Wolin warns, is likely to produce a dangerous kind of political art, especially when it is sworn to an eternal hostility toward politics.

A truly political art . . . would be one framed to deal with conflict and antagonism; to take these as the raw materials for the creative task of constructing areas of agreement, or, if this fails, to make it possible for competing forces to compromise in order to avoid harsher remedies. The business of the political art is with the politics of conciliation; its range of creativity is defined and determined by the necessity of sustaining the on-going activities of the community. . . .[3]

[3] Sheldon Wolin, *Politics and Vision* (Boston: Little, Brown; 1960), p. 43.

There are many ways to distinguish between democratic and totalitarian systems of government, but none is more important than the pre-eminence of politics in the former and its debasement in the latter. In one there is competition for power and disagreement over the uses to which it will be put; in the other there is just power, with those who hold and exercise it intent on implementing what they regard as fundamental truth. In a democracy politics is the process of making decisions about issues that arise out of problems, of selecting among several alternative courses of action, of choosing between the lesser of two evils. In a totalitarian system politics has been abolished for the very simple reason that there are no evils for the people to choose between, lesser or otherwise. Once policy is determined from above, it then flows downward. There is no mechanism through which the people can select their own leaders and influence the formulation of policy. Totalitarian decision-making is simply the process of self-appointed leaders making the right decisions in managing the community's problems and taking whatever action is necessary to bring about the ideal society. The Marxist-Leninist blueprint provides the model; all that remains is for the communist rulers to shape the society in its faithful image.

Someone has said that decision is choice under uncertainty. I take this to mean that in a democracy it is impossible to know in advance the consequences of any given decision or act because the future holds no promises. Political action is always based on imprecise knowledge, never able to take account of all the factors entering into any situation. It can never know all the results after action has been taken. Politics in a democracy deals with the contingent and the unknown. As Michael Curtis has said, "Political solutions are temporary at best, irrelevant at worst." [4] For communist rulers, however, the future has already

---

[4] Michael Curtis, *The Nature of Politics* (New York: Avon Book Division; 1962), p. xxvi.

been promised, revealed from ineluctable truths and principles that need only be translated into communist policies. Once the right course has been charted, there is no room for disagreement. There are no contingent circumstances, only the "scientific proof" of Marxism-Leninism. There are no doubts, only certitude. There are no partial answers, just total solutions.[5]

The key to an understanding of why politics has been eliminated from nondemocratic systems like the Soviet Union or Communist China has to do with the totalitarian notion of order. Order produces stability, and to the totalitarian ruler the disturbing thing about politics is that it leads not to order and stability but to instability and change. The intensity of factional strife, the competition for power among the organized groups of society, the conflict between social classes—these are the products and conditions of a democratic society that undermine the hopes for a tightly managed order and lead instead to an "incessant movement of shifting currents" that make up the flux of political life in a free society. The spontaneity, variety, and continuous unrest of democratic politics is a contradiction of every canon of order. The only order that could flourish in the absence of conflict is the kind that could stifle opposition and subdue discontent. Order thus created, as Wolin makes clear, has surrendered the distinctive qualities of politics. It might be order, but it is not a "political" order. "For the essence of a 'political' order is the existence of a settled institutional arrangement designed to deal in a variety of ways with the vitalities issuing from an associated

[5] For a comprehensive discussion of how Marxism has raised history to the level of a genuine science capable of explaining the nature of every social system and the development of society from one social system to another, see *Fundamentals of Marxism-Leninism* (Moscow: Foreign Language Publishing House; n.d.). According to Communist theoreticians, ". . . Marxism-Leninism gives us an instrument with which to look into the future and see the outlines of impending historical change. This 'time telescope' has revealed to us the magnificent future of humanity freed from the yoke of capitalism, the last exploiting system."

life: to offset them where necessary, to ease them where possible, and, creatively, to redirect and transmute them when the opportunity allows." There can be order in the garrison state just as there is order in the prison camp, for order can always be imposed. But neither of these is a political society. The art of politics can only proceed on the assumption that order is something to be achieved *within* a given society, that is, between the various forces and groups of a community. "The ideal of order must be fashioned in the closest connection with existing tendencies, and it must be tempered by the sober knowledge that no political idea, including the idea of order itself, is ever fully realized, just as few political problems are ever irrevocably solved." [6]

In stressing the fact that conflict is the essence of politics I do not mean to suggest that there is never agreement. One of the functions of politics is to turn unreconciled differences of interest into some kind of agreement that will persist for some period of time. This is the way a democratic system handles its problems. But anything which is done without any disagreement at all, from beginning to end, is not a political act. In the words of the British political philosopher, J. D. B. Miller, "Politics occurs because the diversities in society make themselves felt as disagreements about which government can be made to act, or on which it is accustomed to act." Politics keeps happening because diversity of ambition and opinion is a permanent condition of man's social life. "To say that politics rests on disagreement, and disagreement upon diversity, variety, unevenness or inequality in social conditions and opinions, is not to say that everyone always disagrees with everyone else, or takes political action when he does. It is simply to say that, where political activity does take place, it will be actuated and sustained by diversities." [7] "If I am

---

[6] Wolin, *Politics and Vision,* pp. 43–4.
[7] J. D. B. Miller, *The Nature of Politics* (London: Gerald Duckworth & Co.; 1962), p. 22.

right," Professor Miller adds, "then politics will never stop."
It has become a platitude to say that politics is an art. I would
add to this only what seems to me to be its central meaning: that
politics is the civilizing process of conciliation. It is politics in a
democracy which permits all the differing interests and rival
claims a share in political power. It is in this sense that the true
commitment to politics is a democratic commitment. All the
diverse individuals and groups discuss a given issue not in terms
of what objectively "is" the answer but according to what they
believe to be best for them. The idea of politics as an ever-
changing, ambiguous series of public judgments, where appetite
and ambition openly compete with knowledge and wisdom, con-
tradicts the very notion of order based on truth. The conception
of politics as a continuing flow of compromises between groups,
with the accent on innovation, clashes sharply with the static and
disciplined world of the closed society, where the accent is on
stability. The regulated harmony of a totalitarian society cannot
tolerate the frenzied clash of factions seeking self-interested advantage. Harmony, unity, order—these are the themes which
evoke an anti-political mold. Where power becomes a principle
instead of a commodity, politics has been banished.

But what of the politician? Is he, as is regularly charged, the
corrupter of the democratic process? Is he the price, perhaps
too high a price, a democratic society must pay for its freedoms?
I know it is the fashion to look upon the politician as a shallow,
ingratiating vote-getter who kisses babies (some would consider
that his total effort at paying lip service to the voters), wears silly
hats, and then, on top of everything else, betrays the public
trust for his own private ends. However, the nature and sources
of this popular but limited perspective are not our concern here.
The point I want to stress and develop is the one made by
Maurice Klain over twenty years ago—that the widespread belief that politics is saturated with dishonesty results in "a fantastic

system under which we treat our politicians as unsavory characters while at the same time we charge them with preserving our civilization." [8]

If politics is, as it were, the market place and price mechanism of all social demands, then the politician can rightfully be called the people's broker. There is much talk about the power of politicians, but it is too often overlooked that his is not the power of the autocrat barking orders and commanding obedience. He is a bargainer, a negotiator, a conciliator, and it is a rare occasion when his control is so complete and unchallenged that he can dispense with the very skills on which his position and control depend. To play a decisive role in the formulation of public policy and to help in directing the machinery of government, a political leader must have the consent of a plurality of the voting public. He must convince enough people that his approximate solutions on a wide variety of issues are better or at least more acceptable than those of his opponent. To stay in office the politician must become the champion, articulator, and follower of enough specific issues involving the differences and divisions within society to insure his election or re-election. He must continually be able to create new coalitions of support when his former basis of power weakens. He must have a system of communications that will inform him of the constantly changing demands of his followers and at the same time let his supporters know his own position and actions. He must commit himself to the norms, values, and traditions of the society he serves and play according to the rules of the political world he inhabits. He must try to formulate his own proposals into public policy and he must be able to compromise with his opponents in order to arrive at a partial solution. Thus the politician is an important channel through which those who care enough may in

[8] Maurice Klain, "Politics—Still a Dirty Word," *Antioch Review,* June 1944.

turn help to direct and influence the policies of government. The life of the politician, then, involves a relationship of means to ends, where violation of the former becomes an act of political death and the inability to fulfill the latter satisfactorily can cause political extinction. As Professors Dahl and Lindblom have put it, without the work of the politician "a bargaining society would fly into its myriad separate warring parts—and the pieces would be put together, no doubt, by the strong hierarchical leader who would reduce the need for politicians by destroying the autonomy of social organizations." Because he fulfills the bargaining role, the politician, "the negotiator of alliances," is a key figure in American life.[9]

It is a source of considerable frustration to those who are impatient with the democratic political process that politics seldom means conflict *about* the present system but rather conflict *within* it. Those who are contemptuous of politics place little value on the proposition that the resolution of conflicts in society is essential if the political system itself is to survive. One of the important lessons to be learned from the American Civil War is that there are greater benefits to be gained and more rewards to be won through compromise and conciliation than from hostility and intransigence. In a democratic system politics is something

[9] Robert A. Dahl and Charles E. Lindblom, *Politics, Economics, and Welfare* (New York: Harper; 1953), pp. 333–4. T. V. Smith once made his defense of democratic politics and the politician in these words: "It is precisely that outcome of intergroup conflicts which the democratic politicians shield us from. If they sometimes lie in the strenuous task, it is regrettable but understandable. If they sometimes truckle, that is despicable but tolerable. If they are sometimes bribed, that is more execrable but still not fatal. The vices of our politicians we must compare not with the virtues of the secluded individual but with the vices of dictators. In this context, almost beautiful things may be said of our politicians—by way of compensation, if not by way of extenuation, of whatever vices attend upon the arduous process of saving us from violence and murder." T. V. Smith, *The Promise of American Politics* (Chicago: Univ. Chicago Press; 1936), pp. 248–9.

more than a trivial activity but it is also something less than a matter of life and death. The great variety of individuals and groups who participate in politics can do so without going to each other's throats.[1]

⁓⁓⁓⁓⁓⁓ 3

One can go to many lengths in trying to explain politics. But to explain it is one thing. To understand it, to have a "feel" for it, is something else. Someone once asked Louis Armstrong what "swing" was in jazz. He said, "Man, if you gotta ask, you ain't ever gonna know." In a real sense this applies to politics, too. A leitmotif running throughout these pages is the notion of commitment—specifically, the commitment to politics for its own sake. It is the kind of commitment that eludes a formal explana-

---

[1] It should be mentioned, in passing, that there is a tendency in some quarters of our own democracy to sterilize and even remove politics from the picture. Unlike the totalitarian thrust to obliterate politics altogether, this is a tendency toward personalized government in many of the small communities around the country where it is felt the "public interest" should be discussed in a forum more secluded than the political arena. This is the escape from politics at the grass roots, where it is widely proclaimed that there is no need to disrupt the serene mood of near unanimity by introducing the ugliness of political debate. Conflicting opinions, factions, political parties, everything that is the lifeblood of the democratic process in a constitutional government is replaced by the fraternal spirit of the town meeting, albeit greatly suburbanized. The grassroots ideology is simplicity itself. In the small community there are no serious divisions arising from personal prejudices, individual ambitions, or opposing interests. Nor is there any need to be concerned about the rights of minorities because the mass of citizens are right-thinking people who will resolve any issues that crop up in calm and rational discussion, always operating "at the peak of civic virtue." Partisanship is rejected, the principle of unlimited popular control is embraced, and politics is hustled off into a dark corner. Perhaps the most penetrating analysis of this whole trend is in Robert C. Wood, *Suburbia: Its People and Their Politics* (Boston: Houghton Mifflin Company; 1959).

tion, much less a precise definition. It is an attitude as much as anything else, and involves a matter of feeling, of understanding. For example, those who want to make a "science" out of politics often try to explain it on the basis of their own particular interests, their special principles, and their rigorous methods of investigation. That politics may have little in common with the nature of their usual subject matter seems to be beside the point. In fact, there has arisen today a cult of scientism which claims only to want to improve politics by having the desired ends or goals made clear so that the most efficient means for their attainment can be calculated regardless of their morality. How is this to be done? By applying the scientific method. Who is to apply it? The scientists, since only they understand it. Dr. Albert Szent-Györgyi of the Woods Hole Marine Biological Laboratory has concluded flatly that "The only way out is to apply to political questions the same humble, honest, objective approach that has characterized the development of science." That, to scientism (and many scientists), is politics. But as John Fischer has pointed out, when a scientist does apply his brains to political problems he is all too likely to come up with a "scientific" solution—that is, "one which is mechanistic, tidy, and oblivious to human passions, prejudices, greeds, fears, traditions, and political realities." Fischer cites the example of Dr. Leo Szilard, "a brilliant and charming man" and one of the pioneers in atomic research, who has been "bombarding Washington for the last ten years with Peace Plans—all remarkably ingenious, and all equally remote from the actual world where statesmen have to work." The point is that the "mental set" of scientists is of a different order—more professional than national in character, impatient with ambiguity and imprecision. In the face of established scientific knowledge, politics symbolizes ignorance. In the naïve and simplistic view of scientism, politics is literally a means. In addition to being unacceptable as an explanation of politics, this attitude clearly demonstrates a serious lack of under-standing.[2]

It is not my intention to belittle the value of scientific inquiry in seeking to make the study of politics more meaningful. My concern is that politics be recognized as a special kind of activity and a commitment to the study of politics as a special kind of undertaking. One of the reasons the intellectual is so often mistrustful of politics is that he is unsuited, both by temperament and training, to the politician's job of trying to find workable solutions to pressing problems. The intellectual (I include the writer and the artist) is committed to excellence, not the whims of the masses. A fresco painting, a symphony by Brahms, a poem by Yevtushenko, these are works of the mind and the spirit, and their merit cannot be determined by compromise or majority rule and certainly not by the sanction of political authority. As Pro-fessor John Schaar has said, "The Intellectual lives the most intense part of his life in a spiritual community which has no objective boundaries in space and time. His model is perfection. He tolerates only the pure."[3]

No wonder, then, that the intellectual has often little more than contempt for politics and politicians. His alienation from

[2] John Fischer's comments are from his "A 'Scientific' Formula for Disarmament?" *Harper's*, January 1963, as is the quotation by Dr. Szent-Györgyi. Norman Jacobson has examined the cult of scientism with special emphasis on its implications for political theory in his "The Unity of Political Theory: A Case for Commitment," a paper prepared for a Conference on Political Philosophy and the Study of Politics at Northwestern University, February 24–26, 1955. For another analysis of scientism, see Hans J. Morgenthau, *Dilemmas of Politics* (Chicago: Univ. Chicago Press; 1958), especially Ch. 12.

[3] John A. Schaar, "The Two Republics," *California Monthly*, No-vember 1960, p. 16. My use of the term intellectual is the same as Schaar's: ". . . for those whose dominant interest and objective is the preservation and enrichment of culture for its own sake. . . . As the repository of society's highest cultural traditions, and as the stratum charged with the creation of the cultural future."

the world of politics is, in part, the result of his expecting both too much and too little from the political process. Inclined to ignore what *is*, in contemplation of what *should be*, he harbors the belief that dramatic if not noble results can emerge from the chaos of the political arena, while at the same time he is inattentive to the important, usually unsung, accomplishments that are fashioned in the everyday workshop of politics. The antithesis of intellectual and politician also coincides with the antithesis of theory and practice. The intellectual embraces theory as a norm to which he feels political practice ought to conform, whereas the politician looks upon theory as the easy refuge of an irresponsible dreamer. "It is the eternal dispute," as Sorel put it, "between those who imagine the world to suit their policy, and those who arrange their policy to suit the realities of the world." [4]

[4] Henry Fairlie, a British journalist, contends that the intellectual does not really understand the nature of a political decision because he is seldom confronted with the dilemma of having to dispose of political problems whose nature can only be dimly perceived and the solutions for which are seriously in doubt. He has no real appreciation of the raw materials with which politicians and political leaders must work, e.g., "interests which conflict, and are hard to reconcile; wills which cannot be commandeered but at best only persuaded; resources which are limited but on which the claims are many; support which must be weighed and re-weighed, and may at any time slip away." Fairlie points out that when decisions are made, they emerge from a less than ideal political process which, "burdened by enormous pressures, seeks to interpret and conciliate the forces and factions of public opinion." He records the following observations by "one of Britain's greatest Prime Ministers when I was talking to him at the end of his career:

'I am not sure that there is really such a thing as "power" or "decision." I would certainly find it very hard to give you an example of when I have ever exercised power or taken a decision. Of course, I will try to make it all look very different in my memoirs: and if I am lucky, part of my vision will be accepted by historians, and then I will be called a great statesman.

But it all happens very differently. For one thing, there is just a build-up of big and small events, of big and small factors, and they may not be brought to your notice until the issue has already been decided; and, when you eventually have to decide, it may be in response to the smallest of them all. That is not "power" or "decision";

The temperament of the intellectual mirrors his style of life and mode of thought. This is not said with hostility, but simply to make the point that his commitment to intellectual and artistic integrity has encouraged him to steer clear of the meanness of politics or to scorn it as unworthy of his interest or attention. He is sympathetic to the feelings of Goethe, who expressed his own contempt for politics in "the vow not to take part any more in anything but that which I have in my power, such as a poem, where one knows that in the end one has to blame or praise only oneself." This is a kind of comfortable seclusion which a man in political life will never know. "Do not squander your faith and love into the political world," Friedrich Schlegel advised Novalis at the dawn of the nineteenth century. "Into the divine world of scholarship and art you must sacrifice your innermost in the holy stream of eternal culture." It is more than certain that the politician upon occasion has wished he could exchange his engagement in the ceaseless fire of political combat for the luxury of quiet contemplation.

But the intellectual has not always withdrawn from politics. The pages of history are filled with accounts of intellectuals of all kinds taking direct action to correct the enormous political wrongs for which they have claimed a lack of responsibility, from Thoreau's passionate defense of John Brown and his belief that only direct, indeed violent, action was required to smash the slave system, to the writers and novelists in the thirties who joined the Fascist or Communist party. Intellectuals have often

---

you are too much in the hands of events. For another thing, the in-tray is always full. That is what politics is: trying to empty the in-tray.' "

These comments are from an article by Henry Fairlie entitled "Johnson and the Intellectuals," *Commentary*, October 1965, pp. 51–3. Although I disagree with much of what Mr. Fairlie has to say (I think many of his observations apply more to the European tradition of political theory and political action than they do to the United States or American politics), I found the article useful and perceptive.

preached withdrawal, yet they have also advocated or turned to extra-constitutional methods in their demand that wrongs be righted. The apparent discrepancy rests on a subtle but crucial point: only if direct action is to be equated with political action can the two be regarded as antithetical. In fact, both withdrawal *and* direct action are unmistakable signs of the intellectual's hostility to politics. Professor Norman Jacobson suggests that in the one case he washes his hands of politics, perhaps because the issues are not significant enough or because he is at the moment struggling with other, more personal, concerns. In the second case, he is willing to mount a direct assault because he is persuaded that politics is nothing but the trivialization of great moral issues. He does not become politicized so much as outraged by the failure of the political process itself. In place of the politician's search for public policy through endless debates and compromises, he substitutes the search for truth, an enterprise more appropriate to intellectual than political pursuits. As Jacobson points out, those of the intellectual community who became Fascists or Communists in the thirties were not suddenly awakened by the possibilities of political action. On the contrary, they became completely disenchanted with bourgeois politics which, to them, was a politics of mediocrity and mendacity, lacking above everything else a compelling sense of human destiny. From the standpoint of the intellectual "there is an essence to man, a profound core. Man is not trivial; he has a destiny. The intellectual, the artist, the musician—they want to discover that essence. They want to articulate the fundamental motivations and purposes of men, to lay bare man's destiny, and then build a society which would do justice in its institutions, its practices and its decisions to the inner man."

The point that Professor Jacobson makes is that this all-encompassing view was shared by the Communists and the Fascists alike, although in sometimes strikingly different ways. More important, they acted upon it. Democratic politics, they said, was a sham. It had to be destroyed. In its place systems were erected which would have the capacity to touch men directly. Both the Communists and the Fascists went to the very core of man by substituting mystical community for individual self-interest and, finally, terror for superficiality. Man, they said, was much more than he appeared. His nature cried out for more than bourgeois politics could ever promise him. It is a sad fact, Jacobson says, but one thoroughly confirmed by the history of the past forty years—the politics of truth often leads to the politics of terror. There is no question that democratic politics can be corrupt and that good men can be corrupted by it. But an intolerance of ambiguity, an impatience with parliaments as debating societies, a silencing of opposition—these can corrupt also. In fact, they have corrupted. And no group, concludes Jacobson, proved more susceptible to the appeal against ambiguity and circumspection, at least for a time, than the artists and intellectuals.[5]

It should be made clear that it is not my intention to downgrade the scholars and artists who make up the intellectual community and to elevate the politician. Those who would be prompted to come to this conclusion would be guilty of reducing my meaning and intention to a series of arguments that might well serve their own purposes, but not mine. This is the pitfall of reductionism into which one may fall unsuspectingly, the same snare which can lead to the vulgarizations and distortions of politics which this book sets out to examine and criticize. Nor would I want it to be said that I have made politics out to be "value-free," which is to say without any ethical content at all. This, too, would be a distortion. Politics is very much the story of

[5] For many of the foregoing observations I relied on a remarkably discerning paper (unpublished) by Professor Norman Jacobson entitled "Modern Literature and the Political Sense: George Orwell as Critic." I have drawn heavily on what he has said and how he has said it.

convictions and principles, and the many and various attempts to put them into practice can only be justified by ethically oriented conduct.

But this is a complex matter which is too often reduced to simplistic categories of analysis. My concern here has been with those whose primary approach to politics has been to mistake its very nature by insisting that the political process in a democratic society make as its only order of business the implementation of ethical rules and moral principles. It is not that rules or principles are "wrong" or unnecessary. It is simply, as Michael Curtis has suggested, that political activity which seeks to implement what is regarded as "fundamental truth" or to establish an ideal society may lead to tyranny. This is why politics and legislation cannot be made synonymous with inflexible principles or unattainable ideals. Those who would prefer it otherwise will not appreciate the wisdom of John Morley when he said that "politics is a field where action is the long second best, and where the choice constantly lies between two blunders." Those who would purify politics by removing the politicians and replace them with intellectuals have a distorted view of the former and gross expectations of the latter. Many intellectuals themselves, quick to admit their own deficiencies as would-be politicians, would rather have politics purified "by purging the classes and factions and replacing them with principles and doctrines." Concerning this form of purification, comments Professor Schaar, "Little need be said beyond the melancholy observation that the history of politics in the West since the French Revolution has been the history of ideologies. In our own day the disease has spread to Asia and Africa. Behind each of the great revolutions of modern times there has stood a handful of passionate intellectuals brandishing a doctrine—Natural Law and Natural Right, Liberalism, Bolshevism, Socialism, Nationalism, Fascism, Racism." One wonders if perhaps there is not a touch of good fortune in the American experience in that, for the most part, our intellectuals

have chosen to be "scathingly anti-political, so contemptuous of
the state and its ways as to be almost natural anarchists" rather
than attempting to "transform politics through inaugurating the
reign of the philosopher-kings or the reign of pure principle." [6]

~~~~~~~~~~~ 4

A columnist in San Francisco who is an acknowledged authority on jazz wrote a column not too long ago on Joan Baez, the

[6] Schaar, "The Two Republics," p. 17. It should be noted, I think,
that the other side of the intellectual-political coin—the contempt of the
politician for the intellectual—has been omitted here not because it is
unimportant but because it is not my chief concern. However, the
American version of this conflict is a fascinating one and has been
treated with great brilliance and style in Richard Hofstadter's illuminating book *Anti-Intellectualism in American Life* (New York: Knopf;
1963). Among other things in this wonderfully amusing and scholarly
work, Hofstadter shows how our politicians, in falling back upon a
well-established preconception of the American male, have argued
that "culture is impractical and men of culture are ineffectual, that
culture is feminine and cultivated men tend to be effeminate." The
men of education and culture who became reformers around the turn of
this century were ridiculed as "namby-pamby, goody-goody gentlemen
who sip cold tea" and were "deficient in masculinity," even denounced
as "political hermaphrodites" or as the "third sex." In the words of
Senator Ingalls of Kansas, they were "effeminate without being either
masculine or feminine; unable to beget or bear, possessing neither
fecundity nor virility; endowed with the contempt of men and the
derision of women; and doomed to sterility, isolation, and extinction."
What the politicians relied upon, Hofstadter points out, was the feeling
"accepted then by practically all men and by most women, not only that
to be active in political life was a male prerogative, . . . but also that
the capacity for an effective role in politics was practically a test of
masculinity." George Washington Plunkitt of Tammany Hall derided
the college-educated reformers as "dudes that part their name in the
middle" by which he meant to suggest "anglicism and anglophilia,
while culture suggested femininity." Hofstadter comments that "the
more recent attacks by the late Senator McCarthy and others upon the
Eastern and English-oriented prep-school personnel of the State Department, with the associated charges of homosexuality, are not an altogether novel element in the history of American invective." Ibid., pp.
188–9.

folk singer, in which he applauded her decision not to volunteer payment of the 60 per cent of her income taxes which goes to support the war in Vietnam and the arms race generally. His article was a tribute to her making "a dramatic and meaningful protest against war and against the whole military complex." He was angered by "the blindness of those who make our daily bread out of the Establishment's orthodox position" and he heaped scorn on the newspaper editorial that suggested Miss Baez had much to learn about the nature of conscience. "Stop kidding," he intoned. "Where would this world, this Nation, this State be if, in the past, there had not been dreamers and idealists and impractical citizens willing to take a stand, support an issue, make a gesture and put it on the line where it counts?" Somewhat akin to unctuous moralizing, he then asked, "Render unto Caesar the things that are Caesar's?" Ah yes, he answered, but not if they are to be used to destroy the things that are God's. "Miss Baez," he concluded, "is a better citizen of this country than those who criticize her. Her conscience honors us."

I do not want to dwell on Miss Baez's tax problems, except to say that I think she is acting within her rights in withholding some of her income and that the government is acting properly in collecting it from her anyway. That she is paying an additional penalty of more than $5,000 to the United States for making her point is a curious bit of irony. In any event, she is paying a price for her feeling of moral indignation, an attitude which, while it may not be self-righteous in its motivation, certainly embraces the kind of morality whose logic is simple enough: good is seen only as good and bad only as bad.

On the morning this particular column appeared I asked a student of mine what his reaction was. "Beautiful," he said. "Just beautiful. You have to admire anyone who has a conscience and acts on it."

It is hard to be an enemy of conscience. It is also foolish.

Nonetheless, the metaphysical notion of individual moral conscience as a valid axiom of democratic politics needs to be seriously examined.

One invariably turns to Henry David Thoreau, both as an example and a warning. Like the Bible, the writings of Thoreau can be used to make almost any point or support any position, which is one reason perhaps why he is remembered, justly I believe, as one of the outstanding American spokesmen for the genuineness of each man's soul and conscience. The difficulties and, more important, the inconsistencies arise from Thoreau's insistence that each man's soul and conscience are the only true test of what is politically right and wrong. Let there be no misunderstanding of Thoreau's position: he is making more than the gentle plea for men to strive to do what is right and let conscience be their guide. He has elevated individual conscience to an absolute, transformed it into an inviolable political principle, and asserted that it is the only valid guide in political action. In holding to the same fundamental premise throughout his life, Thoreau could draw conclusions as opposite as day and night. He could champion the cause of political quietism by withdrawing to Walden Pond, or lead the call for violent action in defense of Abolitionism. Anyone who believes that moral justification is simply a matter of conscience can easily justify both passive resistance *and* civil disobedience and, for that matter, almost anything at all.

Thoreau was a moralist, which in itself is neither good nor bad —simply true. But like many dedicated moralists, he was perfectly willing to sacrifice the democratic political process before his own special gods. Acting on moral precepts which, to him, were always self-evident, he struck out in whatever directions they led him. Each man, he felt, could determine for himself what is right and just. Thoreau was only dimly aware that his "transcendental individualism" could have no practical application and that, when translated into politics, individual conscience was inherently deficient. As he commented during the early "unpolitical" stage of his life, "I came into this world not chiefly to make this a good place to live in, but to live in it, be it good or bad."

It is useful, I think, to examine some of the metaphysical assumptions on which the American Transcendentalists based their whole philosophy, especially since they lead, almost necessarily, to ambiguous political consequences. One finds in both Thoreau and Emerson an attack on the skepticism that had grown up in the Age of Reason. In place of rationalism there is a return to faith. God dwells in each individual soul, they said, leading to the emphasis on both individual conscience and individual will. Emerson, the great individualist of his day, lashed out at the materialism he saw manifested all about him, discarded politics, and said men must turn to God. Political institutions should be moral instruments of men, not their corrupters. Like Thoreau, he believed that each individual had the ability to see the truth and make the right judgments on the basis of his own individual conscience. He had the voice of God in himself. Returning to an ancient Christian concept, Emerson proclaimed that all men were morally equal since they each were possessed of the spark of divinity. Democracy, when it meant majority rule, was degrading. Human dignity—that is democracy. The true majority is the majority of one—he who has seen God. Emerson spoke eloquently of "good will," or the sympathetic drive, in all men, claiming it is not necessary to have coercive government. In attempting to democratize Platonism, he said the "absolute good" should rule, and, if left alone, man can find this absolute justice. In his "Essay on Politics" he concluded that every State is morally bankrupt and political action thoroughly corrupting.

Thoreau spoke in the same tones. The State, he said, does not exist. It is an abstraction. Only the individual is real, and only the moral law within the soul of the individual is supreme and binding, not the law of the State. Thus there can be no compromise when the individual's conscience is in conflict with the State. That the practicality of such an individualized moral absolute could never be evaluated by any kind of objectively rational standard was unimportant. Like the doctrine of natural law, conscience is a matter of individual duty. There is no understanding of a means-ends argument or relationship, just as there is no conception of politics as a never-ending process of compromise and adjustment. Democracy is simply defined as a concept of morality held by the individual. There is no allegiance to the democratic process. Instead, Thoreau enthrones the individual and announces, "Any man more right than his neighbor is a majority of one."

I do not mean to detract from Thoreau's effort in all of his writings to rescue the human values of life from the onsurge of materialism, industrialism, organized labor, and everything else he felt was corrupting men's souls. Nor am I attacking the particular goals he sought or the causes he championed. What I am trying to suggest is that a "democrat" must have a loyalty to the democratic political process. One can feel passionately for or against something—a war, integration, capital punishment, the income tax. The question is how this passion is to be handled and how it is to be channeled. For a week or so in October, 1965, a friend of mine was in the hospital during the climactic days of the nation-wide demonstrations against America's involvement in the war in Vietnam. A bitter foe of this country's policy, she had intended to march herself, and it was a blow almost as severe as her illness that she could not. When told that the thousands of marchers in Berkeley, California, had peacefully turned around when confronted by the police at the Oakland line, she was instantly furious. "Why didn't they break the law?"

she asked angrily. "Were they cowards?" Her husband explained to her that they had agreed in advance against such tactics, feeling that civil disobedience there, at that time, could have resulted in a complete disaster. She was not impressed. "I would have broken through the police line," she said. "They should have broken the law." She was told that the marchers had exercised both restraint and wisdom in obeying the authorities and turning around when ordered to do so. They had been peaceful and orderly. It was the hecklers on the sidelines who had cursed them and tried to provoke them into a fight. She thought for a moment, and then asked eagerly, "You mean this *helped* the marchers? Good. Maybe they came out of this stronger." Completely reversing herself, she said, "If it helped the demonstrators, I think they did the right thing."

Not surprisingly, she had missed the point. Her mind was totally closed to any legitimate concern for law and order, the right of peaceful assembly, and the democratic process. Thinking only in terms of moral outrage, she believed an issue to be more important than an institution or a procedure. Her only interest was in defending the demonstrators. If they had broken the law she would have supported them. If they had taken violent action to break through the police lines guarding the nearby military establishment, she would have justified their every move. When they turned around and took the peaceful alternative, she decided they were absolutely right. What mattered to her was not their methods, but their cause. Shorn of any metaphysics, this is the familiar position that when the end is deemed right and just, any means is justified.

A "democrat," I have said, must owe allegiance to politics, at the heart of which is the democratic process. But when certain "truths" are purported to transcend everything and, in addition, every man is to be his own prophet, an impasse has been reached. No one can argue with an individual who proclaims the absolutism of individual conscience and ignores the political institutions of government. "I am not responsible for the success-ful working of the machinery of society," said Thoreau, which made it possible for him to urge on the one hand passive obedience and no political action, and on other occasions the exact opposite to enforce his concept of morality when he felt it was right. He would not vote because he considered the demo-cratic ballot ineffectual for his own purposes. The same man who had turned his back on politics and steadfastly stood for nonvio-lence could later savagely excoriate all those who adopted a nonviolent solution of social conflict.

Those who accept the premise that all governments are cor-rupt give themselves a license to flail away at the democratic political process whenever it stands in their way. There is no recognition of majority rule. The individual is a majority because every man has his own theory of justice based on his own intuitive judgment. Since only the end is important, there is no concern with means. And as I have tried to show, when the ends are the only important consideration, politics can be reduced to manipulation or simply scorned entirely. Professor Eulau has warned of the dilemma into which Thoreau fell and from which he could not escape because he returned time and again to individual conscience as the "ultimate reality." His thought was full of ambiguity and paradox, and he did not realize sufficiently how contradictory and, in fact, dangerous the moral can be. "Granted, he had no fear of consequences in disregarding the law. But there is no virtue in accepting the consequences of an act because the premises from which they flow might be essen-tially good. Thoreau's politics suggests that it is a small step, indeed, from insistence on the principle of morality to insistence on the principle of expediency."[7]

The moralist has no commitment to democratic politics be-

[7] Heinz Eulau, "Wayside Challenger," *The Antioch Review,* Decem-ber 1949, p. 522. This excellent article is one of the few in the literature that deals with the anti-political implications of Thoreau's philosophy.

cause he fails to distinguish between his own concept of morality
and moral realism. Morality is regarded as truth, and truth, wrote
Thoreau, "is always in harmony with herself, and is not concerned chiefly to reveal the justice that may consist with wrong-
doing." In other words, not only is there no understanding of a
relationship between means and ends, but as Eulau points out,
the consequences of any given act are separable and, indeed,
must be separated from its nature. Even truth is thus reduced to
being a matter of individual taste. This is a morality that is
treated simply, dogmatically, and almost always at the level of
abstraction. This is no practical morality because the contingency
of politics is missing. Moral realism, on the other hand, does not
consist of a simple knowledge of good and bad, nor is it a faith
unto itself that becomes a passion for certitude. In contrast to
morality, moral realism is an awareness of the stubborn persist-
ence of the complexities and ambiguities of the human condition
and a knowledge of the anomalies of living the moral life. Many
of the important values inherent in the democratic commitment
are derived from moral realism, not the least of which is the
recognition that ambivalence, not moral tidiness, is a necessary
fact of life. When intricate political questions are reduced to
simple moral ones, they are, in effect, put out of the reach of
practical solution. The price that is paid is a deeper understanding of politics.

In the chapters that follow I have focused on those whose
anti-political temper has led them to reduce politics to something
else. They are widely divergent in their beliefs and values,
running the political gamut from left to right. Preoccupied with
their own social diagnoses and cures, they are distrustful of
politics. They cannot abide its mediocrity and are unconcerned
with accommodation and conciliation. They have little interest
in searching for acceptable solutions to difficult problems, in

many cases preferring instead to impose their own preconceived solutions *on* problems. Like political religionists of every faith, they insist on the best possible good and will not settle for the best good possible. They are devoted to their own hard and fast principles and regard political compromise as no less ignominious than moral compromise.[8]

They reject politics as a way of getting things done because it does not represent unequivocal evidence of moral excellence. They fail to understand that politics is nonmoral. As J. D. B. Miller has observed, politics can be made to serve as the means of carrying through a moral obligation derived from some social situation, but it does not constitute a moral obligation in itself. Politics is often infused with a strong sense of moral urgency, but it does not provide this urgency from its own processes.[9] Those who insist that the feeling of moral urgency should come directly from politics reveal an antagonism to the political discipline of compromise because it requires a patience and sense of proportion they are not likely to possess. With the exception of the chapter on psychology, in which I have discussed a different variation on the theme of anti-politics, I have sought to show that those who see the world in terms of "either-or" leave no room for maneuvering in between, and that by some strange inversion their political judgments have tended to become more absolute at the very same time that moral judgments have grown more relative.

[8] Henry Clay, who knew that compromise was the cement that held the Union together, once declared, "Let him who elevates himself above humanity, above its weaknesses, its infirmities, its wants, its necessities, say, if he pleases, 'I never will compromise'; but let no one who is not above the frailties of our common nature disdain compromise."

[9] Miller, *The Nature of Politics*, p. 23.

CHAPTER TWO

Politics and Conspiracy: *The Moral Crusade of the American Right Wing*

> . . . *the Communists have contrived an elaborate, calculating and scientific technique directed at rendering a generation of American youth useless through nerve-jamming, mental deterioration and retardation. . . . The destructive music of the Beatles merely reinforces the excitatory reflex of the youth to the point where it crosses the built-in inhibitory reflex. This in turn weakens the nervous system to a state where the youth actually suffers a case of artificial neurosis. The frightening, and even fatal, aspect of this mental breakdown process is the fact that these teenagers, in this excitatory, hypnotic state can be told to do anything—and they will.*
>
> DEAN DAVID A. NOEBEL *of the Christian Crusade Anti-Communist Summer University, Manitou Springs, Colorado*

> *The whole country [United States] is one vast insane asylum and they're letting the worst patients run the place.*
>
> ROBERT WELCH *of the John Birch Society*

༄༅༅༅༅༅༅ 1

A number of years ago I was invited to debate a prominent
member of the John Birch Society before an overflow university
audience that had come to listen to a "real live Bircher" defend
the policies and general outlook of his organization. It was clear
from the start that his purpose, and indeed his solemn obligation,
was to list the sorry details of America's sell-out to its enemies—
the United Nations, Chief Justice Earl Warren, the Socialists,
Communists, pinks, punks, psychopaths, and other assorted scum
who constituted the real menace to the land of the free and the
home of the brave. It was a chilling performance, and I remember being worried for a few uneasy moments as I sat on the stage
watching the grim, unsmiling faces of those who clenched their
fists, pursed their lips, and then released all of their pent-up fury
in frantic applause when their "leader" pounced on the name of
a public figure, exposed a domestic plot, or revealed a hidden
secret. It occurred to me at the time that if these red-faced, angry
young men were really serious about wanting America to launch
a "freedom invasion" of Communist China, they would be stirring candidates and my personal nominees for the first wave to
be sent ashore.

I learned something that afternoon, however, which I have
since come to believe without reservation. The extremists of the
right do not like to be kidded or poked fun at. After being
introduced, I remarked that I had recently come across a way of
differentiating between right-wing extremists and Goldwater
conservatives. The distinction had to do with survival shelters,
which at the time was a subject of heated debate in many
quarters. I pointed out that the Goldwater conservatives, according to my information, will deny the right of the government to
interfere in anything as personal as survival and will insist on
digging their own shelters. This was in keeping with their strong

commitment to free enterprise, for it was really a kind of under-
ground individual initiative, or digging one's own grave. But the
John Birchers, on the other hand, will simply not trust shelters
built by a government as Communist-ridden as ours. I went on
to say that I had discovered that the John Birch Society was
conducting a national essay contest, the winners to be awarded
seats in the shelters since it was obvious that everyone could not
possibly be saved. Some of the suggested topics for the Birchers
included "Why I Deserve to Survive," "Why My Breeding
Entitles Me to Special Consideration," and my particular favorite, "Why, If I Survive, I Would Impeach Earl Warren If He
Survives." The audience roared with laughter—except, I remember, for a hearty band of Birchers who sat in the front row, their
eyes fixed on me with a kind of white heat that left no doubt of
their anger. Later that evening I received an anonymous phone
call at home telling me, among other things, that I was a "rotten
American," "undoubtedly a nigger lover," and, in some remarkably terse but colorful language, the offspring of some dubious
forebears. None of this was surprising, and the whole episode
merely reaffirmed what many others have also discovered—that
the right-wing extremists are an angry lot who seldom see anything to laugh at. Theirs is a humorless, sanctimonious, and
stultifying world, and they see nothing funny about liberals,
smutty books, or fluoridated water. Eric Goldman once remarked
that what we too often lack in this country is self-mockery, an
essential part of self-criticism. As the self-appointed guardians of
our morals, virtues, and whole way of life, the right-wingers do
not have the ability or the time to laugh at themselves. Fortu-
nately, most of us have preserved our sense of humor, and in so
doing have maintained an important quality and ingredient of a
free, democratic society.

Anyone who has ever engaged a right-wing extremist in a
serious conversation about American politics inevitably has felt
a deep sense of personal frustration. There is never any agree-

ment on any of the issues, and the bitter disagreements tend to degenerate into the most primitive emotions. But more important, what is missing is a meeting of the minds on the "rules of the game" which are basic to a democratic society. These rules have nothing to do with the substantive issues around which one expects and hopes that there will be a strong division of opinion. Liberals and conservatives are keen political opponents who, no matter how widely they are separated in point of view, recognize and accept the political legitimacy of the other and thus occupy a necessary place in a democratic polity. The rules have to do with democratic boundaries, and their central function is to confine political conflicts to peaceful solutions. Extremist groups, however, alienated from a society they themselves have disavowed, do not easily accept or welcome a consensual system of politics. They are convinced that America has fallen into the hands of corrupt and even pernicious politicians (most of whom are Democrats, but not exclusively so) who have subverted our basic traditions and deserve nothing less than full condemnation. In sum, their indictment is of the "give-and-take" nature and efficacy of our democratic political process. Robert Welch, leader of the John Birch Society, has put it bluntly:

We are at a stage, gentlemen, where the only sure political victories are achieved by nonpolitical organizations; by organization which has a surer, more positive, and more permanent purpose than the immediate political goals that are only means to an end; by organization which has a background, and cohesiveness, and strength, and definiteness of direction which are impossible for the old-style political party organization.[1]

Mr. Welch then gets down to cases:

As you look more and more carefully into the hopes that have been bred, and the disappointments that have followed . . . you come increasingly to realize the wisdom of the old advice: "Put not your

---

[1] Robert Welch, *The Blue Book of the John Birch Society* (Belmont, Mass.; 1958), p. 111.

faith in politicians . . ." I am thoroughly convinced, however, that we cannot count on politicians, political leadership, or even political action. . . .

Actually we are going to cut through the red tape and parliamentary briar patches and road blocks of confused purpose with direct authority at every turn. The men who join the John Birch Society . . . are going to be doing so primarily because they believe in me and what I am doing and are willing to accept my leadership anyway. . . .[2]

With this modest assessment of himself out of the way, Mr. Welch spells out what he has in mind:

What is not only needed, but is absolutely imperative, is for some hard-boiled, dictatorial, and dynamic boss to come along and deliver himself as follows:

". . . You fellows, over there, all of you, get the heaviest clubs you can find, spread yourself out no more thinly than you have to along the whole length of this wall, and don't hesitate to break the heads of any saboteurs you find monkeying with it. Don't even hesitate to break the heads of those you find creeping towards the wall, if you are sure of their evil intentions, just as a warning to the rest of the dirty gang. . . ."[3]

Much of the right-wing extremists' ill-temper toward democratic political procedures is an outgrowth of one of their bedrock convictions, namely, that the United States is being led into Communist perdition by liberal international-minded politicians who are bent on scrapping American constitutionalism and individual freedom. They are extremist in their shrill reaction to the multiple forces at work in this country today because, in their missionary zeal to save not merely the American way of life but its very soul, they are convinced there is no time left for the double-talk of politics, that it is one minute to midnight before the lights go out all over the American republic. With such a

[2] Ibid., p. 161.
[3] Ibid., p. 117.

burden on their shoulders they are unable to share that sense of
affinity to political leaders and attachment to political institutions
which help maintain what has rightly been called the "fragile
consensus" underlying the American political system. It is well to
remember that what is "radical" about the right wing is not its
opposition to foreign aid, income taxes, or the "mental health
racket," but its hostility to the democratic framework of American politics—in the apt phrase of Edward Shils, "the politics of
civility." The right wing, aware of its social and political displacement in the world it no longer comprehends yet feverishly
strives to rebuild in its own frenzied image, is ready "to jettison
constitutional processes and to suspend liberties, to condone
Communist methods in the fighting of Communism." It is in this
sense more than any other that the ideology of the right wing
threatens the politics of American civility.[4]

2

In the latter half of the seventeenth century the people of
Lord Baltimore's colony in Maryland became convinced that a
take-over of the government by the Catholic population, in the
name of the pope, was imminent. Lord Baltimore himself was
persecuted, and groups of citizens banded together to enact legislation to prevent Catholics or Catholic sympathizers from holding office. Without a break, from 1660 to the present day,
American political history has been marked by scores of groups
predicting the immediate destruction of the "American way of
life" by some highly organized conspiracy. Today the cry is from
such organizations as the John Birch Society's Robert Welch:

Communist influences are now in almost complete control of the
federal government. These same influences are very powerful in the

[4] Daniel Bell, *The Radical Right* (New York: Doubleday; 1963),
p. 2.

top echelons of our educational system, our labor-union organizations, many of our religious organizations, and of almost every important segment of our national life. Insidiously but rapidly the Communists are now reaching the tentacles of their conspiracy downward throughout the whole social, economic and political pyramid.[5]

On first glance it might appear that Welch's outlook on life typifies a position and posture that can be dated as, roughly, post-1917. Yet if one looks at the contemporary right wing against the backdrop of the various self-styled "anti-conspiracy" groups that have come to the surface down through American history, it becomes evident that, far from being simply a unique product of twentieth-century complexity, it is very much a part of our political tradition and heritage. Today's right-wing "anti-conspirators" share a number of moral, political, and intellectual roots with other groups, sects, and movements which have viewed their own times through conspiratorial lenses. The focal points seem to fall into five general categories: [6] (1) a fear of take-over of the government by "the people"—the uneducated, the unwashed, and the unprincipled; (2) fear of the West's becoming an all-powerful force for an un-Christian democracy; (3) fear of a Catholic coup; (4) fear of an immigrant (also Jewish, Negro) coup; (5) fear of a Communist revolution. Each succeeding phase, it appears, adopts most of the last and adds a new point of its own, which then becomes its concentrated focus. Although the many regional and national groups convinced of the serious danger of imminent crisis have never been able to unite themselves in a single all-encompassing organization, at any one time they all fear the same conspiracy, each working its

[5] *Supplement to Bulletin for February, 1961,* The John Birch Society (Belmont, Mass.), p. 13.
[6] Listed in a rough chronological order as they took their places in American life.

prejudice into the larger framework of the currently popular conspiratorial theme.

The representative rightist groups geared to stamping out conspiracies are matched in numbers only by their diversity. In the seventeenth century no one group can be cited as representative since most "anti-conspiratorial" activity was organized around a particular incident rather than oriented to a long-range plan. Religious intolerance bred fears that drove Catholics and Quakers from colonies which were fearful of attempted coups against the government. Some historians have asserted that these prejudiced fears contributed to some of the unity that enabled the American Revolution to succeed. References to the Order of the Cincinnati, in the 1780's, are found in Jefferson's papers and in his letters to Washington. The Order was a group formed after the Revolution, initially as an opportunity for soldiers to get together. As fears began to mount that the order was the beginning of a military class, Washington found it necessary to denounce it. For its part, the Order feared a government of the people, feeling—in the red-white-and-blue fashion of the American Legion today—that since it had fought the Revolution, it knew best its true meaning.

In the next decade the fear of conspiracy is found in various Federalist groups and individuals who looked with dread on the emergence of Jeffersonian democracy. Hamilton and his followers claimed that Jefferson had been opposed to the Constitution and its adoption, that he did not support the program of the administration, and that he was responsible for political intrigue disparaging the government.[7] More directly, conspiratorial fears were fanned by the influx of aliens, culminating in the Alien and

[7] This instance of "conspiratorial politics," it should be noted, was not the action of a fringe group trying to subvert the mainstream, but was initiated and took place squarely within the mainstream of political activity.

Sedition Acts which, subsequently, were followed by the Kentucky and Virginia resolutions against them.

The Essex *Junto,* a conspiracy in itself, grew out of the fears of the Federalists that the states of the western territories would inevitably change the political balance of power in Congress, leading to the ascendancy of the agrarian frontier interests over the northeastern commercial and industrial interests. The name was first applied by John Hancock in 1781 to a group in Essex County, Massachusetts (who were later anti-French Federalist extremists), under the leadership of Senator Timothy Pickering. They had considered a (protective) establishment of a northern confederacy including five New England states, New York, and New Jersey.

In 1827 anti-Jackson forces capitalized on the disappearance of a defecting Mason, along with a hue and cry against Masonry, to form an Anti-Masonic party. A good portion of the party was merely playing a political game for John Adams, but there was a hard core that feared the secret society, attributing to it a plot to take over the government. The party attracted a sizable reaction to the forces of Andrew Jackson.

In 1836 the outcome of the response to the publication two years earlier of Samuel Morse's anti-Catholic Foreign Conspiracy was the formation of the Native American Association. Eventually, the association broadened from anti-Catholicism to anti-foreigners in general in a relatively successful attempt to broaden its base of support.

During the next ten years a variety of rightist groups made their appearance. In 1840 the formation of the American Republican party, an outgrowth of the Native American Association, saw nativism wielding a definite effect as it assumed its first clear role in national politics. Its platform stressed opposition to voting and office-holding privileges for Catholics and foreigners. The first Nativist convention, held at Philadelphia in 1845, gave birth to the Native American party. Four years later, after the slavery issue destroyed the two major parties, the Order of the Star Spangled Banner was formed and led, in turn, to the American party or, as it came to be called, the "Know-Nothing" party. However, it would be a mistake to view nativism as a movement culminating in the Know-Nothings. The first native American associations were theologically oriented, fearing mostly a western conspiracy, and led to the founding of the Home Mission Society and its counterparts to distribute Bibles, preachers, and the words of the gospel.

The first Ku Klux Klan, formed in 1865 to destroy "radical political power" and establish white supremacy, was formally disbanded in 1869. The second Ku Klux Klan was formed in 1915 as a secret nativist organization patterned on the rituals of its predecessor and active against minority groups (Negroes, Catholics, Jews, immigrants) as well as certain tendencies in modern thought such as birth control, pacifism, internationalism, Darwinism, and prohibition repeal.

During the early years of the New Deal the initially respectable American Liberty League was organized as a conservative revolt against Roosevelt that eventually came to regard the New Deal as a Marxist conspiracy, with the President as a dictator and income tax "communizing" the nation. In addition to the American Liberty League a bevy of anti-New Deal groups was formed during the period with some individual "heroes" rising to power, including Gerald L. K. Smith and Huey Long. Many anti-New Dealers, screaming of a Marxist conspiracy, joined with members of various anti-Semitic organizations which had just reached a peak, blending into a reaction against organized labor and immigrants. In 1940–1 the America First Committee attempted to counteract the imminent entry into war which it regarded as a conspiracy on the part of the anti-Germans and anti-Americans, the so-called "powerful elements" who were leading the United States into war. Once the war ended, the growth of the current anti-Communist organizations followed close on the heels of the anti-New Dealers and increased as American dollars became more and more involved in foreign aid and international agreements. It has been estimated that there are "approximately 1,000 voluntary organizations in the United States today which may be called rightist and which regularly publish or distribute great quantities of right-wing literature." [8]

There is a tiresome dreariness in chronicling the order of appearance of some of the right-wing anticonspiratorial organizations that have vented their ill will in virtually every period of American history. But the fact is that in discussing today the phenomenon of McCarthyism, the John Birch Society, or the Oklahoma radio evangelist Billy Hargis calling into battle the "Blood Redemption Christians," we are talking of attitudes that reach all the way back to the early and middle decades of the nineteenth century and in some cases even earlier. Today the principal evil is communism, but in other days it was the pope, foreigners, city women, Jews, Wall Street, and Darwin. "The radicalism of the right," Senator Fulbright has remarked, "can be expected to have great mass appeal. It offers the simple solution, easily understood, scouring the devil within the body politic or, in the extreme, lashing out at the enemy." At a meeting of the "Congress of Freedom" in the spring of 1961, convened by the Soldiers of the Cross, the American Coalition, the Committee to Impeach, and the Constitution party, a woman arose in the audience at the conclusion of the featured speech by Senator Strom Thurmond of South Carolina and shouted, "I don't know why all this time is being wasted in talk. The best way to get rid of our problems is to kill all the damn niggers and Jews." Other

8 Ralph Ellsworth and Sarah Harris, *The American Right Wing* (Washington, D.C.: Public Affairs Press; 1962), p. 2.

speakers attacked fluoridation, immigration, the movie *Exodus,* urban renewal, the income tax, and the Federal Reserve Act. One said, "If Eichmann is calling for witnesses, let them take the six million Jews out of New York and send their ghosts back as witnesses."[9] A cartoon by Justus in the Minneapolis *Star* showed a wild-eyed man labeled "Lunatic Fringe" carrying a heavy poster on which is printed countless times the one word "Hate." As he marches along shouldering his placard, he mutters angrily to himself, "Sometimes I Even Hate Myself."

The perplexing mystery of the right-wingers is not simply *what* they believe, but *why* and *how* they believe what they do. Early in our history fear of a "democracy of the people" was the motivating force behind those who lashed out against what they felt was the "conspiracy of the immigrants." The first fears (in the early and middle 1800's)—that Catholic immigrants still held allegiance to a foreign ruler—provided the basis for the many conspiracy theories that surrounded later immigrations of other groups. The first predictions of "Rome's design on the West" came in the 1820's when the religious press began to warn that "unless Protestants sent missionaries and Bibles to the Mississippi Valley, Rome would occupy the region and 'build up a system of ignorance, priestcraft, and superstition such as now casts a blight over some of the fairest portions of Europe'."[1] This propaganda told of a plot jointly arranged by the pope and the despotic monarchs of Europe to secure control of the Mississippi Valley. Eventually the entire United States would be under Catholicism, immeasurably increasing the strength of the papal church and at the same time relieving the despots of the Old World from the constant threat of revolutions inspired

[9] Quoted in Tristram Coffin, "The New Know-Nothings," *The Progressive,* December 1961, p. 10.

[1] New York *Observer,* October 20, 1827, cited in Ray Billington, *The Protestant Crusade, 1800–60: A Study of the Origins of American Nativism* (New York: Macmillan; 1938), p. 119.

by the example of freedom and liberty offered by the young American republic. This was to be accomplished "by sending Catholic immigrants to the West until their numbers assured them control of that region. They would then rise in armed revolt and establish Popery and despotism in America."[2]

It is important to point out that, just as in today's charges of a "Communist conspiracy," there was a grain of truth to the cries of a "Catholic conspiracy." The truth, however, invariably gets tangled with many more falsehoods, and it is these unequal proportions that enable a small group of "true believers" to attract nation-wide support. This is a significant clue to an understanding of the right-wing mentality and its uncontrollable need to see a plot or conspiracy at every turn. In his *Foreign Conspiracy*, F. B. Morse linked immigration and Catholicism and made both equally objectionable in American eyes. By proving that the Roman Church had been consistently hostile to political and religious liberty, and by offering evidence of her unchanged character, Morse and the Protestant clergy who adopted his conclusions had advanced a long way toward arousing the American Protestant community.

But Morse insisted that there was a definite plot against the United States, by which Austria was fomenting the collapse of the American republican system. The Leopold Society had been organized upon recommendation of Cardinal Rudolph, brother of Emperor Francis I, and was placed under his protection. The all-powerful Metternich endorsed it, the Emperor assented, and Pope Leo XII blessed it. . . . These were the facts, but they alone could not prove the existence of a conspiracy. Neither could the existence of such a conspiracy be deduced from the letters of American Catholic leaders to the Leopold Foundation, but that did not deter Morse. . . .[3]

The basic insights of the Protestant "crusaders" were correct. Allowing for the fictitious nature of Morse's "foreign conspiracy"

[2] Ibid., pp. 118–19.
[3] John R. Bodo, *The Protestant Clergy and Public Issues, 1812–1848* (Princeton, N.J.: Princeton Univ. Press; 1924), p. 72.

and, writes Bodo, "condemning unreservedly the perpetrators of the Maria Monk hoax and all other similar excrescences, we are left with several indictments whose validity has been proved by the subsequent history of our country." But the existence of a conspiracy could not be proved because it did not exist. "Whether Morse himself believed in its reality, or whether he merely used it as a device to attract attention, we cannot tell. . . ." [4]

Even before the ferment of nativism in the mid-1800's the Anti-Masonic party took it upon itself to expose what it felt was the conspiracy of its time. Although a great part of its backing can be explained in terms of anti-Jackson political strategy, a solid core of adherents were fearful of a secret-society, Masonic conspiracy. The ever-present grain of truth which forms the catalyst for the formation of anticonspiracy groups found its way into the anti-Masonic movement with the murder of a Mason, allegedly by fellow Masons in retribution for breaking an oath. But the real source of anti-Masonry stemmed from a fear of rule by the people—the masses. Its beginnings may be traced to 1800:

The New England anti-Masons and anti-Masons elsewhere of New England affiliations viewed the Revolution in France with suspicion and distrust. They had a horror of any sort of a democracy which would lead to disorder or atheism. . . . It was well known that secret societies had played a large part in all the French democratic struggles. The facts furnished the anti-Masons in America with good ammunition at a very opportune time. As early as 1828 the LeRoy Convention passed a resolution "That we discover in the ceremonies and obligations of the higher degrees of Masonry principles which deluged France in blood, and which led directly to the subversion of all religion and government." [5]

[4] Ibid., pp. 82–3.
[5] Proceedings of a convention of Delegates opposed to Freemasonry, LeRoy, Genessee County, New York, March 6, 1828, cited in Charles McCarthy, "The Anti-Masonic Party: A Study of Political Anti-Masonry in the United States, 1827–1840," in the Annual Report of the Ameri-

Two major points must be clearly established if the self-proclaimed "anti-conspirators," both of the past and the present, are to be seen in their proper perspective. The first is that those who invariably look for and find plots—Catholic plots, Jewish plots, Communist plots, or whatever the latest may be—regard the plotters with a thoroughgoing anti-political animus. The conspirators are not looked upon as simply another group of political opponents to be opposed at the polls, or the proverbial "rascals" who must be thrown out of office at the next election. One cannot deal with conspirators through the political process or by political bargaining. By definition a conspiracy cannot be compromised with. Thus the anticonspirators are impatient with the normal channels of political discourse and procedure because, as one of their favorite clichés has it, "you have to fight fire with fire." Whether they see conspiracies at every turn because they are badly out of step with the tendencies of the modern world, or, as some would have it, out of step with the times because they see conspiracies everywhere, the fact remains that the "logic" of their position—on its own circular terms—is so airtight that it is self-confirming either way. It is this tautological bind of the anticonspirators which places them at odds with the logic of democratic politics. The exasperation we have all felt in arguing with right-wing extremists is a reflection of their inability to talk our language—or we, theirs. Their conspiratorial theory of American politics cannot be tested in the marketplace of ideas or exposed to rational discourse because—again on its own terms— it is not capable of being controverted by empirical evidence. In short, the conspiratorial thesis of the right wing, because it cannot be tested in any way, cannot be disproved. A contemporary twentieth-century scientist, committed to the strict canons of the scientific method, runs into much the same problem when he

---

can Historical Association, 1902, Vol. 1 (Washington, D.C.: Government Printing Office, 1903); p. 486.

confronts a "true believer" in astrology. They cannot communicate because they are worlds apart. They must of necessity talk "past" each other because they cannot agree on any common criteria of proof; this is the crux of the problem, for the right-wing extremist as well as the astrologer, for if there are no clear criteria according to which a theory can be disproved, then that theory is little better than metaphysical or polemical doctrine.

The second point has to do with the conspiratorial outlook itself and deserves particular attention. I have already said that there is likely to be a degree of reality in the exaggerated charges of those who hold a conspiracy view of life, and it is important that my meaning be neither confused nor distorted. Franz Neumann has called the conspiracy theory "a theory of history characterized by a false concreteness." This view of history, he says, is quite evident:

Just as the masses hope for their deliverance from distress through absolute oneness with the group, so they ascribe their distress to certain persons, who have brought this distress into the world through a conspiracy. This historical process is personified in this manner. Hatred, resentment, dread, created by great upheavals, are concentrated on certain persons who are denounced as devilish conspirators. Nothing would be more incorrect than to characterize the enemies as scapegoats (as often happens in the literature), for they appear as genuine enemies whom one must extirpate and not as substitutes whom one only needs to send into the wilderness. It is a false concreteness and therefore an especially dangerous view of history.[6]

The danger lies in the fact that the conspiratorial view of history is never completely false, but always contains a grain of truth and, in fact, must contain it if it is to have a convincing effect.

[6] Franz Neumann, "Anxiety and Politics," *Dissent,* Spring 1955, pp. 133–43.

"The truer it is, one might say, the less regressive the movement; the falser, the more regressive." [7]

W. H. Auden has labeled the present period the "Age of Anxiety," by which he meant what many others have also described—a time of individual loneliness and isolation in a world that is moving uncertainly in many directions at a frantic pace. We are living through one of the most climactic eras in the history of man, with no assurance at all that we will, in fact, live through it. Is there any reason why man should not be anxious about the present and apprehensive of the future? His anxiety is real enough because his worries and fears are equally real. But there is another kind of anxiety that does not reflect the same fears which all of us know and share. This is the anxiety of persecution. In this case the individual's fears arise out of emotions of the most intense kind, ranging from a resentment of others who are unlike himself to a hatred of self for what he himself has become. [8] In political terms this persecutory anxiety manifests itself in denunciations of those who are accused of being responsible for the distressing state of the world, a formidable list that is likely to include political leaders, world statesmen, government agencies, and international organizations. There is a strong tendency, particularly in times of crisis, to associate every crime, misfortune, or danger in the world with groups or organizations that hold positions of public trust. Plots of one kind or another are continually uncovered because the charge of conspiracy is apt to stir up public opinion. The intensification of anxiety through manipulation, identification, and false concreteness, Professor Neumann has said, make up the sequence of the basic models of conspiracy theories. For example,

---

[7] Loc. cit.

[8] In a similar vein Karen Horney discusses some psychological variations on this theme in her *The Neurotic Personality of Our Time* (New York: W. W. Norton; 1937).

the pages of history show that all kinds of crimes were attributed to the Jesuits, from the outbreak of the Thirty Years' War to the assassination of Henry III by Jacques Clement. "That these tales should have been believed is naturally connected with the significance of false concreteness in politics. There is some truth in many of these accusations. It is precisely in this element of truth that the danger of these views of history lies."[9] As we have already seen, the denunciations of the freemasons followed in the same pattern.[1]

The classic model of our time is the theory of the Communist conspiracy. Starting with the Russian October Revolution itself, communism and Communists have been distorted beyond recognition by those who, for one reason or another, find it easier and more convenient to reduce historical change and complex political crises to the more simplistic theory of a conspiracy. Thus the Russian Revolution is seen as the conspiratorial work of two sinister men, Lenin and Trotsky, plotting secretly to seize power. Again, the partial truth of the charge is enough to provide a full-blown explanation for those who prefer their revolutions neat and tidy and uncluttered by the complication of severe social and economic conditions. Lenin, it is true, was a militant leader with a plan and a passionate believer in his goal. But the success of the revolution went far beyond the simple notion of some revolutionary committee, secretly and in a hidden back room, plot-

---

[9] Neumann, "Anxiety and Politics," p. 135.
[1] Neumann writes: ". . . the English believed the Jacobite conspiracies to be the work of freemasons; the French Revolution was ascribed to a mysterious group of Bavarian Illuminati, and this view of history again is closely connected with the anti-Jesuit one, since the Bavarian Illuminati had been founded by Adam Weishaupt in 1776, in order to combat the influence of the Jesuits. Again these assertions have some truth in them. Most of the Encyclopedists were freemasons and more than half of the members of the Estates General belonged to freemasonic lodges. But . . . no detailed discussion is needed to show that the conspiracy theory represents a blurring of history."

ting and scheming as if they were about to rob the biggest bank in town. Furthermore, the same conspiracy theory is invoked to explain the Soviet conquest of the satellite countries in eastern Europe: the men in the Kremlin conspired to seize power, made their move, and were successful. Once again another small and sinister group is charged with leading a conspiracy against good and virtue. Few would deny that the Communists in each of the satellite countries conspired, but it is a mistake to give them either full blame or credit for their undisputed efforts. The Communists were able to take over the government because the Red Army, representing military muscle and power, stood behind them, and—in strict Leninist terms—because the "objective situation" was "ripe."

The anticonspirators, in their zeal to extirpate the enemy, are impatient with the hair-splitting and theorizing of intellectuals who can never see things in the stark colors of black and white. The conspiracy theory, whether it be applied to international or domestic affairs, serves the unquestioned purpose of reducing complexity to simplicity. As Neumann has pointed out, those who adopt the conspiratorial model as their explanation of the way the world is run are strongly under the influence of Pareto's facile antithesis between the elite and the masses. The result is that democratic politics, which is the endless and patient process of reconciling diverse individual and group interests in society, is viewed as nothing more nor less than the manipulation of the people by their leaders. Seen in this way, politics is reduced to the technique of manipulation. From the point of view of those who clamor for direct action instead of words and whose total program amounts to repeated demands for "positive steps" and "standing up to the enemy," it matters only that the "right" people become the manipulators. This, it need hardly be said, is the perversion of politics.

Conspiratorial theories, of course, are not the exclusive possession of the right wing, a point that will be underscored in the next chapter.[2] The Populist movement of the 1890's saw a number of its leaders spreading the notion that everything that had happened in the United States since the Civil War was the result of a conspiracy by the international money power. However, the qualities of a conspiratorial frame of mind found among some of the Populist leaders should not lead to the conclusion that the Populist movement and the John Birch Society or other contemporary right-wing organizations are cut from the same political cloth. Today's radical rightists, while they share some of the views of the "Populist lunatic fringers" who poured venom on the eastern-educated Anglicized elite, lack the "generous, idealistic, social reformist instincts that partly justify the original Populists."[3] The point being stressed here is that the outlook of the Populists demonstrates that the persistent cries of conspiracy are not just a right-wing phenomenon but a reflection of the pervasiveness of this way of looking at things. Robert Welch has charged that President Eisenhower was "a dedicated, conscientious agent of the Communist conspiracy."[4] A half century earlier South Carolina's Ben Tillman, in his maiden speech to the Senate in 1896, charged that President Cleveland had conspired with the "gold ring of New York" to secure his nomination in 1892 and was "either dishonest or the most damnable traitor ever known."[5] Mr. Welch has accused President Franklin Roosevelt of "plain unadulterated treason." Sermoniz-

---

[2] The Russian Communists have long held the theory of capitalist encirclement, in which Wall Street personifies the imperial arm of American capitalism.

[3] Peter Viereck, "The Revolt Against the Elite," in Daniel Bell, *The New American Right* (New York: Criterion Books; 1955), p. 95.

[4] Robert Welch made this comment in *The Politician*, but I most recently came across it on p. 5611 of the *Congressional Record*, April 12, 1961.

[5] Francis Simkins, *Pitchfork Ben Tillman* (Baton Rouge, La.: Louisiana State Univ. Press; 1944), pp. 315–22.

ing from another pew in the same church, the Populist party candidate for president in 1892, James B. Weaver, attacked the United States Supreme Court for its "stupendous crimes." [6] Today Welch calls for the impeachment of Chief Justice Earl Warren because "he has taken the lead . . . in converting this republic into a democracy and democracy is a weapon of demagoguery and a perennial fraud."

The lengths to which the anticonspirators can go in their fomentations are endless. In 1894 a cartoon in W. H. Harvey's *Coin's Financial School* showed "The English Octopus—It Feeds on Nothing but Gold." The head of the beast was the British Isles—labeled "Rothschilds"—and its tentacles reached all over the world, ensnaring Russia, Australia, South Africa, South America, and the United States in its grasp. In 1960 a film called *Communism on the Map* appeared, a product of the National Education Program sponsored by right-wing Harding College of Searcy, Arkansas. A map depicts the United States, West Germany, Formosa, and Switzerland standing alone in a world of Communist or Communist-influenced nations. Venezuela is a "Communist satellite," Ireland is "deep in socialism," Hawaii is controlled by Communists, Iceland is a full-fledged Communist country, and in the United States Communists are "deep in the heart-mechanism of our nation." During the heated campaign of 1890 Mrs. Mary Elizabeth Lease of Kansas told her audiences:

Wall Street owns the country. It is no longer a government of the people, by the people, and for the people, but a government of Wall Street, by Wall Street, and for Wall Street. The great common people of this country are slaves, and monopoly is the master. The West and South are bound and prostrate before the manufacturing East. Money rules, and our Vice-President is a London banker. Our

[6] Edward Lewis, *A History of American Political Thought* (New York: Macmillan; 1937), p. 295.

laws are the output of a system which clothes rascals in robes and honesty in rags.[7]

The familiar refrain is heard again as Senator Joseph McCarthy addresses his audience in Wheeling, West Virginia, on February 9, 1950:

The reason why we find ourselves in a position of impotency is not because our only potential enemy has sent men to invade our shores, but rather because of the traitorous actions of those who have been treated so well by this nation. It is not the less fortunate, or members of minority groups who have been selling this nation out, but rather those who have had all the benefits the wealthiest nation on earth has had to offer—the finest homes, the finest college educations, and the finest jobs in the government that we can give.[8]

College graduates were denounced as "drones and vagabonds" by Ben Tillman in 1885. When he became governor he subjected the University of South Carolina to drastic reform: it was changed to South Carolina College and lost a portion of its faculty, including a Unitarian professor of philosophy whose religious beliefs did not meet Tillman's requirements.[9] Almost seventy years later Senator McCarthy attacked Harvard University as that "sheltered sanctuary" of the Fifth Amendment, and for the next ten years a barrage of bitter attacks was directed toward the "pink" Ivy League schools and constant pressure was put on education in general to purge itself of left-wing professors and "Communist" reading material. Manifesting its own persecu-

[7] Quoted in John Hicks, *The Populist Revolt* (Minneapolis: Univ. Minnesota Press; 1931), p. 160.

[8] Quoted in a chapter by Seymour Martin Lipset entitled "The Sources of the 'Radical Right'" in Daniel Bell, *The New American Right,* pp. 210–11.

[9] Simkins, op. cit., p. 177. Discharging of professors in state universities was common when the Populists came to power. In Harvey's *A Tale of Two Nations* (Illinois: Coin Publishing Co.; 1894), pp. 16, 106, the colleges are pictured as being under the control and in the pay of high finance.

tion complex, the right-wing extremist today blasts away at the "leftist" press, the "pink" universities and professors, the religious establishment, and the Supreme Court. One is reminded of the John Birch Society's self-characterization as a movement of the "revolted, misinformed, deceived, abused, angry Americans."[1]

The Populist movement at the end of the nineteenth century was also led by some angry, misinformed Americans, a fact which, until recently, has been generally overlooked by most teachers and students of American history. It still comes as something of a revelation to learn that the anti-political, conspiratorial orientation of the American right has much in common with some of the twisted strands of American Populism. I am not talking of shared objectives or compatible economic and social programs but of an outlook and frame of mind that follows a straight line from Ben Tillman and William Jennings Bryan to Huey Long, Father Coughlin, Senator McCarthy, and Robert Welch.

The Populists, along with the Progressives, have been traditionally pictured as economic and political liberals who constituted the direct forebears of the New Deal. John D. Hicks, whose classic work on American Populism has been used in schools all over the country, has boiled down the Populist philosophy to two fundamental propositions: ". . . One, that the government must restrain the selfish tendencies of those who profited at the expense of the poor and needy; the other, that the people, not the plutocrats, must control the government."[2] Given the fact that Hicks's approach was almost exclusively

---

[1] From *American Opinion,* quoted in Alan Westin, "Deadly Parallels: Radical Right and Radical Left," *Harper's Magazine,* April 1962, p. 28.

[2] John D. Hicks, *The Populist Revolt* (Lincoln, Nebr.: Univ. Nebraska Press; 1961), p. 466. The first edition was published by Univ. Minnesota Press.

economic and political (the more or less traditional approach for the 1930's) there is nothing surprising about his conclusion. He stressed what the Populists did, or said they would do, to implement their program of wider distribution of the fruits of the economic system and more direct control of the political machinery and government by the people. But he had relatively little to say about how the Populists interpreted the origins of their problems or viewed the nature and fabric of the society in which they lived. His approach, in other words, was neither intellectual nor sociological.

Richard Hofstadter's book *The Age of Reform,* published in 1955, represents the most comprehensive attack on this older and traditional view of American Populism. His approach, fundamentally different from Hicks's, is of particular importance here because it points up some of the Populist values and qualities which were to reappear in the garb of the American right wing many years later. Going far beyond a simple interpretation of agrarian grievances, Hofstadter probes the Populist view of the historical process in general and American society in particular. He concludes that "Far from being progressives, the Populists looked back with longing to the lost agrarian Eden." "What they meant," he said, "though they did not express themselves in such terms, was that they would like to restore the conditions prevailing before the development of individualism and the commercialization of agriculture." [3]

Hofstadter maintained that five themes formed the ideology of Populism: the idea of the Golden Age, the concept of natural harmonies, the dualistic nature of social struggles, the doctrine of the primacy of money, and the conspiracy theory of history. The concept of natural harmonies and the view of social struggles as dualistic are two sides of the same coin. The Populists felt, on the

[3] Richard Hofstadter, *The Age of Reform* (New York: Vintage Books; 1955), p. 62.

one hand, a natural, indeed an invariable, conflict between the producing and the nonproducing classes. "It is a struggle," said Sockless Jerry Simpson, "between the robbers and the robbed." [4] Or, as Ignatius Donnelly wrote in the preamble to the Populist platform of 1892, "From the same prolific womb of governmental injustice we breed the two classes—tramps and millionaires." For the Populists history was a conspiracy of the nonproducing, chiefly moneyed classes against the producing classes. This was the Populist way of accounting for relatively impersonal events in highly personal terms. Given the importance the Populists placed on the question of money, it was inevitable that their "conspirators" would be big bankers, particularly international bankers. Who were the international bankers? They were the Jews, operating out of England. As Hofstadter has remarked, "In Populist demonology, anti-Semitism and Anglophobia went hand-in-hand." [5] Nor was this conspiratorial theory confined to a hatred of Jews in Great Britain. It radiated out to embrace nearly all who were alien to American agrarianism and ruralism. Thus the counterpart of anti-Semitism and Anglophobia was nativism and nationalism.

In this light several of the progressive aspects of Populism take on a different hue. More direct democracy, for example, does not imply an abiding faith in the individual. It means that only certain individuals belonging to a particular socio-economic class are to be trusted. Direct democracy, rather than being a protection for individual liberties, becomes an instrument by which one class can come to dominate another. Economic reforms, which the Populist platform of 1892 made clear were to center on the monetary system, became not so much a remedy for the plight of the farmer but a weapon that could be used against Jewish bankers. The economic reforms suggested by the Populists might have eradicated some existing evils, but the farmer in the west-

[4] Ibid., p. 64.
[5] Ibid., p. 78.

ern sections of such states as Kansas and Nebraska was farming a
marginal area that had gone bad. Beginning in 1887 and lasting
for about a decade, these areas received little rainfall for successful dry farming.[6] Moreover, improved transportation facilities
meant cotton and wheat from Russia, Argentina, and Australia
were moving into the eastern markets. With more rainfall and
an increased world demand for agricultural products in the late
1890's the farmers' position improved markedly and remained
good through the First World War. The point to be made is that
the reforms of the Populists were largely abstract. They could
not be aimed at the heart of the farmers' problems, and so they
were aimed at the enemy of the farmer—as Populist folklore
depicted him.[7]

It would be foolish to deny that the Populists were reform-
minded. But one can question the nature of their reforms in
relation to the problems they faced. So, too, can their liberalism
be questioned. Suffice it to say that Populism contained the
strains of economic reform and direct democracy as well as
conspiratorial fears, nativism, anti-Semitism, and Anglophobia.
Thus Populism as we have been talking about it here is not the
exclusive possession of the left, and it is not confined to the
lower classes. It speaks with many voices and carries its multiple
appeals to a mixed assortment of political groupings.

There are certain Populist features that have been incorpo-

[6] It has been noted that there was a strong correlation in Nebraska
between the percentage of Populist vote and the degree to which an area
was drought-stricken. See John D. Barnhart, "Rainfall and the Populist
Party in Nebraska," *American Political Science Review,* Vol. XIX
(1925), pp. 527–40.

[7] Arthur Mann, in a related observation, says that Hicks "misled a
generation in asserting that, because many Populist planks later became
law, nineteenth-century agrarian radicalism was the grandfather of
twentieth-century reforms. One could say just as easily that the American income tax is Marxian in origin because in 1848 Karl Marx
proposed it as a levelling device . . ." Arthur Mann, "The Progressive
Tradition," in *The Reconstruction of American History,* ed. John
Higham (New York: Harper; 1962), p. 160.

rated into the right-wing pattern of ideas and predispositions
which serve to underscore the anti-political nature and posture of
the far right. I have in mind the undisguised hostility of Senator
McCarthy and his followers to the conservative aristocracy of
New England. It was no accident, for example, that Harvard
University was a continual target of McCarthy's most strident
denunciations. In the celebrated Army-McCarthy hearings it was
entirely fitting that the man who ultimately pointed the finger of
shame at the Senator from Wisconsin, Joseph Welch, was a
distinguished and respected Republican attorney from Massachusetts. McCarthy's antagonism to these established "institutions" of conservatism was in the best anti-intellectual tradition.
One could see again the deep distrust of those who had been
reared and educated in the effete East, of those who had gone to
Harvard, Yale, or Princeton and later emerged as successful and
often influential members of Democratic and Republican admin-
istrations in Washington. It was not only that they represented
wealth and social standing, although this was certainly part of it.
The sharper bone that stuck in the throat of Senator McCarthy
was their "fancy upbringing" and "Ivy League intellectualism,"
along with all of the refinements and subtleties accruing to
persons who have learned poise and self-confidence. To Mc-
Carthy these were the "overeducated" and the "egg heads," and
in his mind they formed the core of the "fuzzy-minded liberals"
who had gone to Washington in the early days of the New Deal,
"infiltrated" the State Department, and then proceeded to "sell
out" the United States to the Communists. These were the "soft-
headed" men with woolly ideas who lacked the "guts" to stand
up for their country. They were "soft," Senator McCarthy reminded us, because they were reared on etiquette and eastern
upper-class pretensions and knew nothing of the real world of
hard-headed experience. They were "soft" because, for all of their
college degrees, they lacked the tough-minded, old-fashioned

"horse sense" which is the common touchstone of ordinary people on every Main Street throughout America. The trouble was that the smart "college types" and eastern "do-gooders" had succeeded in removing the government from the control of the people. The high and the mighty had ensconced themselves comfortably in the seats of power and prestige, with barely time now and then for a glance at the lowly people. Thus Senator McCarthy could score one for the home team—the "American team"—of plain people everywhere who knew nothing of upper-class manners but could look a man straight in the eye—by publicly demanding an accounting from all those who had taken the government away from the "little people," the very ones who make up the heartland of this star-spangled country. It was a moving appeal, familiar to anyone who remembered how others in another day had also thundered at the invidious "interests," "cliques," and "inner circles" in the government for stripping the people of their rights. From Senator McCarthy and his followers just as from the fervent spokesmen of agrarian Populism there came the same bitter cry: the people and their government must be protected from conspiratorial secrecy. The will of the people, representing nothing less than justice, virtue, and morality, must once again take its rightful place as the ultimate guardian of the American way of life.[8]

As we have already said, it is difficult to carry on a responsible discussion with anyone who unleashes such a torrent of charges, innuendoes, and abuse. For one thing it is never easy under any

---

[8] In this account of the many faces of Populism I am not unmindful of the true concern for the people and their problems on the part of such genuine humanitarians as George Norris and Robert La Follette who, in their advocacy of many progressive reforms, urged that power be given back to the people. But these populist expressions of democratic hopes and beliefs are not to be confused with other strains of populism which can also be found in everything from fascist to communist appeals to the "will of the people."

circumstances to stand up to an onrushing windstorm. Often, the most one can do is to stand aside in sheer wonderment and quiet agony. But a more serious problem arises in trying to respond intelligently and judiciously to a persistent anti-political theme that runs through the invective of the right wing. I say anti-political rather than antidemocratic because the major point I want to stress is that the constant appeal of the rightists to "the people" is misperceived and misunderstood if it is not clearly seen that this appeal is made not on democratic grounds but in the belief that the "will of the people" is somehow supreme over our legal and political institutions. The ring-wing appeal to the people to set things right once and for all should be recognized for what it is—an arrogant attempt to brush aside the established political standards and institutions of society and, in their place, to enthrone the will of the people. There is no genuine commitment to the American people on the part of the rightists, no basic democratic belief that their wishes and interests should serve as a guide to peaceful and progressive change. One need only recall that Hitler repeatedly invoked the will of the people to justify his own actions and to demonstrate that he was really working in their behalf, "for their own good." One also remembers that it was in their name that he rooted out the remaining vestiges of the abortive democratic experiment in Germany in the 1920's and, ultimately, did away with all of the political institutions and procedures which are the bedrock of any democratic political system. These are the anti-political overtones which, to one degree or another—and, admittedly, Hitler's Nazi regime is an extreme example—are characteristic of the rightist onslaught on institutional traditions and boundaries. These are the emotions and resentments which lead to the repeated demands for no-holds-barred investigations of Communist subversion in the public schools. These are the anti-political sentiments, nourished in the soil of suspicion and contempt, which culminate in the insistent cries that sex and pornography be banned. These are the expressions of an anti-political outlook throughout the country which result in the cruel browbeating of the town librarian for her "different" ideas and "eccentric" ways. In short, these are the restless and tireless passions of Populism which, when they are swept up in the angry orgy of the right wing, are destructive of the fragile system of democratic politics.

Edward Shils has written that Populism seeks substantive justice. It is an important and penetrating observation because it reaffirms our major contention that the Populist philosophy is, in significant respects, anti-political in orientation and outlook. Shils points out that Populism has no concern whatsoever with the traditional rules and areas of life outside its own immediate sphere. It looks upon the legal system as a trap for the innocent, a system of "outdoor relief" for lawyers and judges. It regards administration as a vast swamp sucking in the unwary and the virtuous. Its hostility to politics and politicians, however, is the most extreme of all.

It regards politicians as artful dodgers, as evaders of responsibility, as twisters with fine words but ready to compromise away the interests of those for whom they stand. . . . Populism regards parliamentary politicians as very inferior beings with no inherent virtue in themselves or in their institutions. Politicians are at best errand boys with little right to judgment on their own behalf if that judgment seems to contradict Populist sentiment.[9]

The Populist quest for substantive justice does not depend on politicians who live off a system that is corrupt and immoral. Yet Populism still has need for leadership, and this it finds in the spellbinding appeals and promises of those who possess the emotional fervor to move the multitudes and, as Shils says, bend them to their own will. But there are Populists and there are

[9] Edward Shils, *The Torment of Secrecy* (Glencoe, Ill.: Free Press; 1956), pp. 102–3.

Populists. When Norris and La Follette spoke of the people, they addressed themselves to the serious problems of the poor. But when Bryan, the great silver-throated orator, spoke to his audiences, he shook his angry fists at the moneyed classes of the city for despoiling the dreams of the plain people of the countryside. His was the cry for simple rectitude and love of God, the plain man against the eastern banker. Today the right-wing spokesman of Populist sentiments is a Senator McCarthy or a Robert Welch. When a leader of the John Birch Society talks of cutting through the "road blocks" of parliamentarianism and explains how those who join up with him will be doing so "primarily because they believe in me and what I am doing and are willing to accept my leadership," he is simply giving the latest expression, albeit perhaps a little crude in its formulation, of contempt for our political procedures and institutions. This is the voice of the present-day demagogue heard perennially throughout the land, scornful of the formalistic barriers erected by lawyers and bureaucrats and contemptuous of the niceties of institutional responsibilities. Mr. Welch is not the first and he will not be the last to offer his personality, resources, and ideas as the last remaining route by which "the people," if they will only push aside the needless torment of political chicanery, can reclaim their government.

3

One of the reasons the extreme right wing in the United States is so often misperceived is that it is too quickly bracketed with American conservatism. Part of the problem arises from the limitations of our political vocabulary. Right-wingers are certainly conservative, and Senator Goldwater, "Mr. Conservative" himself, is vociferously championed by the radical right. Thus the line that separates them appears fuzzy and blurred, allowing many observers to join them together for better or for worse. The difficulty with this political union is not simply that the right wing is badly miscast in this company, but that neither the rightists nor the conservatives are seen in the full light of their respective political colorations. Frequently this is the fault of those who find it easier to fit political groupings and philosophies into ready-made pigeonholes—and the fewer the better. According to this mentality liberals are neatly lumped together with all of the political wreckage on the left, and by the same token, conservatives are easily tossed together with the vast assortment of political wild life on the right. The result is the grossest form of political reductionism and distortion.

The political character of the right wing, if it is to be carefully delineated rather than conveniently labeled, should be viewed not as the inevitable extension of conservative thought but as a distinct core of ideas and attitudes whose central meaning and purpose is subversive of the major tenets of true conservatism. The extreme right wing is angry at almost everything that has happened to the United States in the last thirty-five years because it is violently at odds with the main drift of the world of the twentieth century. It feels about this country and what it has become much as a bitter parent feels about his son who, suddenly grown up and "different," has become a stranger in his own home. The measure of right-wing bitterness is its ability to attack the responsible leaders of our government as agents of perfidy or, at the very least, as unknowing dupes. Yet the calumny directed at a former president or a chief justice, or at the churches or the schools, reflects not so much a disagreement with policies and programs as an implacable dislike and suspicion of all constitutional authority. As Richard Hofstadter has observed, the extreme right wing "is constituted out of a public that simply cannot arrive at a psychological modus vivendi with authority, cannot reconcile itself to that combination of acceptance and criticism which the democratic process requires of the relationship between the leaders and the led." [1] This is a key that helps to distinguish the extremists from the nonextremists, the wordy abuse of the right-winger from the legitimate opposition of the conservative.

But the distinction is even deeper than this. Implicit in the idea of democratic opposition—in England the party out of power is given the title of "loyal opposition"—is the basic premise of commitment. For example, in the United States the intensive activity of pressure groups presupposes as its most fundamental condition a stable and widely accepted political system. It is this political consensus that gives the system its legitimacy and widespread support. Any group that "presses" on the government is itself committed to the government. Those that are disaffected in our society—the extremists who are aliens in our midst—have little use for the leadership of the government because what they dislike and distrust is what the whole system has become. The fact of the matter is that any leadership that falls short of their own prescriptions and demands must be vilified, not opposed; overthrown, not endured. The extreme right, comments Hofstadter, is "incapable of analyzing the world with enough common sense to establish any adequate and realistic criterion for leadership. The right wing tolerates no compromises, accepts no half measures, understands no defeats. In this respect, it stands psychologically outside the frame of normal democratic politics, which is largely an affair of compromise." [2]

Our political pantry is full of examples of right-wing pronouncements, pamphlets, and personalities so that we need not review here their general paranoia item by item. For myself, I

[1] Richard Hofstadter, "Pseudo-Conservatism Revisited: A Postcript —1962," in Daniel Bell, *The Radical Right,* p. 85.
[2] Ibid., p. 86.

have long felt that simply to call the roll of the staggering array
of right-wing organizations that have been spawned across the
country and recite their incredible statements and accusations is
to overlook their real significance. For every ludicrous charge
pointing to the betrayal of the United States by our elected
officialdom there are twenty others that are even more revealing
of the range of their fantasies and the pathological state of their
fears. But even an updated cataloguing of these charges would
not enable us to understand "the Manichaean style of thought,
the apocalyptic tendencies, the love of mystification, the intolerance of compromise that are observable in the right-wing
mind." [3] The missing link, as Hofstadter, Weston, Danzig, and
others have pointed out, is an understanding of the history of
fundamentalism in the United States—or, in more contemporary
terms, "the fundamentalist revolt against modernity." [4] The hostility to democratic politics on the part of the right wing is in
large measure the result of its fundamentalist roots.

We have already seen that throughout American history there
have been countless groups that have viewed their times
through conspiratorial glasses and have shared a common antip-
athy to the democratic political process. Their conspiratorial
outlook derives from the belief that the "politicians" will be the
first to compromise, to give in, and—what is worst of all—to betray the fundamental truth. The political system itself is viewed
as the product of those who would deceive the people. The idea
that the truth is uncompromisable and indivisible is part of a
rigorous fundamentalist orthodoxy among whose basic doctrines
are the infallibility of the Bible, salvation by faith alone, and the

---

[3] Hofstadter, loc. cit.
[4] Hofstadter's own admission on this point is important: "If this
essay were to be rewritten today (referring to his article written in
1955), there is one force in American life, hardly more than hinted at
in my original formulation, that would now loom very large indeed, and
that is fundamentalism."

pre-millennial return of Christ. These religious truths are also
literal truths, and they are not to be tampered with by revision-
ists or "modernists." Many of the small fundamentalist sects
insist on the commonplace and the ancient in theology, practice,
and manner of life. They seem to believe, as Elmer Clark has
said, that all persons must think alike, and that departures in
minute details of doctrine are sufficient to cause lasting schisms.

The conservatism which resists change of every sort is one of the
clear marks of sectarianism. . . . Worship of the remote past, coupled with mistrust of modernity, is found in many sects. . . . A
deep-seated suspicion of all others save themselves is a characteristic
of many sects. Only a handful will enter upon any real program of
cooperation with other bodies. . . . Very many small sects are inim-
ical to modern scholarship, which they call "modernism." [5]

The emphasis on literalness and purity of doctrine in religious
matters has its counterpart in the world of politics. The fundamentalist is as suspicious of pragmatists and pragmatism in
political society as he is of heretics and "atheistic radicals" for
their work in spreading false religious doctrines. The give and
take of democratic politics is reduced to a politics of conspiracy
because the fundamentalist, a prisoner of his own rigidity when it
comes to the religious truth, is equally determined to do God's
work in combating all those who would pervert and destroy
social truth. "The true fundamentalists in our midst," affirmed
Robert Welch in the John Birch Society's *Blue Book,* "whether
Catholics, Protestants or Jew, are the moral salt of the earth." [6]
In politics as in religion, there are the forces of good and forces

[5] Elmer T. Clark, *The Small Sects in America* (New York: Abingdon-
Cokesbury Press; 1927), p. 223.

[6] Welch, *The Blue Book,* p. 79. He goes on to say, "And nothing I
say now, nor any of the plans I outline tomorrow, is intended to question,
weaken or disturb any fundamentalist faith in the slightest; or to dis-
count one iota its tremendous worth as a core of strength for all that
we might hope to do." Quoted in Edward Cain, *They'd Rather Be
Right* (New York: Macmillan; 1963), p. 74.

of evil, those to be saved and those to be damned. For the right-wing John Birch Society the fight against communism in America is much more than a political or economic conflict. It is a conflict of faiths, not power blocs, and for this reason is part of an unending struggle between good and evil. The danger in this country, says Welch, is almost entirely internal—that is to say, from the corrosion of faith by sinister forces at home.[7] The real danger, now that the virtually sacred socio-economic doctrines of nineteenth-century capitalism have been undermined and corrupted, is collectivism—in David Danzig's words, "the modern fundamentalist's secular counterpart of atheism."[8]

In his perceptive analysis of the John Birch Society, Professor Alan Westin makes the important point that right-wing fundamentalism spans a broad spectrum.[9] At one pole are those who make up the hatemongering right, led by the American Nazi George Rockwell and other similar outcasts who preach violence along with their anti-Semitism, anti-Catholicism, and anti-Negro diatribes. They stand alone, thoroughly discredited in the country they hate. At the other pole is the "semi-respectable right"—the Daughters of the American Revolution, the Committee for Constitutional Government, and a variety of political and educa-

[7] "When any man tells you today that the danger of Communism, to America, is not from within our country, but from without, that we should stop worrying about the Communists and their sympathizers in our midst and worry only about their armies and their possessions outside, he is either a pro-Communist, completely uninformed, or naieve beyond reason." Robert Welch, "The Life of John Birch," *American Opinion*, Vol. III, No. 3, March 1960, p. 73.

[8] David Danzig, "The Radical Right and the Rise of the Fundamentalist Minority," *Commentary*, April 1962, p. 292. I have drawn heavily in this discussion of fundamentalism on Mr. Danzig's excellent article.

[9] Alan F. Westin, "The John Birch Society: 'Radical Right' and 'Extreme Left' in the Political Context of Post World War II—1962," in Daniel Bell, *The Radical Right,* op. cit. In my own reflections and for purposes of this chapter I have returned to Professor Westin's article many times. I consider it one of the best in the literature dealing with extremist politics and attitudes.

tional organizations which are dissatisfied with the major currents of American political and social life. However, these groups do not wish to disengage themselves completely for fear of becoming isolated and thereby losing their "semi-respectability." [1] The John Birch Society, Westin believes, stands between the "hate" right and the semi-respectable right.

The advantage of such spectrum analysis is that it provides a useful measurement by which to differentiate among the various right-wing complexions. The handful of misfits who constitute the "hate" fringe of society and openly flaunt the law need not concern us. But the other rightist groups to one degree or another share in the basic fundamentalist belief that the social order of the United States is being poisoned by insidious "collectivist" doctrines masquerading as "liberalism" and "internationalism" whose only purpose is to carry the country down the road to appeasement, socialism, and, ultimately, surrender. The gentle ladies of the DAR need not be made to resemble the not-so-gentle activists of the John Birch Society to see that each in its own way wants a return to the pre–New Deal era of free enterprise, self-help individualism, and an undisturbed trouble-free isolationism. This glorification of the political past in American life has qualities of that old-time religion which in itself reveals a good deal about the nature of rightist politics. There is little in the heated dialogue of the right wing that reflects a serious interest in the practical day-to-day problems of the ordinary citizen. The program of the right wing is not directed to the area of material needs to which the politician in a democratic society must give his attention. The politics of the right rests on frustration and fear and, in sounding their alarms to the American people, the right-wing evangelists insist on speaking in tones

---

[1] Although Professor Westin includes the White Citizens Councils of the South in this "semi-respectable" category, I would put them in the company of the John Birch Society.

of moral certainties, patriotic pieties, and emotional satisfactions. Thus the John Birch Society or the Reverend Billy James Hargis of the Christian Crusade or the Reverend Fred C. Schwartz of the Christian Anti-Communist Crusade have nothing concrete or positive to say about how to confront such urgent problems as unemployment, automation, discrimination, or a host of other society-wide ills. They prefer instead to attack the whole social and economic direction of the country as the culpable handiwork of irresponsible political leaders who have sold their shoddy wares to an unsuspecting and gullible people. Traditional politics, by which I mean the pluralistic politics which must accommodate conflict and diversity, cannot and does not see every issue as a moral struggle between irreconcilable alternatives. The democratic mentality believes that the alternatives fall within a narrower range and that small achievements and successes are not only expectable but valued. The political differences that separate opposing parties in a particular dispute can be peacefully accommodated because the solutions rarely require a choice between salvation or damnation. Democratic politics is marked by moderation, not because it is weak or ineffectual but because it places realistic limits on its demands and accepts and encourages a common attachment to its supporting institutions. In contrast, the right-wing extremist is inflexibly attached to a given value or evil and holds the passionate belief that nothing less than its complete fulfillment can be tolerated. Thus he is impatient with compromise, and in his impatience feels free to disregard the rules and boundaries of the political order which, in his zealous view, stand in his way.

Consider the program of the John Birch Society for counteracting "the enemy." As with other groups throughout our history which have felt it necessary to take on the responsibility of fighting conspiracies in our midst, the Birchers reveal a distinct similarity of approach in their various plans of militant action against the Communist conspiracy and their related attitudes toward the democratic governmental process. The John Birch Society, as with their right-wing compatriots as well as their ancestors, fix upon a Messianic purpose. "We are fast coming to a point, gentlemen," warns Robert Welch, "when we've got to offer something that people are willing to die for." [2] Already he has surpassed the appeal and purpose of democratic politics, in whose name no one is asked to give his life. "But this is no cream-puff war we are in, and the stakes involved are not those of a pillow fight, we have to face squarely up to the solid truth— that unless we are willing to take drastic steps, a lot of them, and very drastic indeed, we haven't a chance in the world of saving our lives, our country, or our civilization." [3]

First you categorically define the state of the nation and the world: imminent disaster. Then you provide the only remedy sufficient to meet the task ahead: drastic action. The implication is clear: the ways of traditional politics and democratic procedures are for the timid—and besides, there is not time. Welch has asserted that there are "more Communists and Communist sympathizers in our government today than ever before." Communists, he would have us believe, are at the heart of all our problems. The "trouble in the South over integration is Communist contrived"; the Supreme Court "is one of the most important agencies of Communism"; the "very idea of American foreign aid was dreamed up by Stalin, or by his agents for him"; the Federal Reserve system is a "realization" of "point five" of the *Communist Manifesto,* calling for centralization of credit in the hands of the state. Everywhere, says Welch, the Communists are winning—in "the press, the pulpit, the radio and television media, the labor unions, the schools, the courts, and the legislative halls of America." Welch and his "board of experts" have

[2] Robert Welch, *The Blue Book,* p. 116.
[3] Ibid., p. 103.

published a "score board" rating all the nations of the world (since 1958) according to the "present degree of Communist influence and control over the economic and political affairs of the country." This country's red fever chart is alarming, if one is to believe Mr. Welch: in 1958, the United States rated 20–40 per cent under Communist control; in 1959, the United States rated 30–50 per cent under Communist control; in 1960, the United States rated 40–60 per cent under Communist control. At this rate, we will be close to completely communized before the Republicans and Democrats are ready for the next presidential election!

But there is a larger and more important point to be made about the radical right in the United States than their hyperthyroid anticommunism. The right-wing extremist stands apart from both the liberal and the conservative in that he lacks a full commitment to the democratic process. It is in this sense that he is radical, which is to say that he approaches this country's problems with not only an alien mood and temper but an unmistakable hostility to the complex procedures by which our political differences are normally resolved. The conservative and the liberal differ seriously in their views on everything from the nature of man to the necessity and desirability of social reform. One is more prone to rely on instinct and tradition while the other prefers reason and planning. Nor are these unimportant differences, for their implications ramify out into every corner of our political life and generate wide and often serious divisions among a multiplicity of groups and factions in the country. Yet both liberals and conservatives, Republicans and Democrats, moderates and progressives—the labels are endless—are generally committed to the democratic processes of accommodation and reconciliation. The right-wingers' acerbity of language has no place in this commitment because it is alien to the style of democratic discussion which has as its rationale the belief that intelligence and understanding are to be valued far more than abuse and denunciation.

I have mentioned the style of democratic discussion because it bears directly on the commitment to the democratic process. For one thing, it reflects a sense of affinity to the politics of civility that is in sharp contrast to the right-wingers' rancor and intolerance. But there is still another sense in which this notion of democratic style, for all of its ambiguity and imprecision, has an important meaning and carries a special significance. The extremist of the far right subscribes to a politics of fanaticism that goes far beyond the particular preachings which make up his passionate beliefs. The right-winger is an absolutist whose commitment is to his own inflexible form of perfection, and like all perfectionists he cannot accept anything less, abhors any hint of moderation, and will use and justify any means to realize his uncompromisable goal. The style of the radical rightist is that of the extremist everywhere who relies upon intense emotion and excessive righteousness in demanding the complete and absolute fulfillment of his sacred goal of rigid doctrine. He has the absolute and complete answer from which the slightest retreat is viewed as moral cowardice. It is in this light that Mr. Welch's disdain for the democratic style of political inquiry and debate is especially illuminating. In the John Birch Society's *Blue Book* he has offered the following observation:

The folly of the two-sides-to-every-question argument is emphasized in a brief story we have told elsewhere and often. The minister has preached a superb sermon. It has moved his whole congregation to a determination to lead nobler and more righteous lives. Then he said: "And that, of course, is the Lord's side. Now for the *next* half hour, and to be fair, I'll present the devil's side. You can then take your choice." [4]

It is not surprising that the right-wing extremists have expended their greatest energy in combating what to them is the

[4] Ibid., p. xv, footnotes to the 4th edn., No. 26.

subversive philosophy of education in the United States today. There are, it is true, a seemingly endless number of American programs and policies to which the radical right is unalterably and loudly opposed. The John Birch Society, for example, has included the following among those it regards as either wicked or Communist but in any event dangerous to the country:

— Reciprocal trade agreements
— The "useless and costly" NATO
— "So-called defense spending"
— All foreign aid
— Diplomatic relations with the Soviet Union and all other Communist nations
— The National Labor Relations Act
— Social security
— The graduated income tax
— The Rural Electrification Administration
— The Reconstruction Finance Corporation
— The Tennessee Valley Authority
— "Deliberately fraudulent" United States bonds
— Urban renewal
— Fluoridation
— "The mental health racket"

And this is only a partial listing that demonstrates again the right-winger's dislike of the present and the desire to re-create his ideal past. But it is important to point out that the right-winger's image of the past is based less on what it actually was than on what he wants the future to be, which is one reason why he has entered the field of education with a vengeance.

In keeping with their fundamentalist faith, the right-wing extremists look upon education as a mirror of what has been happening to traditional American principles of government in the last twenty or thirty years. Liberals may advocate a program of federal aid to education in their belief that nothing less than a full-scale national effort will bridge the gap between present performance and future potential; conservatives may staunchly oppose any program that will lead to further intrusion of the federal government into this country's educational system. The continuing debate along these lines is both legitimate and necessary, and from it ultimately will emerge something close to a national consensus. But those who roam the range of the far right strike their discordant tones because they look upon the schools and colleges in the United States today as leading the betrayal of the fundamentals of "Americanism" and "undermining allegiance and faith."

No one who has watched closely what has been going on in our public school system in America these past two decades can escape the feeling that something drastic—and rather terrible—has happened to it. What is more, it is difficult to believe that it has happened by accident, that there has not been a planned, slyly executed and almost successful attempt to deliberately under-educate our children in order to make them into an unquestioning mass who would follow meekly those who wish to turn the American Republic into a socialist society.[5]

The attack, of course, is on progressive education, the *bête noir* of those who see "revolutionary educationists" instilling in every schoolboy a tolerance of "ideologies completely foreign to American traditions, in place of love of home, flag and country."

These subversive ideas had to be sneaked over on the teachers and through the teachers on the students. . . . It was put over on our schools by the same men, the same groups, the same organizations bent on building "the new social order" of socialism in America through the schools. . . . All over America the seething and the striving has been rising in volume and in numbers. But never reckon without the progressivist revolutionaries. . . . They have one more fatal tool in their kit which, if they can get it used, will give them finally and forever a stranglehold on the public school system of the

[5] Rosalie M. Gordon, "What Happened to Our Schools?" pamphlet entitled *America's Future, Inc.*, published in New Rochelle, New York, 1956, pp. 4-5.

American states. This tool is embodied in the sweet-sounding phrase "federal aid to education." [6]

It is interesting to note that the conservative National Association of Manufacturers does not share the right-winger's feeling that the educational system in this country is subverting the American way of life. In 1953, when Senator McCarthy was at the peak of his Communist-hunting career, the NAM's president announced his opposition to any "wholesale indictment" of American colleges and universities by anti-Communists. He went so far as to say that the fact that some college faculties probably include professors with "Communist leanings" or who expound "socialist ideas" in the classroom "should not cause a general condemnation of our educational system." Increased support of higher education, he contended, is the "positive approach to the left-wing problem." [7]

In February 1954 the NAM issued a pamphlet entitled *This We Believe About Education*.[8] It is a perceptive document, and many of the statements within its pages are models of restraint and reason in comparison with the bitter and emotional pronouncements of the right wing.

It is the responsibility of Education to support, and frequently to lead, the necessary and continuing fight to preserve freedom of expression and freedom of inquiry. Even tolerance of intolerance must be safeguarded. . . . All educators should oppose any attempt by either government or public opinion to repress expression of honest views or to curtail scientific studies and researches. An educator must stand ready to fight for his right to pursue knowledge in the true scientific spirit. Because education has a centuries-old familiarity with the struggle to achieve and maintain freedom for

[6] Ibid., pp. 8, 9, 13, and 18.

[7] San Francisco *Chronicle*, April 15, 1953.

[8] *This We Believe About Education*, A Statement Concerning Education in America, by the Educational Advisory Committee and the Educational Advisory Council of the National Association of Manufacturers, New York, February 1954.

the human mind, the American people rightfully look to educators for leadership in that continuous battle.[9]

Every teacher in America, the NAM declares, should have the "unquestioned right to impart knowledge objectively concerning all matters related to the subject he teaches." Completely objective teaching, however, especially for the social sciences, "while a desirable goal, can scarcely be expected or achieved in actual practice by teachers who are also thinking human beings; reasonable deviation from this absolute standard should not expose any teacher to attack, intimidation, or insecurity of his position." Short of advocating the overthrow of the government, "no attack on any teacher, or on his teaching because of his individual ideological convictions, should be supported or condoned." Furthermore, the NAM believes that "businessmen, the public, and educators should view with proper and customary caution sweeping charges made by any group which studies the educational system and publishes adverse findings as to its methods, purposes, or practices, or as to the ideological loyalties of some of its leaders." [1]

The NAM, contrary to the spokesmen of the far right, feels that with few exceptions all the major goals and objectives of American education have been endorsed by a sufficient percentage of the American people to assure those goals a "justified place in the over-all design." It would seem wiser, the NAM advises, if all persons concerned with education would recognize the advantages of a "heterogeneity of ideas as to the purposes of education." [2] But this is the kind of advice which the right-wing extremists consider to be little better than dangerous nonsense. They regard the current trend in education as something to which all patriotic citizens must be forcefully alerted, and to this

[9] Ibid., p. 16.
[1] Ibid., pp. 29–30.
[2] *This We Believe . . . ,* loc. cit.

end one right-wing organization established a Committee on Education, one of whose principal projects was to examine the contents of textbooks through its own quarterly publication, *The Educational Reviewer.*

Once again the antidemocratic style and temper of the radical right is clearly revealed. Mrs. Lucille Cardin Crain, secretary and editor of the *Reviewer,* explained why the need for such a publication became urgent. In a radio interview she cited the case of a father who was "shocked when his daughter came home from college full of un-American doctrines. . . . He looked into the textbooks that his daughter had been made to study. The history books were slanted toward the revolutionary 'new order.' The textbooks on government pleaded for 'change' and for giving more power to government." He "hit the ceiling," Mrs. Crain said, when he discovered that his daughter had been taught "a lot of economic nonsense" in textbooks in which he found "general condemnation of the system of which he is a part."

BILL SLATER: Then what did he do?

MRS. CRAIN: First, he read the economic textbooks used in the high school of his home town. Then he asked his school officials why they used them. They said there was nothing better—that there hadn't been a sound, new textbook on economics for high school pupils in the last ten years.

BILL SLATER: That's about the story all over the country, so far as I've heard it. But this man found a way to do something, did he?

MRS. CRAIN: Yes. Mutual friends brought us together and we planned the work of *The Educational Reviewer.*

. . . . .

BILL SLATER: What about the argument that's heard these days about presenting "all sides of every question"?

MRS. CRAIN: I'm awfully glad you brought that up. One of my favorite teacher-reviewers gave me her interpretation of that trick —it is a trick—and I shall be eternally grateful to her for her answer.

BILL SLATER: How did she explain the trick?

MRS. CRAIN: She pointed out that giving the same emphasis to all points of view, good and bad, and letting immature minds make decisions without guidance, is just what the propagandists want. And I remember her adding something like this: "Truth and falsehood are *not* equal; there is no equality between right and wrong."[3]

The subversion of American principles taking place in the classrooms is seen by the far right in much the same way that it has viewed the destruction of individual initiative and personal liberty throughout society since the inauguration of President Roosevelt in 1933. The radical right, in the tradition of its anticonspiratorial outlook, is convinced that left-wing educators, sometimes known as "frontier thinkers," are moving step by step in their scheme to demolish faith and belief in our political principles and traditions in order to pave the way for the "new society." One right-wing organization urged every precaution possible to prevent anyone who subscribes to "any of the ideologies of Communism or any other governmental philosophy at variance with our form of government" from being appointed to a position of trust or influence. "Only Americans," it said in a burst of patriotism, "should be employed to handle government affairs and to teach our youth; only those persons who are glad to turn their faces toward the rising sun every day and swear allegiance to our country, are suitable for such employment."[4]

In contrast to conservative organizations like the National Association of Manufacturers which have expressed strong confidence in our schools in the practical belief that prosperity will continue as long as the nation has greater production, better education, and better leadership, the right wing has deep fears

[3] Excerpts of a radio broadcast entitled "What Is Taught Your Children," reprinted in *The Educational Reviewer,* Vol. II, No. 2, October 15, 1950.

[4] *Report of Proceedings,* Conference of American Small Business Organizations, Eleventh National Session (Washington, D.C.: March 27, 28, 29, 1951), p. 40.

that American education will subvert our sacred values and ideals. If one continuously thinks and talks in terms of plots, he will ultimately find them. Thus W. P. Strube, Jr., vice-president of the right-wing Christian Anti-Communism Crusade, can say in all seriousness that "one dedicated Communist at a strategic position at a crucial moment could literally have the population at his mercy. The number is almost insignificant."[5] This is the frame of mind that is totally divorced from the basic political sanity of the United States. "Almost every day," cries Robert Welch, "I run into some whole new area, where the Communists have been penetrating and working quietly for years, until now they are in virtual control of everything that is done in that slice or corner of our national life."[6] This is the voice of the right-wing extremist expressing his basic convictions, and it is these very convictions which make his participation in democratic politics a precarious venture. This is the conspiratorial view of the world, distrustful of the democratic political process and of politicians in particular, that would have us believe (again in the words of Robert Welch) that this country received "the exact Communist line from Jack Kennedy's speeches as quickly and faithfully as from the *Worker* or the *National Guardian.*" Anyone who can believe this can believe anything.

Many Americans, without thinking too long or hard about it, have adopted the formula that "if the Communists are for it, we ought to be against it and vice versa." But now even this formula, certainly not the last word in reason and logic, has been ruined by Mr. Welch's extraordinary contribution—his "principle of reversal."[7] This is the Alice-in-Wonderland concept that

[5] W. P. Strube, Jr., *Communism—A Monopoly,* undated pamphlet, pp. 8–9.

[6] Welch, *The Blue Book,* p. 5.

[7] For this particular point I am indebted to the analysis of the John Birch Society prepared by the office of the attorney general of California and submitted to the governor in a 15-page letter dated July 7, 1961.

says, "Many of the things the Communists profess to be for, they
are really against. They only *say* they are for it so we will be
against it." Some examples show how it works: (1) Mr. Welch
characterized the late United Nations Secretary General Dag
Hammarskjöld as "one of the most contemptible agents of the
Kremlin ever supported by the American taxpayers." When
Khrushchev became frantic and angry over Hammarskjöld, Mr.
Welch explained that the Soviet leader did so because he wanted
us to defend Hammarskjöld, thereby keeping him at his post.
(2) Mr. Welch claims that many American organizations generally supposed to be anti-Communist are really Communist.
"Some of them have no more harmful purpose than merely to
drain off, into innocuous wastefulness, money and effort which
might otherwise find its way into really patriotic and anti-Communist activities. Others are primarily designed to offer protective coloration to Communists who can thus get themselves as
active in anti-Communist organizations." [8] (3) Mr. Welch believes that the real reason the Russians sent Sputnik aloft was
that they wanted us to increase our defense spending! "Although
our danger remains almost entirely internal, from Communist
influences right in our midst and treason right in our government," he writes, "the American people are being persuaded that
our danger is from the outside, is from Russian military superiority. And under the excuse of preparing to match that military
might, or defending ourselves from this threat of outside force;
in other words, under the guise of fighting Communism, we are
being stampeded into the biggest jump ever towards, and perhaps the final jump right into socialism and then the Communist
camp." [9]

The result of all this is a "heads they win, tails we lose"
proposition of incredible proportions—and an insult to all the

[8] Welch, *The Blue Book,* p. 160.
[9] Ibid., p. 32.

respective criteria of rational, democratic decision making. If the United States increases its military might to resist the Soviet Union, it is playing into Soviet hands. If it reduces its military might it is playing into Russian hands. It can hardly escape notice that by the logic of his own principle of reversal, Mr. Welch himself stands convicted of being the most unscrupulous Communist agent of all. It is no wonder that Welch and the John Birch Society, "frantic in their self-induced terror," can conclude ". . . that unless we can reverse forces which now seem inexorable in their movement, [we] have only a few more years before [the U.S.] will become four separate provinces in a world-wide dominion ruled by police-state methods from the Kremlin." [1]

On a Saturday in April 1962, a few small civic groups in southern California sponsored an open town meeting at which a film and public discussion were planned. Without giving notice of their intent, seventy to eighty members of the John Birch Society invaded the meeting and broke into cheers and boos on signal, shouting the word "republic" whenever a speaker referred to "democracy." The intruders completely disrupted the meeting by throwing insults not only at the speakers but at the audience as well. The following day this performance by a similar group of invaders, seventy-two in all, disrupted a peaceful meeting of a club in Encino, California, at the local community center. The Birch members were so vocal and abusive in their interruptions that it became necessary to call public officers in order to prevent physical violence.[2]

---

[1] Ibid., p. 9.

[2] A report to the governor of California about the activities of the John Birch Society, op. cit., p. 9. "Members of the Birch Society," the report continued, "have indicated that they learn about these meetings by means of 'infiltration' into legitimate political organizations, and that the invasion and disruption of peaceable assemblies of citizens is part of their program of action."

Robert Welch has given encouragement to members of the John Birch Society to use whatever anti-political means seem effective to accomplish a particular mission or reach its ultimate goal. One looks long and hard for an unambiguous statement in any of its literature expressing allegiance to the democratic process. The whole internal structure of the society itself mirrors its antidemocratic bias.[3] The allegiance of the John Birch Society is to its version of the absolute truth. Put in the simplest authoritarian terms, there is one truth, and it resides in one man, one group, or one principle. This has always been one of the major tenets of antidemocratic thought, and it is from this basic precept that the right-wing extremists maintain that those who are in possession of the truth and know the right goals are free to use any means to achieve them and to ignore or silence all opposition to either their means or ends.

It is important to distinguish the antidemocratic thought of the right-wing extremists from the more paternalistic and aristocratic notions of the conservatives in the tradition of Edmund Burke. The latter, believing that men are not created equal, harbor a distrust of the common man and question his abilities to make reasonable and right decisions. They prefer to place their trust in the elite, either as a group or a single member of the

---

[3] "The John Birch Society is a monolithic authoritarian organization with the policy dictated from above and no dissent permitted in its ranks. The Communist Party is a monolithic authoritarian organization with policy dictated from above and no dissent permitted in its ranks." Welch, *The Blue Book*, p. 10. Welch himself has made no attempt to conceal this: "The John Birch Society will operate under complete authoritative control at all levels. . . . There are many reasons why, in the fight immediately ahead, we cannot stop for parliamentary procedures, or a lot of arguments among ourselves. . . . Men who join the John Birch Society will be doing so because they believe in me [Robert Welch] and what I am doing, and are willing to accept my leadership. We are going to use that loyalty, like any other reserve, to the fullest possible advantage. . . . Those members who cease to feel the necessary degree of loyalty can either resign or will be put out." Pp. 161–2.

group, in the belief that it can best pursue the correct policies. Change is unwise and unnecessary, democracy is undesirable. History abounds in examples of aristocratic thought and rule. The bases of determination of the elite have been numerous and varied, including age, sex, wealth, power, property, heredity, race, education or training, religion, and profession. In most cases the leader is elevated by circumstances rather than by achievement; in all cases he is not to be questioned or opposed. Elements of aristocratic thought and allegiance are evident even in basically democratic societies. Thus sex and race have played a central part in determining (albeit by popular election) who will rule in the United States, and certain professions and training are generally held to be more preparatory to the art of leadership and the conduct of government. Even within the democratic process some traces of aristocratic thought are present. To the degree that he can resist the temptation and pressures of the extremists of the far right, the aristocratic conservative may be defined as one who has a highly developed sense of tradition and order in social and political life.

But the antidemocratic character of the right-wing extremist is something else again. If the Burkean or moderate conservative seeks to remind us of the continuity and universality of certain traditional values, the radical rightist, in fusing his own values with fundamentalist religion and morality, makes absolute judgments about them and demands their total acceptance. It is this dogmatism and certitude, the very antithesis of open inquiry and toleration, that is subversive of the democratic process. The inherent religiosity of those who demand total passion and total commitment has no place in politics. As Camus has pointed out, "Politics is not religion, or, if it is, then it is nothing but the Inquisition." The political revivalists of the far right are but the latest breed of extremists to polarize good and evil in their search for the omnipotent. Those who stand in their way are their enemies. They project their "God-devil axis" into every nook and cranny of American life and—not surprisingly—discover every evil under the sun: communism, socialism, liberalism, welfare-statism, fluoridation, professors, scientists, churchmen, foreigners, to mention only a few. The energy that a century ago was directed to organized religion has been transferred to the politics of right-wing fanaticism, with a kind of Messianic radicalism demanding sweeping changes in the political and social order and, for some, an apocalyptic vision calling for a return to past utopias.[4]

As we have seen, the right-wing extremist has a longing for safety, definiteness, and authority. His "island of safety" mentality, which fears the future and the unknown, seeks protection from the menace that seems to be present on all sides. His is basically a threat-orientation to life, which when translated into political terms leads him to object to democracy because it fails to maintain the strict order and dominance of authority he feels is necessary for the operation and survival of society. Thus there is a denial of the supremacy of public opinion because the prevailing authority must be in the name of the *right* principle, and the only recourse is to the *"right* man, the leader, he who not only knows what is right but is strong enough to assure it."[5]

---

[4] David Riesman has pointed out that "the growing minority of old people who feel rejected, disoriented, impoverished and resentful are ready to applaud an anti-political movement that promises to reorganize the world so that the old folks can understand it again. Many of them . . . are grateful for the simplistic, evangelistic messages of anti-Communism, which affirm to their hearers that the latter are the really good Americans. . . ." Riesman, "The Intellectuals and the Discontented Classes: Some Further Reflections—1962," in Bell, *The Radical Right,* p. 119.

[5] David Spitz, *Patterns of Anti-Democratic Thought* (New York: Macmillan; 1949), p. 12. His aggressive attitude is revealed, T. W. Adorno reports, in his agreement with this statement: "There are some activities so flagrantly un-American that, when responsible officials won't take the proper steps, the wide awake citizen should take the law

For the right-wing extremist, safety is sought in the creation of a rigid, two-value world. In this world, as we have already indicated, there are no grays—only black or white, good or bad, weak or strong people, superpatriots or Communists. "Right" and "wrong" are the clear bifurcations in this person's thinking, equipped with ready-made slots into which everyone and everything must be fitted. Consequently, his usual way of responding to people is either approval or disapproval—or, to put it differently, responses are evoked "subcortically" without any attempt to understand the issues at hand. A moralistic emphasis predominates in everything from sex to politics, thus setting him apart from the more "open" individual who is more concerned with human relationships and can accept his own mixed and often conflicting feelings and attitudes. The right-wing extremist finds individuality disconcerting and looks for a clear hierarchy in society whereby power arrangements, instead of shifting unpredictably, are definite and set. The result is an unbending devotion to "truth" and "right principle," a familiar posture of all antidemocrats. In the interest of the total success of this "right principle" it is not important what methods are used or at what cost. "Do you think," asks Robert Welch, "that by strictly political means . . . there would be the slightest chance of success?" [6] There is only one goal, one principle—and one authority to which all else must yield. In the Calvinist tradition, everything

into his own hand." Adorno, et al., *The Authoritarian Personality* (New York: Harper; 1950), p. 237. However, the willingness to accept and submit to authority simultaneously conflicts with the strong desire to rebel and to obtain power. "The data on these functional items give us indications of a strongly ambivalent feeling toward leaders. . . . They accept direct authority but, when given half a chance, react to it with vigorous hostility." Fillmore H. Sanford, *Authoritarianism and Leadership* (Philadelphia: Stephenson-Brothers; 1950), p. 70. This is one reason why all right-wing extremists have never been able to organize themselves into a national movement with a unified system of direction and control.

[6] Welch, *The Blue Book*, pp. 111 and 120.

must be sacrificed to the fulfillment of God's will according to the supreme authority of the Bible. "Unregenerate and sinful men must have no share in God's work. The Saints must not have their hands tied by majority vote." [7] To the right-winger, who is one of the supreme moralists of our time, if the democratic political process corrupts mankind, that process is evil and must be opposed. Morality must be preserved at whatever cost. The anti-Communist is willing to give up all his other freedoms in order to silence and destroy the enemy. The serious harm to democratic procedures takes place when the extremists act on their implict belief that any means are justified if they will bring about what is "right" and "true." [8]

The extremists of the far right belong to that discontented company of alien men and women in quest of self-identity who are in but not of present-day American society. Like the small

[7] Adorno, op. cit., p. 227.

[8] The right-wing extremist finds in clear-cut institutional memberships the definiteness and security he needs. "For him nationalism is a positive anchorage: it is his country right or wrong. This isolationist 'patriotism' or hyper-Americanism is highly correlated with the rejection of various out-group minorities—Jews, Negroes, etc. [The extremist's] kind of patriotism is often a part of a broad cluster of 'anti' attitudes: anti-integration, anti-United Nations, anti-sex education, and anti-labor. The 'safety islander' is vigorously loyal to his particular ingroup—his Church, fraternity, family, and over everything, his nation. In general, there is suspicion toward those unlike himself, and he distrusts people until they prove themselves trustworthy. Consequently, we should expect groups which attract to themselves a great many authoritarian personalities to have much inner dissension and many struggles for power. Such seems to be true in the case of the John Birch Society, by their own admission and literature." Roy W. Fairchild, "To Whom Do 'They' Appeal?" *Dialogue,* May 12, 1961, p. 3. I have found this excellent Special Issue on "The Radical Right Wing" extremely useful, although I have certain reservations about the "authoritarian personality" approach to politics as Chapter Five attempts to make clear. *Dialogue* is a fortnightly newspaper published by the Publications Board of the Student Association, San Francisco Theological Seminary.

fundamentalist sects they so much resemble, they are a religious people who are separated from the rest of mankind for the great purpose of preserving and propagating the true religion. In their own special blend of Apostolic Christianity that combines true Americanism with Puritanism and Protestantism, they have fashioned an "Uncle Sam's religion" that substitutes the Constitution for the Bible and glorifies a Fourth-of-July patriotism. Worship of the past is coupled with a mistrust of modernity. Besides resistance to change of every sort, one of the clear marks of their political sectarianism is the belief that all must think alike. Departures in important details of doctrine are enough to cause lasting schisms. Their deep-seated suspicion of everyone but themselves merely underscores their belief in the betrayal of the American Dream by hidden conspiracies and reaffirms their fervor for immediate and total solutions.

The point should not be misunderstood. All progress in society does not come from the "radical middle" or what has been called the "national anti-Communist consensus." New ground must be cleared of the confusing and distracting carry-overs from the past, for the weary doctrines of liberalism and conservatism will not be sufficient to meet the crises of our times. For this we will need searching criticism and visionary ideas—in short, the powerful acid of radical dissent. The all-important distinction, as Alan Westin has said, is that these constructive criticisms, instead of resting on cries of "soft on communism," allegations of traitorous leadership, and dangerously millennial proposals, be made instead "within the framework of rational discourse and civic responsibility." [9]

A few days after the 1964 Republican convention in San Francisco I found myself in conversation with one of the many "true believers" who was still rejoicing in the triumph of Senator Goldwater's nomination for president.

[9] Westin, op. cit., p. 224.

"So you're one of those political scientists," he said with a wry smile. "How did you like our convention?"

I told him I thought it had resembled something of a revival meeting.

"What the hell does that mean?" he asked, with more than a hint of anger in his voice.

I explained that I agreed with James Reston who had written in *The New York Times* a day or two before that the Goldwater movement was not a normal Republican political campaign but a counterrevolution, and that Barry Goldwater was looked upon by his ardent supporters not so much as a candidate but as a prophet.

After a few well-chosen epithets directed at "that pinko Reston," he really warmed to his subject. "I'll tell you something," he began. "This isn't going to be any ordinary political campaign. We want a big victory and we've been waiting a long time for it. There isn't going to be politics as usual. This is going to be a campaign to save this country's soul. I suppose that sounds pretty corny and old-fashioned to you," he added.

I told him I thought it was a little bit frightening, but that I always got upset at those who want to foist a new morality on the country.

"Listen," he went on, "it's about time we had a whole new moral attitude in this country, if that's what you're talking about. You don't change thirty years of un-American ideas and leadership with the same old political guff we've all been used to at every other election. This is going to be a crusade to restore the American faith. You know, all those eastern big shots like Rockefeller and Lodge and Scranton thought they could come out here and smooth things over with their soft talk and hard money and have it their way all over again. But this time they were wrong. This was our year—one of the delegates called it our Year of Judgment. You've heard Goldwater talk about a total victory against the Communists? Well, this was the beginning right here. Make no mistake about it." [1]

The ideological extremists of the right are not at home in the world of pluralistic politics. The adoption of extreme positions by its very nature places them poles apart from the vast majority of American people and dictates instead that they turn their efforts to those aspects of politics where numbers are not crucial. Thus the rightists are less successful in national elections where the outcome depends on the votes of millions, but are much more effective in trying to take control of the state party organization, pressuring the local school board, or, in a nonurban, unpopulated state like Wyoming, marshaling their forces to defeat a Democratic senator in his bid for re-election.[2] These are

[1] In writing about the Goldwater presidential campaign in 1964 Professor Aaron Wildavsky observed that the distinguishing characteristics of the Senator's most loyal followers included "their emphasis on internal criteria for decision, on what they believe 'deep down inside'; their rejection of compromise; their lack of orientation toward winning; their stress on the style and purity of decision—integrity, consistency, adherence to internal norms." The Goldwater style "represented a virtually complete privatization of politics. The private conscience of the leader rather than his public responsibilities became the focal point of politics. Internal criteria—possession of, devotion to, standing up for private principles—became the standard of political judgment. . . . Problems are met by stating one's principles first and assuming that they must be relevant to whatever is in hand. . . . If only one has principles and stands up for them, this position seems to suggest, the messy world of politics—compromise, bargaining, exceptions, modifications, inconsistencies—will disappear. Political style thus becomes a substitute for politics itself." Aaron Wildavsky, "The Goldwater Phenomenon: Purists, Politicians, and the Two-Party System," *The Review of Politics* (July 1954), pp. 395, 399, 401–2.

[2] It has been speculated that all of the states where the radical right is most active "have in common a political characteristic that is conspicuously lacking in the Northeast, where the right is feeblest. Where the radical right flourishes, political party organizations are weak and lack continuity. Control of a major party is an important inducement to right-wing activity in a number of states. But where party organizations are strong, where established leaders have formidable resources for protecting their positions from challengers, and where the rewards for

the arenas where the radical rightists, in focusing their attention on a specific ideological goal, need not be concerned with accommodating a plurality of values or a diversity of interests. In the conviction that they possess the solid truth they stand apart from those who look upon democratic politics not as a passion for certitude or a moral crusade for inviolable truth, but as a creative process of peaceful and practical reconciliation.

---

political action run more toward tangible benefits than ideological satisfaction, the difficulty of taking over the party discourages potential right-wing activists. The presence of a strong party organization also impedes other radical-right activity like the intimidation of school teachers and librarians." Raymond E. Wolfinger, et al., "America's Radical Right: Politics and Ideology," in *Ideology and Discontent*, ed. David Apter (Glencoe, Ill.: Free Press; 1964), p. 287.

CHAPTER THREE

Politics, Power, and Ideology: *The Distorted Perspectives of the American Left Wing*

> *We usually see only the things we are looking for—so much so that we sometimes see them where they are not.*
>
> ERIC HOFFER

> *In terms of policy and institutions, it is impossible to think of any important way in which this country would be different today if there had never been a Socialist party. . . . We have had a few socialists of some note and interest, but they never did get around to building a real political party.*
>
> RICHARD H. ROVERE

1

Several years ago three graduate students from the Soviet Union who were touring the United States and visiting a number of colleges and universities in different parts of the country requested permission to attend the weekly seminar I was giving that spring in American politics. Needless to say, I quickly agreed. The eight Americans, undergraduates and graduate students in political science, welcomed them warmly, thoroughly delighted at the prospect of having three "live" Communists seated around the table for two hours. The Russians were in their twenties, and through their spokesman, who was an active Communist youth leader in the Soviet Union with an almost perfect command of English (the other two could speak English only a little better than we could speak Russian), told us that they were working for advanced degrees in economic and social history. We exchanged pleasantries for a few minutes, and it soon became evident that our visitors were not only charming and friendly but witty and bright. When the afternoon's spirited discussion was finally ended some four hours later, all agreed that we understood a good deal more of each other's general position and point of view.

In order to take full advantage of the limited time we had with our Russian guests, I suggested they begin by asking us any questions they might have about the American political system. They were more than willing to oblige, and through their spokesman immediately placed the Marxist stamp on what turned out to be their major theme of the afternoon. "We have read much about the two political parties in your country, the Democrats and Republicans. You Americans say you have a two-party system, but it does not seem to us that one party is very much different from the other. What real choice do your citizens have when each political party accepts the capitalist system and tries to surpass the other in defending the unjust economic arrangements which, as everyone knows, serve only to strengthen the monopolists at the expense of the people? Your presidential candidates have no important differences in their programs because each embraces an economic system which permits the means of production in America to remain in the hands of the few who are wealthy. Your two parties are really only the political instruments of big business corporations like General Motors. It does not make much difference what name you give them since they are both friendly to the ruling class. We do not think you can ever have a real political choice until you have a party that speaks for the progressive forces in the United States and will work for a new and just social order. As it is now, your politicians and your political parties speak with one voice."

The Russian Communists were more than faithful representatives of the Soviet Union. Throughout the afternoon they gave an impressive performance in the dexterous art of Marxist analysis and left no doubt that they had learned their catechism well. The point they made about the American political system was clear and unequivocal: politics cannot be separated from economics in a capitalist system because it is the economic piper that constantly calls the political tune. They took a jaundiced view of our political parties because they saw the whole two-party system as a device to blunt the sharp edge of conflict between the working class and the ruling class. They insisted that the American political system, far from educating the workers to their "real" interests, blurred any feelings of class-consciousness and succeeded only in reducing the natural and inevitable conflict between worker and capitalist. There were no other issues which compared in importance to the necessity of increasing the division and tension between the two antagonists. Thus to our Marxist critics, the significant political issues were economic issues. In the Marxist idiom, the real issues are class issues. Any others are of no real importance and can be safely left to the politicians who, in turn, can be trusted to handle the unimportant skirmishes for the ruling elite. Through the ideological lens of a rigid determinism, politics in the United States, and, for that matter, politics as it is generally understood in most democratic societies, is reduced to nothing more than an epiphenomenon of economics.

The intellectual stimulation we derived from the comments and criticisms of the Russian students was at the same time admixed with a feeling of almost total frustration. In addition to tossing back and forth the many disagreements between us, we spent a good part of the afternoon simply talking past each other. There was no common ground we could share, and there were few mutually acceptable standards of reference we could employ to explain ourselves. Words like "democracy," "change," and "conflict" were infused with such widely divergent values that we found it difficult to make clear, much less communicate, our respective meanings. The American political system was not only held in considerable contempt by our Marxist guests—this was predictable—but appeared to be something of an enigma to them as well. The end result was that their understanding of the political process in this country, although completely consistent with their own ideological outlook and self-confirming of their inevitable Marxist presuppositions, was badly distorted and bore little resemblance to the way we conduct our political affairs. Encumbered by iron-clad determinist assumptions which re-inforced each other at every point, they were unable to perceive the nonideological, pragmatic, consensual character of American politics.

It will be a major contention of this chapter that the failure of the left wing in the United States to win any substantial support from the American people reflects not only its basic hostility to American society but its ideological distance from the realities of our political life.

꼬꼬꼬꼬꼬꼬꼬꼬꼬   2

One of the myths that dies hard is the notion that most of the important political decisions in the United States are made by so-called powerful and influential members of a ruling clique. The right-wing version of this theme, as we have already seen, is that America is run (and run down) by men in high office who are bent on destroying the sacred principles of our way of life by turning this country into a socialist or communist society. Wherever they look they find their evidence—in the schools, in the churches, in the State Department, even in the Tarzan books which an enterprising group in Los Angeles has discovered are subverting the youth of the country because in all of their jungle madness Tarzan and Jane, as it turns out, were never married.

For the left wing the idea of a ruling clique is given its most contemporary expression in the elitist implications of C. Wright Mills's provocative book *The Power Elite.*[1] Here is described the pyramidal structure of American society at the top of which is a triumvirate of business, military, and political "influentials" who are presumed to be in command of the major decision-making centers in the country. The same general picture is presented in miniature by Floyd Hunter in his study of the community power structure of Regional City (Atlanta, Georgia) where again a ruling group is said to be making the important decisions.[2] Hunter discovered some forty members of the community who, in effect, ran the city. Not surprisingly, the forty influentials were the economic notables of the city, the leading members of the business community who exercised their power more in private than in public and in a way that came close to a kind of benevolent manipulation. The point is that these economic interests in Regional City—and in large part, for C. Wright Mills, throughout the United States—were seen to be the "real" determinants of political action. Like the proverbial iceberg that is nine-tenths submerged and out of sight, the major economic forces of the community are somewhere "behind the scenes" pulling strings and in general making the community hum to

[1] C. Wright Mills, *The Power Elite* (New York: Oxford Univ. Press; 1959).

[2] Floyd Hunter, *Community Power Structure* (Chapel Hill: Univ. of North Carolina Press; 1953).

their own self-interested tune. Thus another variation on the theme of economic determinism has once again reduced politics to a level of secondary importance.

I have overdrawn the picture to make a central point. In the view just outlined, the diversity of our political institutions and decision-making procedures is denied, and in its place is substituted a monolithic structure of power and influence. Political decisions, far from being regarded as the outcome of a complex interaction of competing demands on political leaders by a myriad of claimants, are seen instead as the conditioned by-product of a power structure run by economic influentials. The general theory that animates this position deserves consideration and elaboration because in its own way it has characterized much of the left-wing approach to American society in general and American politics in particular.

The earliest investigations of American communities were done by sociologists, and of these none have received more widespread attention than the classic and pioneering *Middletown* studies by the Lynds.[3] They represent one of the first attempts to investigate an entire community and are still regarded as among the significant contributions toward understanding the interrelationship between power, economic position, and social status. In his later writings, as well as in his almost three decades of teaching at Columbia University before he retired, Robert S. Lynd made clear his belief that power is the axis on which one can solidly orient himself toward society. My purpose in examining Lynd's position here is not only to describe the basic elements of his ideas on power, but to evaluate his approach with essentially two questions in mind: (1) To what extent does his use of power as a framework of analysis contribute to an understanding

---

[3] Robert S. and Helen M. Lynd, *Middletown* (New York: Harcourt, Brace; 1929); and *Middletown In Transition* (New York: Harcourt, Brace; 1937).

of the American political process? and (2) What are some of the implications of his power orientation for politics in a democracy? I have chosen to focus on Lynd at the outset for two reasons: first because many of the values and premises which form the foundation of the intellectual position of the left wing in the United States stand sharply revealed in his own writings; and second, because the major thrust of his argument is in the tradition of many other left-wing critics who have insisted that political power in this country is concentrated in the hands of an economic and social class. By examining the configurations of Lynd's analysis of power, we will be able to see how other power perspectives proceed from many of the same assumptions in arriving at a general theory of elite control in America.

Clearly explicit in all of Lynd's major writing is the conviction that the promise of democracy and the harsh reality of capitalist "undemocracy" are fundamentally in conflict, with the result that our whole way of life is dominated and manipulated by the organized power of big business. Any notion that political power, or politics, can be independent of economic power represents a convenient escape route, a way of avoiding the fact that in a capitalist society there is a heavy tendency for power to be located in the economic axis. "Actually," Lynd told a United Auto Workers' Education Conference, "economic power is political power. There is only one fundamental power in industrial society, no matter what political tags you pin on the society. Don't let anybody fool you about that. Economic power is direct political power." [4] Politics, to Lynd, is the outgrowth of economics.

But Lynd's image of power involves some other presuppositions about American society and, in particular, the ways in

[4] Robert S. Lynd, "You Can Do It Better Democratically," an address delivered at the Fourth Annual International Education Conference, UAW-CIO in Milwaukee, Wis., January 1949.

which important political decisions are made. Professor Seymour
M. Lipset has pointed out that various power approaches can be
distinguished from each other by the difference between those
which emphasize the composition of the power holders and those
which stress access to power.

Concern with the composition or social backgrounds of the decision-
makers is in part based on the assumption that actions flow logically
and directly from the narrowly defined self-interests of those who
hold power. Thus if one knows the salient group affiliations of
decision-makers, one knows who will benefit from their decisions.
The access approach assumes rather that the decisions of men in
power like those of men in any other role are determined by a
complex analytic calculus of the consequences of decisions.[5]

In line with this analysis, power, to Lynd, has what might be
called a substantive mold to it. It visualizes and implies a close
correspondence between a pyramiding of control and influence in
society *and* the dominating social, economic, and political position of the American business class. At the same time it suggests
a direct *access-success relationship* to the important decision-
making points in the United States which business groups (economic power) are presumed to dominate as a result of both their
controlling position in the United States and the built-in features
of a capitalist society. However, a close examination of Lynd's
theory reveals that it is so constructed it cannot help but confirm
itself. That is to say, the social and economic arrangements of a
capitalist society are such that business power (like class power
in the strict Marxist version) is supreme; business power is so
supreme, Lynd's argument continues, that other power contend-

         [5] Seymour M. Lipset, "Old And New Frontiers of Political Sociol-
ogy," a paper delivered at the August 1957 meeting of the American
Sociological Society in Washington, D.C., reprinted in substantially the
same form under the title "Political Sociology" in Robert K. Merton,
Leonard Broom, and Leonard S. Cottrell, eds.: *Sociology Today* (New
York: Basic Books; 1959).

ers (in this case the labor movement) by implication are unable to do much more than play business's game and "ride the tail of business profits." Therefore, Lynd concludes, "The aces are in the hands of private business" and "democracy" is seriously threatened. Given its own premises, it is an airtight argument. The problem is where and how to break in on this iron-clad, neatly formulated theory whose own self-confirming logic has the facility of proving almost anything it wants to.

Lynd's main premise, shared by many of the left-wing analysts of the United States, is that the social structure of a capitalist society automatically favors the position and power of the privileged economic class. When it is pointed out that labor, through organization and mobilization of its members, has gained considerable political power in the last thirty years in terms of increased access to the major "tension points" of our legislative process, Lynd will reply that labor has merely contented itself with "pressing steadily for a bit more and then a bit more of the business take" to the point, for example, where the "garment unions have actually wedged themselves into the position of being co-partners with the owners and managers of that industry." How long, he asks, can labor continue to assume that "things will go on indefinitely substantially as they are, with industry cashing in and with labor shaking it down time after time as the two of them ride the glory train together?" [6] But the increased power of the American labor movement in the United States today, one may insist, is clearly evident by its political successes at the polls, or in such important triumphs as the defeat of "right to work" laws in the congressional elections of 1958 in the five out of six states where labor had a strong voice. Lynd has an answer to this kind of argument. The depression of 1929 hurt business power and alerted it to the fact that the economic system was ailing. When the government stepped in on business

[6] Lynd, "You Can Do It Better Democratically," op. cit.

through the New Deal, business became thoroughly aroused. So, today, Lynd writes:

Government is the prize, the game is "for keeps," and business is in Washington to stay, with the armed forces as its closest ally. I do not believe that business will allow another New Deal, with its free-wheeling populist sentiment, to happen. As to the new strength of organized labor, this should be borne in mind: next to, and as an adjunct to, control of the government, organized business today is out to destroy organized labor power; and despite the growth of organized labor from less than four million in 1932 to fourteen million to fifteen million today, I believe the estimate may be hazarded that the *relative* position of labor in the power struggle today is weaker than it was twenty years ago. The development of labor-management training centers in our universities is a deceptive device aimed at pulling the teeth of potential leaders. This is industry's answer to the dangerous dilemma pointed out by Gunnar Myrdal in his *American Dilemma.* According to Myrdal, vertical mobility of able men out of the working class is being slowed up in America, but meanwhile increasing popular education is making these men better equipped to exercise leadership. If, he says, they are blocked from moving up in the industrial structure, they will in time turn to leadership of their own class.[7]

I have quoted Lynd's comments here at length to indicate the difficulty, if not the impossibility, of controverting his position, given the terms on which he bases his argument and analysis. Lynd has stated his concept of power in such a way that it is incapable of disproof, and until it is known what it takes to disprove a proposition—any proposition—we cannot be certain that it is correct. In Lynd's view business clearly has the power advantage in the United States. Labor's power is essentially

[7] Lynd, "Who Calls The Tune?" *Journal of Higher Education,* Vol. XIX, No. 4, April 1948, pp. 169–70. In connection with Lynd's continued reference to "business power," it is worth noting that in none of his writings is there any real attention given to power struggles *within* the business community. Big business is treated as a homogeneous entity.

nullified because the business system of power and control remains unchanged. In Lynd's opinion the economic rigidities of a capitalist society are so pervasive that the "power struggle" can be viewed in one of two ways: (1) It can be seen as a series of unimportant contests *within* the capitalist structure which, because that structure is dominated and manipulated by business, are really only meaningless "rear guard" thrusts that do not upset the existing power relationships; or, (2) It can be viewed as pointing to an all-out, full-scale attempt to unhinge the jaws of the capitalist vise, and then proceeding to use power for what Lynd conceives to be democratic goals. The circular aspects of Lynd's position are evident once again: no important changes in the power relationships of society can be made without a deep-seated class conflict that will threaten the entire social system itself; any changes which do take place in a peaceful and democratic manner are, by the terms of his own definition, unimportant.

In abbreviating Lynd's approach to power, I have wanted only to stress that his very tight and inflexible description of what he sees as our power-controlled social structure leaves little room for any consideration of the procedural aspects of American democracy.[8] His theory of power makes it difficult for him to be sympathetic to the ambivalences and contradictions of a political system such as ours which, in his view, is never certain of "where it is going." Translated into Lynd's ideological language, this means that our political system is not pushing ahead hard enough with a program of social change and planning that satisfies his version of a democratic future. A serious limitation of his power approach—an approach that regards power as a positive instrument seeking major alterations in the entire social structure of capitalist America—is that it looks upon politics as

---

[8] I have given fuller treatment to Lynd's position in "The Commitment to Power of Robert S. Lynd," *Ethics,* January 1961.

largely superstructure. For Lynd the real determinants of change
in the United States are "beneath the surface," inexorable forces
(largely economic) at work in our society which, when they are
revealed and unmasked, disclose ultimate political realities. His
concentration on power—"real power"—is intended to put the
lie to the presumably naïve notion implicit in democratic pluralism that economic interests can be restrained by, and even made
responsible to, our political institutions. Furthermore, it is intended to point up sharply the bankruptcy of what has been
called our "nonsense politics," a politics concerned with compromise and consensus. Lynd has little respect for the fumbling
nature of our politics and points out that the best we can normally do is "throw the welfare of all of us under the feet of a
knock-down and drag-out battle royal among power interests."
Indicating again his general impatience with democratic processes, he says, "I submit that that is a disorderly and grossly inef-
ficient way for a democracy to try to secure continuing welfare
here in the middle of the twentieth century." [9]

It is important to emphasize that the rationalism in Lynd's
theory of power places it outside the mainstream of our empiri-
cist politics. Rationalism, as I am using the term here, embodies
two essentials: one is consistency, and the other is proceeding
from assumptions to an end or conclusion through a complete
theory. What is missing in this approach is room for compromise, since compromise comes about as the result of empirical
observations. For example, American political parties prefer to
compromise rather than follow a strict, uncompromising rationalism on a given issue or controversy. The premium in rationalism is its logic and "truth," and because of such an emphasis the
rationalist must insist on absolutes rather than on the processes
of compromise. Thus when Lynd talks about the possible uses of
power, he spells out with a high degree of certitude what must be

[9] Lynd, "You Can Do It Better Democratically," op. cit.

done to move society in the direction he approves. Since it is clear to Lynd what program of positive action is required to attain the truly democratic social order, the only remaining problem is somehow to *get* society there. "How"—and this is an implicit danger in Lynd's analysis—is less important and is given little attention. But it is precisely this question of *how* a democratic society reaches its goals that constitutes the tactics and strategy of politics. Democratic politics involves a commitment not only to desired goals, but to precepts and practices that will relate these goals to democratic methods. The politics of a democracy, in short, involves a relationship of means to ends.

But Lynd is not alone in his minimal concern for the procedural aspects of politics. It has been said of C. Wright Mills that he had no difficulty in knowing what he was against and in deciding what he was for. His difficulty lay in locating the means of radical change. In an important sense this is a discerning statement of the dilemma of many left-wing social critics. Description of the ills of American society was easy for Mills, and his prescription for its cure was not much more difficult. But prescription does not automatically follow from description, and the former is less likely to be reliable if the latter reflects a basic antagonism to the subject at hand. Mills's difficulty in locating the means by which some fundamental changes in American society could be made rests to an important extent on his unequivocal criticism of the United States. He had no respect for American political parties because he regarded them as the products of a bankrupt society. He disliked the American political system in its entirety because he recognized its central function to be that of holding together the very social order he condemned. One of Mills's supporters has put it this way:

Unlike many critics of American society, Mills, in this as in many other respects, went the whole hog. He was not a critic of this or that particular aspect of American society, of this or that evil in

American life—he was against the American condition as a whole, against the way America went about making a living, against the way it treated people, against the way it conducted its political affairs, against the values, rhetoric apart (indeed, rhetoric included), by which it was guided; he was against what America was doing to itself, and what it was doing to the world. The point must not be burked: in relation to American society, Mills was wholly alienated and utterly unsentimental; his commitment, in a negative sense, was total.[1]

For Mills, politics in the United States was essentially an enterprise in perpetuating the trivialities of American life. For him to associate in any way with the main political parties or public leaders was to compromise the utopian elements of his socialism.

In *The Power Elite* Mills was engaged in an all-out attack on American pluralism. Many of the assumptions which are pervasive in the outlook of Lynd are restated in Mills's elitist theory of the nature and structure of power in the United States. In purporting to get at the "real" picture of how important decisions are made, he develops a picture of concentrated power in relatively few hands—in essence, those who belong to the upper class.

The power elite is composed of men whose positions enable them to transcend the ordinary environments of ordinary men and women; they are in positions to make decisions having major consequences . . . for they are in command of the major hierarchies and organizations of modern society. They rule the big corporations. They run the machinery of the state and claim its prerogatives. They direct the military establishment. They occupy the strategic command posts of the social structure, in which are now centered the effective means of the power and the wealth and the celebrity which they enjoy.[2]

[1] Ralph Miliband, "Mills and Politics," in *The New Sociology,* ed. Irving Louis Horowitz (New York: Oxford Univ. Press; 1964), p. 78.
[2] Mills, *The Power Elite,* pp. 3–4. In this same paragraph Mills makes a curious statement about the "power elite." He writes: "Whether they [the "power elite"] do or do not make such decisions is less important

The picture that emerges is of a unified power elite, largely dominated by business groups which, with the possible exception of the military, constitute the major decision-makers in the United States. According to Mills, it is their economic power that dictates political power. One looks in vain for any hint by Mills that this country's political leaders play a significant role in the making of public policy. His power elite does not include even the important leaders in the Senate of the United States. Congress itself is relegated to a secondary level of influence, the "middle level" of the power structure. Mills was interested in one grandiose question: Who runs the United States? Given his own a priori premises, he had a grandiose answer: the power elite.

One of the basic problems of Mills's analysis is that he took for granted precisely what he never bothered to prove. He begins by describing who belongs to the power elite—the Ivy Leaguers, the well-to-do, those with high standing in social and economic circles, and so on. He describes what these people are like, how they go to private schools together, intermarry, and generally remain in close contact with each other. But a little sleight-of-hand has been played here, because in the whole process of describing the power elite Mills presumes that its existence has been demonstrated. In fact, it has not. To assert that there is a power elite and to sketch out the pyramidal structure it is supposed to dominate does not make it true. Mills tells us that these men are the important decision-makers in the country. He does

than the fact that they do occupy such pivotal positions: their failure to act, their failure to make decisions, is itself an act that is often of greater consequence than the decisions they do make." The difficulty here is that there is no way of testing this assertion. If the "power elite" make decisions, this shows they are powerful; if they do not, this also shows they are powerful because they decided not to make decisions. Either way Mill's notion of a "power elite" is established. As was similarly pointed out in our discussion of Lynd, any proposition that is not capable of being refuted is not scientifically acceptable.

not make clear the kinds of decisions they make. He points to an elite that is rich, well-born, prestigious, powerful—but he does not indicate "what the power elite does and precisely how it does it."[3] The rationalism in Lynd's power outlook is no less explicit in Mills's, for he has also developed a consistent theory complete unto itself which he has pushed to a predetermined end. But, as was the case with Lynd, what are missing are any empirical observations. As Robert Dahl put it, it is "remarkable and indeed astounding" that Mills did not "examine an array of specific cases to test his major hypothesis."[4]

These criticisms, however, are ones of approach and methodology. The more pertinent consideration for our purposes here is the extent to which certain elitist power analyses distort the political process in the United States by reducing its procedural elements to categories of economic determinism. Thus Lynd, Mills, and Hunter, having identified in their respective studies those who have money and belong to the upper class, go on to state that these are the people, *because of* their class position, who "run the city" or make up the "power elite." But they have missed an important point which is crucial to an understanding of democratic politics in the United States: namely that the relationship between class position and influence behavior is not automatic or inevitable. Stated another way, they have not grasped the *indeterminate* relationship between class position and class action. It is impossible to predict, for example, how power will be used simply from a knowledge of who has power. It may be known that so-and-so or such-and-such a group has power, but from this information alone we cannot tell how this power will be exercised or how the so-called struggle for power will come out. Why? Because, as Reinhard Bendix has pointed out, we

[3] Alexander Heard, *Annals of the American Academy of Political and Social Science,* May 1957, p. 170.

[4] Robert A. Dahl, "A Critique of the Ruling Elite Model," *American Political Science Review,* June 1958, p. 466.

cannot always determine how, when, or whether political factors —i.e., politics—can or will use these major elements in the struggle for power.

It would be foolish to deny that some people have more power than others. Many of the leading studies of American communities have clearly demonstrated that differences in power or influence are related to social stratification and economic class. (The lawyer or real estate broker who has an office, a secretary, and a telephone is certainly better able to arrange an important meeting or carry on some political transaction than the factory worker who, by comparison, is tied to his eight-hour job.) Differences in personal resources and in public prestige lead to different opportunities to engage in the exercise of power. As Kaufman and Jones have indicated, given any substantial degree of social and economic stratification in a society or community, we would expect to find those exercising power more frequently in the "higher" as opposed to the "lower" strata. There is considerable evidence indicating that more so-called "power behavior" takes place among the people in the upper strata than among members of the lower strata.[5]

It is precisely at this point, however, that one must be cautious. To project by inference a "political class" of decision-makers from a "social class" is simply to assume a continuity and correspondence that may not be warranted by the facts. The left-wing critics of American society who translate directly social class into political class are crossing a bridge of their own making to serve their own purposes. They have overlooked if not disregarded the importance of citizenship and political participation in a democratic society as positive instruments of protest and reform which have been used to undermine the inequality in our class position that at one time represented a *total* inequality. In giving little attention to politics as a process, they have been

[5] Herbert J. Kaufman and Victor Jones, "The Mystery of Power," *Public Administration Review*, Summer 1954, pp. 205–12.

unable to see that the creative development of our democratic political institutions has largely been responsible for making concentrated economic power in the United States more and more the servant of society rather than its unchallenged master. One does not have to claim we have reached the Promised Land to show that arbitrary "class justice" has been severely weakened or that the decision-making process has been opened up by the many political forces in the country which make it possible for people of widely differing backgrounds and resources to engage in effective competition for political power. Those who see political power as emerging directly from the position of the upper class in the social structure of a given community or of the United States as a whole proceed from the dubious assumption that those individuals with the greatest opportunities for using power consistently make use of the opportunity. Yet anyone who either understands or is sympathetic to the ways of politics in this country knows that many businessmen, bankers, and other "elite" members of the community are very often too indifferent to public affairs for the simple reason that they are too busy making money.[6]

It is not by accident that the left-wing social commentators who claim that America is being run by some ruling elite or class have a low regard for democratic politics. As we have had occasion to point out before, they are impatient with its halfway measures and solutions and alienated by the irrationality of its practices and appeals. In its most elemental sense politics has to do with people deciding for themselves what is in their own self-interest and then trying to get as much of what they want as they can. To the idealogue of the left, however, the process is self-defeating because the people, though they may arrive at their decisions democratically, do not make democratic (i.e., the right) decisions.

[6] Ibid.

When Marx talked of the "real" interest of the working class —what he called their true class interest—he meant their collective interest as a revolutionary movement whose purpose and mission, as assigned to them by Marx, was to overthrow the capitalist class. This was Marx's view of what the working class should believe and, ultimately, should do for its own good. But it is important to keep in mind that Marx was expressing his own ideological views and not necessarily those of the working-class members themselves. As history has demonstrated many times, the working classes around the world have rejected Marx's revolutionary advice and, more often than not, have formed trade unions or a labor party, or both, and have pressed their grievances through vigorous political activity within the existing social order. The Marxists would say they have not yet discovered, much less acted upon, their "real" or true class interest. In their own language, they suffer from a "false" class consciousness. In other words, according to the gospel of Karl Marx, they know not what they do—and only the Marxists know what they *should* do. It is one of the classic forms of reductionism whereby self-interest is reduced to class interest.

The lack of enthusiasm for the ways and means of democratic politics in the United States on the part of the left-wing power analysts reflects their own ideological disagreement with the political predispositions and choices of the American people. For this reason it comes as no surprise that they are less than sympathetic to the political system itself. Much of their own view of the power structure in the United States rests on their strong belief that the "wrong" decisions are made because they are made by the "power elite." It is another one of those assertions that is difficult to deal with because, on its own terms, it cannot be tested. It can be neither proved nor disproved. If it is pointed out that on a given decision the so-called "power elite" was defeated and did not get its way, the claim is made that this merely proves that the "big boys" were not interested enough to use their "real" power. The "power elite" exercises its power only when important issues are at stake. Question: What is the test of an important issue? Answer: An important issue is one where the "power elite" uses its real power.

An important insight into the ruling elite writers gradually emerges: power is defined in terms of their own assertions. Power consists of having the most favorable distribution of those values and preferences which are assigned by the ideological view of the ruling elite writers themselves.[7] What they say is that the present system of allocating values favors certain powerful groups. What they propose is a different system which would benefit groups which are presently victimized. Thus they describe how power is distributed in the United States by showing how those values which they do not like are distributed. The extreme example cited by Professor Polsby makes the point: Some ruling elite writers argue that since the "real" and true values of the masses will be brought about by socialism and since the upper class profits most by keeping the present system, preservation of the status quo is on first appearance evidence of the superior power of the business elite.[8]

The point that Polsby is making is that to those who see a power elite ruling in the United States, the index of power is not the outcome of specific cases where important decisions are made. The index of power is the distribution of values. If the social values you personally believe in and support are not distributed throughout American society in the way you would have them distributed, then you maintain that those whose values *are* being

---

[7] I am indebted to Nelson Polsby for the elaboration on this particular point. See his *Community Power and Political Theory* (New Haven: Yale Univ. Press; 1964).

[8] Polsby points out that it is assumed that the interests of the upper class and the working class are irreconcilable—i.e., if the business class is indulged, the working class is deprived, from which it is concluded that it is utopian and incorrect to believe that any event or decision could benefit both classes.

distributed have the power. If it is shown that a situation favorable to the supposed ruling elite is not a result of the activities of that group, the answer, says Polsby, is that if this favorable situation did not exist, the ruling elite would see to it that it did.

The elitist framework of analysis gives men like Lynd, Mills, and Hunter little incentive to be concerned with American political parties. From their point of view the two-party system does not deal with the important issues in the United States. Most of the conflicts which divide the Democrats and Republicans, they would insist, do not involve the real interests of the power elite. If these party issues were really important, the upper-class businessman, who, Mills asserts, "knows the actual power set-up," would not permit them to be handled by the politicians. Just precisely what issues would immediately and directly touch the vital interests of the business class are never made explicitly clear by any of the elitist writers. Methodologically this is important, for as Polsby points out, when such a statement is not forthcoming, this argument can be used after the fact to explain any business defeat as involving an issue too trivial to engage the attention of the elite. But what does become clear is that the ideological beliefs and values of the ruling elite writers not only determine their perception of the power structure in the United States but heavily influence their view of American politics.

As dedicated socialists, both Lynd and Mills have found little to be optimistic about in the refusal of Americans to move toward socialism. The reluctance of the people is explained in one of two familiar ways: (1) The people do not always know what is best for them. As Mills observed in his *White Collar,* "What men are interested in is not always what is to their interest"; [9] (2) if the people do not know what is good for them, their ignorance is the result of clever manipulation by the power elite. Therefore Mills regards American politics as part of the

[9] Mills, *White Collar* (New York: Oxford Univ. Press; 1953), p. xix.

manipulative process by which the ruling elite perpetuates its own power and position. The American party system, Mills explains, "is ideal for a people that is largely contented, which is to say that such a people need not be interested in politics as a struggle for the power to solve *real issues*." [1] What are the "real issues"? They are those which will awaken the working class to its true responsibility. Real issues are class issues. Mills's major complaint about American politics is that it has not confronted what he terms the "conflicts within the social structure."

The U.S. political order has been continuous for more than a century and a half, and for this continuity it has paid the price of many internal compromises and adjustments without explicit reformulations of principle or symbol. . . . For a hundred and sixty years parties have argued over symbols and issues concerned with who got what within the prevailing system. There has been no relatively successful "third party" which questioned that system. . . . [2]

The position of Lynd and Mills is abundantly clear. The political system in the United States has blunted the important issues, which is to say it has produced no significant political movement that has threatened the very fabric of our social order. American politics, in other words, has not bred the substantive policy preferences and values to which the left-wing ruling elite writers themselves are committed. To put it still another way, the American people and their political leaders, deflected by the lure of "practical" politics, have failed to practice the politics of truth.

〰〰〰〰〰 3

It has been a characteristic of left-wing political parties in the United States to include in their fervent appeals for mass support

[1] Ibid., p. 356. (My emphasis.)
[2] Ibid., pp. 344–5.

a demand for radical action—now. In doing so they have never satisfactorily resolved the problem of how to relate their ideological program to the temper and style of American politics. The problem of radical action anywhere has always involved the relationship between doctrine and conduct, between ultimate goals and immediate methods. It is what Irving Howe and Lewis Coser have in mind when they talk of the relationship "between the pressure for ideological exclusivism and the pressure of political activity." [3] The twentieth century alone provides abundant examples of left-wing parties in this country which, in their strict adherence and devotion to their own programmatic ends, have overlooked and frequently scorned the importance of democratic means. Viewing themselves as leading a mass withdrawal from a decadent capitalist America, they have put orthodoxy ahead of opportunism in anticipation of their chosen collective millennium. The merits of their programs are not here in dispute, if for no other reason than that lack of success in achieving their goals is not alone a sufficient test by which to invalidate the justice of their cause. The more serious and pertinent issue is the repeated failure of left-wing parties to make contact with the American political and social environment.

A case in point is the bankruptcy of socialism as a successful political movement in the United States. Whatever personal honor has come to Norman Thomas in recent years as the elder statesman of American Socialists, there can be no mistaking the fact that for decade after decade the Socialist party has been unable to obtain the support of the working class in this country. It has found itself isolated from the American labor movement because its deterministic analysis of social and economic conditions has evoked an appeal that has always been more moral than political and more intellectual than realistic. The socialist

---

[3] Irving Howe and Lewis Coser, *The American Communist Party* (New York: Praeger; 1962), p. 104.

ideology, forecasting the inevitable rise of a socialist society and encouraging its supporters to dedicate themselves to that goal, was basically a European import and inappropriate to the United States. Will Herberg has outlined its three basic postulates: (1) the inevitability of the class struggle and the central role of the proletariat in that struggle; (2) a faith in a future social order and thus a lack of reliance on immediate demands; and (3) a commitment to the "cult of popular absolutism." [4] In refusing to compromise the purity of its doctrine, the Socialist party misperceived the reality of economic conditions in the United States. Its strict ideological outlook left no room for such fundamental considerations as the absence of a feudal past to obstruct the development of American capitalism, the good fortune of a bountiful storehouse of nature's resources, the pace and scope of geographic, demographic, and industrial expansion, and, above all, the fluidity of class lines and the remarkable ease of vertical mobility.[5] Instead the Socialists stressed the theme of class consciousness, never able to understand that such an appeal was too narrow to encompass the common and differential interests that made up the heterogeneous American community. Nor did they learn what the earliest trade union leaders in this country either knew by instinct or learned by hard knocks: that the American workingman was oriented not to a distant millennium but to immediate and concrete economic demands. Even the democratic institutions which the American political experience had developed to curb the excesses of an omnipotent state and to protect individuals and minorities from the intolerance of majorities were regarded by the doctrinaire Socialist leaders, in their inflex-

[4] Will Herberg, "American Marxist Political Theory," in Donald D. Egbert and Stow Persons, *Socialism and American Life* (Princeton, N.J.: Princeton Univ. Press; 1952), Vol. I, pp. 494, 511.

[5] For an elaboration of these points, see Paul M. Sweezey, "The Influence of Marxian Economics," in Egbert and Persons, op. cit., p. 484.

ible belief in "popular absolutism," as merely instruments of capitalist rule and "reactionary restraints on the popular will."[6]

Socialism in the United States first developed nationally with the founding of the Socialist Labor party. It was also perhaps the most dogmatic form of socialism ever to appear in this country. In its relations with labor as well as the whole political process the Socialist Labor party isolated itself by capitulating to the policies of Daniel De Leon. In adopting a sectarian trade union policy it became indifferent to the nonideological but very real bread-and-butter demands of the workers. It not only fostered a deliberate policy of dual unionism in the labor movement, but harbored a deep-seated hostility to any and all alliances between workers and nonworking-class elements. As early as 1873 the Socialist Labor party declared in the most militant terms that it would have nothing to do with any trade unions unless they completely endorsed socialism. Trade unionism, said De Leon, would lead to acceptance of bourgeois values, blur the ultimate goal of socialism, and invite corruption. The political and economic revolutions must occur simultaneously.[7]

In contrast to the SLP, the Knights of Labor were generally pragmatic in their outlook and sought "to secure for the workers the full enjoyment of the wealth they create." Their demands were immediate and short-term, ranging from public lands for settlers to government possession of transportation. By the

[6] Herberg, op. cit., p. 511.

[7] Morris Hillquit, an early twentieth-century American Socialist theoretician, has pointed to still another failure of the Socialist Labor party:

"Its highly centralized form of organization did not suit the political institutions and traditions of the country, and its rigid adherence to all canons of dogmatic socialism and strict enforcement of party discipline were not calculated to attract the masses of newly-converted Socialists."

Hillquit, *History of Socialism in the United States* (New York: Funk and Wagnalls; 1910), p. 359.

1880's, however, the Knights were on the decline, riven by
factional strife between the rank and file and the leadership.
Philip Foner points out that the SLP remained entirely aloof
from the struggle until the Knights were merely an isolated
group, most of their membership having withdrawn. The demand of the Socialist Labor party for ideological purity prevented it from infiltrating the Knights of Labor and making
political overtures to its departing members, with the result that
the SLP was left with an empty organization that could provide
no entry into the working class.[8]

The story of the Socialist Labor party is essentially an account
of its repeated failures to integrate itself into American political
life. Its disdain for alliances and accommodations in seeking
political goals was matched only by a determination to maintain
the purity of its socialist principles. When Henry George ran for
mayor of New York in 1887 as the candidate of the United
Labor party who would bring together all the labor and leftist
groups, the SLP withheld its support because he did not attack
the capitalists and was not a socialist. Convinced of "the futility
of fusion politics," the SLP followed its own class-conscious
approach to American politics. The doctrinaire militancy of its
socialist outlook was the fundamental barrier to its understanding what the American Federation of Labor grasped from the
beginning, that the labor movement in the United States would
win the support of the American worker only if it oriented itself
to his current practical needs and carried on its political activity
as an effective pressure group rather than a radical force for
social revolution. Thus Samuel Gompers set the tone and direction of the AFL when he spoke of Labor's need to work for
limited economic goals rather than devoting its energies to "an
end however beautiful to contemplate . . . the way out of the

[8] Philip Foner, *History of the Labor Movement in the United States*
(New York: International Publishers; 1955), p. 92.

wage system is through higher wages." [9] Gompers had seen that
Marxism would not work in America. The realities of politics in
this country, he felt, would allow labor to try to change the
American economic scene by becoming a part of it rather than
withdrawing from it. The greatest testament to his understanding
of both American labor and the political process in this country
is that the AFL was the "first labor group to accept its role as a
permanent class within American society and to create an institutional framework for its continual existence." [1] Although Gompers did not live to see it, the AFL became the largest labor
organization in America.

The Socialist Labor party, ever faithful to its socialist sectarianism, sponsored the Socialist Trade and Labor Alliance as a
rival union to the AFL. Stressing political activity over economic, this rigorously ideological union required all socialists
and socialist unions to affiliate as a sign of their loyalty, hoping
eventually to attract what they were convinced were the increasingly class-conscious workers. The end result, however, was to
deepen the conservatism of the great majority of American
workers and to isolate once again the militant minority from the
main body of organized labor.

De Leon and others attacked Gompers and the AFL for embodying the basic principle of the pure and simple trade unionist,
whose basic demand was always for "more, more, more, now" in
terms of higher wages and shorter hours. For their part, the
militant socialists were so concerned with the supreme mission of
the trade union that they ignored, for all practical purposes, its
immediate objectives—its daily bread. Gompers was oriented to
the here-and-now, and fashioned a union movement that set its

[9] Quoted in Daniel Bell, *The End of Ideology* (New York: Collier;
1960), p. 283.
[1] Daniel Bell, "The Background and Development of Marxian Socialism in the United States," in Egbert and Persons, op. cit., p. 492.

sights on what was economically necessary and politically possible. De Leon and his supporters, obsessed with the final dawn of the socialist Utopia, narrowed the Socialist Trade and Labor Alliance until it virtually lost all semblance of a labor organization and became "a small sect on the economic field, as impotent as the political sect which ran it, the SLP." [2]

The Social Democratic party, which was shortly to become the Socialist party, was started in 1897 to bring socialism more in line with the realities of American political life. But it soon found itself isolated from the workers and farmers, who were more preoccupied with silver, tariffs, immigration, and imperialism than with such socialist demands as wage guarantees and cooperatives. The 1901 Unity platform of the Socialist party succeeded in isolating it still further, inasmuch as it refused to allow the party to support candidates of any other party or to receive endorsements from any other party. Eugene Debs, as a "good socialist," justified the party's position by announcing that the worker was *outside society* and thus could have nothing to do with the capitalist parties. As Daniel Bell has observed, he could afford his political purity because of his boundless confidence in the future of a socialist America. Not too many years later it was Debs himself who was alienated when an extremist faction that favored revolutionary activity took control of the Industrial Workers of the World. Ending its militant life as a small and isolated anarchist faction of the labor movement, the IWW never learned how to keep the workers permanently organized for "bread and butter" while at the same time firing them up with socialist ideals. Many another radical party has foundered on the same dilemma.

The Socialist party, however, fell on better times in the period of 1902 to 1912. By 1911 it held over one thousand elected offices

[2] Nathan Fine, *Farmer and Labor Parties in the United States* (New York: Rand; 1928), p. 163.

in the country, most of which were municipal, but much of this success was due not to the Socialist party's determinist analysis of conditions in the United States but to the tempering of its socialist line to the point where it now had more of an appeal to the undogmatic middle class.[3] Notable, too, was the spectacular success of the Socialist party in Wisconsin, where in 1910 Victor Berger was elected mayor of Milwaukee. However, Berger was an unusual and independent socialist who not only attacked the SLP for its dogmatism and won substantial political support from the trade unions, but had a shrewd sense of the practical when it came to ward and precinct politics. Nonetheless, the victory of President Wilson in 1912 reaffirmed the popular acceptance of the major two-party system in this country.

Although Debs won more than nine hundred thousand votes for president, the Socialist party suffered a severe loss of membership after the election as party control went to the more revolutionary left. Debs expressed their feeling: "We can have a vote-getting machine and go to perdition with it; or we can have the cooperative commonwealth and working class government. But we cannot have both."[4] It was this kind of doctrinaire socialism that broke the back of the Socialist party in the First World War. While most of the country rallied behind President Wilson in 1917, the Socialists, true to their economic analysis of war as an imperialist battle between crumbling capitalist nations, opposed American participation in the war in the hope that labor would see their "real interests" and go along with them. By 1921 the Socialist party was a mere shell of its former self.

When Norman Thomas took over as leader of the Socialists, he made a deliberate effort to orient the party to the American temperament. When the policy of moderation failed in the wake

[3] Bell, "The Background . . . ," op. cit., pp. 283–4.
[4] Quoted in William B. Hessaltine, *The Rise and Fall of Third Parties* (Washington, D.C.: Public Affairs Press; 1948), p. 42.

of President Roosevelt's great popular appeal, Thomas joined the party militants who urged revolutionary action, violence, and a workers' dictatorship. They were convinced capitalism was doomed and that victory was assured. The consequence was an even more pronounced decline in electoral support in 1934 and 1936. Once again their determinist doctrine and prescription blinded the Socialists to political reality. They preferred instead their own dialectical version of the bright socialist future they alone saw ahead. All the workers need, they said, are "a few more defeats," and they will rally to the Socialist banner. While Socialists waited, American labor closed ranks behind the New Deal.

It was not until the 1950's that the Socialist party began to show some understanding of the American political process. In a pamphlet entitled *Democratic Socialism*,[5] Thomas declared that he was not a Marxist and that politics in the United States could not be correctly diagnosed in Marxist terms. Instead of a deep-seated class conflict in this country, he pointed out, a large middle class had arisen for reasons as closely related to psychology as to productive capacity. Rather than classes alone, he said, there are many kinds of groups in America, and these are not merely economically determined but are also affected by nationalism, religion, race, and the like. The triumph of socialism in America will depend on the ability of the socialist to convince the people that "socialism affords a better way of life than any other form of economic or political organization"—and they must continue to use the "democratic processes of government." Finally, said Thomas, because the two-party system is so deeply rooted in America, the Socialists cannot become a mass party, but must make every effort to capture the Democratic party to advance their program.[6]

One of the ironies of American socialism is that the Socialist

[5] Norman Thomas, *Democratic Socialism* (New York: League For International Democracy; 1953).

[6] Ibid., pp. 6, 7, 30, 37.

party discovered America about twenty years too late. For most of its life it has failed to understand that politics in the United States is more a contest of individuals running for public office than a struggle of masses over principles. It has been politically impotent because its imperturbable left-wing assumptions about capitalist control and power have served only to distort the pluralist nature of American politics.

For the Communist party, however, the discovery of America has still to be made. Created out of the ashes of the Russian Revolution in 1917, the American Communist party has spent a good part of its life in slavish devotion to the Bolshevik model of social upheaval. Lenin's conspiratorial success in overthrowing the Kerensky government in Russia seemed to prove to the early American Communists that a handful of determined revolutionists could achieve power in the United States in much the same way. The only requirement was that they maintain "revolutionary zeal and purity of doctrine." [7] Thus the party immediately endorsed the concept of "mass action," whereby "every means, economic and political, should aim at the revolutionary seizure of power." In the face of the imminent, inevitable revolution the Communists had no taste for the less dramatic but more democratic methods of peaceful electoral activity and, paradoxically, no time to waste on the more earthly demands of the masses for higher wages and decent working conditions.

The strategy and tactics of the American Communist party were never devised to meet American conditions, but rather as a set of responses to Comintern demands and as an appendage to Communist revolutionary power. In persistently advocating the inevitability and necessity of violent revolution and preparing the workers for armed insurrection as the only means of overthrowing the capitalist state, the Communists succeeded only in winning the enmity of the American people. Only on the orders

[7] Theodore Draper, *The Roots of American Communism* (New York: Viking; 1957), p. 102.

of the Comintern did the American Communists attempt to adapt their program to American conditions. But their political association with various indigenous progressive movements such as the Farmer-Labor party or the La Follette Progressives never endured because inevitably they placed a higher premium on preserving their ideological doctrine and militancy than on coming to realistic terms with the traditions of American politics. What was true of the left-wing Socialists was true of the Communists, only more so. Bound to their own rigid preconceptions, they were unable to gauge either the practicalities or possibilities of a given political situation. They operated on the assumptions they wanted to believe rather than those required by what actually was happening in the country. They could not understand the importance or relevance of democratic parliamentary procedures that looked to the long-run accommodation of competing political interests and demands.[8] Their revolutionary eye was fixed on a doctrinaire program that would lead first to political irredentism and, ultimately, social chaos.

During the so-called "Third Period" of Communism (1928-1935) the Communist ideology isolated the party even further from its potential support. The Soviet Comintern demanded dual unionism as a labor policy, and to this end the Communists dutifully set up dual unions in mining, textiles, and the needle trades, with the result that they were prevented from gaining any real strength among mass-production workers. In strike situations, such as in Gastonia, North Carolina, in 1929, the Communists "thought first of the political uses to which they could put the strike, and second of the interests of the strikers themselves . . . [they were] indifferent to the dignity and needs of the human beings whom they involved and then manipulated in the interests of ideology."[9] The early period of the depression

[8] Howe and Coser, op. cit., p. 142.
[9] Ibid., p. 259.

was a time of extreme dogmatism for the Communist party. They could see only the final and irreversible conflict on its way. They called for "revolutionary offenses" and expected the workers to "tense for the revolution." But the workers, alienated and demoralized, turned a deaf ear.

When the Comintern changed its line and switched to the Popular Front in 1935, the American Communist party reached the height of its influence. By playing down its ideology, by working in the CIO and various "front organizations," and by giving "silent approval" to President Roosevelt in 1936, the party was able to play on the emotions of antifascism and thereby take advantage of the popular mood. An attempt was made to change the party image, to make it American:

Until we Americans are ready to go forward to socialism, the first stage of communism . . . it will be necessary to adopt emergency measures to keep our people from social poisoning and degeneration. . . . We have won the respect of our enemies and the sympathy of millions of friends. . . . Our party has been able to become so thoroughly American precisely because it has nurtured itself upon the teachings of the greatest thinkers of the world, Marx, Engels, Lenin and Stalin. . . . Communism is the Americanism of the Twentieth Century.[1]

Through the American League Against War and Fascism, the National Negro Congress, the American Student Union, the American Youth Congress, and numerous other fronts, the Communists were able to use many well-meaning citizens as a platform to give their ideas an audience, taking advantage of the yearning "felt by so many middle-class and semi-intellectual Americans to take their stand on the right side." [2] Infiltration into government agencies, particularly the Treasury and Agricul-

---

[1] Earl Browder, *The People's Front* (New York: International Publishers; 1938), p. 86.
[2] Howe and Coser, op. cit., p. 373.

ture Departments and the National Labor Relations Board, was also accomplished during this period.[3]

By 1939, the Communist party had achieved some influence in the CIO, among the youth and intellectuals, and in a few major cities across the country. The Hitler-Stalin pact nullified most of its success, but when Germany invaded Russia in 1941, the American Communists again returned to favor. The Second World War, which brought the United States and the Soviet Union together as allies against the common enemy, afforded the American Communist party its greatest opportunity to leap into American life. Earl Browder now sought to integrate the party into American politics as thoroughly as possible. Acknowledging the compromise basis of American politics, the party became a "political association" and sought to work through the major parties. "In the United States," said Browder, leader of the American Communist party, "national unity can be achieved only through compromise between the conflicting interests, demands and aspirations of various class groupings."[4]

After the war, however, Moscow dictated an abrupt change in policy for the American Communist party. In keeping with Stalin's all-out attack on the capitalist societies everywhere, Browder was replaced by William Foster, and once again the party, forced into taking extremist positions, became an isolated, doctrinaire movement. The CIO leadership eliminated all high-level traces of Communist influence, and by the mid-1950's the party had only a marginal status in the unions and, in terms of popular acceptance, in the country at large.

Thus the American Communist party, too, foundered on the rocks of ideological dogmatism. There have been other barriers in its path—an electoral system which has worked against minor or third parties, the immense wealth of the United States and its expanding economy, a creed of classlessness which, if not an

[3] Bell, "The Background . . . ," op. cit., p. 357.
[4] Quoted in Howe and Coser, op. cit., p. 426.

altogether objective sociological fact, has nonetheless robbed the Communists' call for revolution of any serious or widespread appeal—and nothing that has been said here is intended to minimize their importance. However, the failure of communism in the United States cannot be explained by the structural difficulties in the American political system. The Communist party failed because its Marxist-Leninist orthodoxy repelled the very masses it was seeking to attract. But even more fundamental than this, the separation in communism of ends and means reflects the tendency to suppose that "the means stand in no need of short-run justification if it is once agreed that they serve morally valid ends of revolutionary action." [5] The role of the Communists was to spearhead the polarization of American society into two antagonistic classes and preach revolution to the larger of the two, the proletariat. Thus, except for periods of time when it served other Stalinist purposes, it was not necessary for the party to adapt itself to the accepted channels of political activity in the United States in order to achieve its goals. It could stand outside and apart, ideologically pure and awaiting only the alienation of the working class. This tactic demanded everything from dual unionism to third parties, on the assumption that the dissatisfied workers throughout the country would rally around in increasingly militant numbers. As it turned out, however, the workers directed their efforts at achieving economic gains within the American political and social system, through "pure and simple" unionism and by political action as a vital and dynamic pressure group. To the repeated dismay and disappointment of the Communist leadership, they preferred to redress their legitimate grievances through the give and take of our pragmatic politics rather than by a series of wars to the death.

I have talked about the importance of ideology and its relationship to the tactics of the American left wing. Specifically, I

[5] Ibid., p. 485.

have wanted to show that the style of ideological thought that has motivated and pervaded the militant leadership of the Socialist and Communist movements in the United States has been so ambitious and sweeping in its demands that all democratic political activity is necessarily sacrificed for these "higher ideals." Dedicated to a fixed set of beliefs—they would call them "fundamentals" about which there can be no disagreement—the idealogues of the left have fastened their eyes on a single future harmony which is both noble and determined. As the capitalists aggressively take more and more control of society, the masses, developing a true class consciousness and revolutionary feeling, will overthrow the tyranny of the minority and thereby bring both social control and justice to the majority. These are the inexorable laws of capitalist development, indeed of all history. In holding out for nothing less than the precise goals of their own ideology, they have mounted a total onslaught on democratic politics. The certitude of an ideology stands in sharp contrast to the ambiguities of democratic politics. There can be no freedom when everything is inevitable and certain. A basic proposition of this book is that politics, for all of its uncertainty and contradictions, is an activity which provides the governance of free societies and cannot be reduced to a system of beliefs and goals. Politics is not a "grasping for the idea" any more than it is a "freezing of tradition." It is a continuous activity, a process— "lively, adaptive, flexible and conciliatory." [6] Politics is politics, and it is in this sense that I have argued here that the ideology of the American left wing has been militantly out of step with our democratic political cadence.

Max Weber, in his essay on the concept of politics, laid particular stress on what he called "two fundamentally differing and irreconcilably opposed maxims": conduct that is oriented

[6] Bernard Crick, *In Defense of Politics* (Chicago: Univ. of Chicago Press; 1962), p. 50.

either to an "ethic or ultimate ends" or to an "ethic of responsibility." [7] The conduct that follows an ethic of ultimate ends—that is, as Weber pointed out, in religious terms "The Christian does rightly and leaves the results with the Lord"—is in complete opposition to conduct that follows the maxim of an ethic of responsibility, where one has to give an account of the foreseeable results of one's action. The former is characterized by a dedication to absolute ends, as in the case of an idealogue or ideology; the latter, in contrast, has as one of its guiding principles the acceptance of limits. Weber offers an example:

You may demonstrate to a convinced syndicalist, believing in an ethic of ultimate ends, that his action will result in increasing the opportunities of reaction, in increasing the oppression of his class, and obstructing its assent—and you will not make the slightest impression on him. If an action of good intent leads to bad results, then, in the actor's eyes, not he but the world, or the stupidity of other men, or God's will who made them thus, is responsible for the evil.

But a man who believes in an ethic of responsibility

takes account of precisely the average deficiencies of people: as Fichte has correctly said, he does not even have the right to presuppose their goodness and perfection. He does not feel in a position to burden others with the results of his own actions so far as he was able to foresee them; he will say: these results are ascribed to my action.[8]

The only "responsibility" the believer in an ethic of ultimate ends feels is in seeing to it that "the flame of pure intentions is not quenched"—for example, the flame of Communist protest against the injustice and moral decay of the capitalist social

[7] Max Weber, "Politics As A Vocation," in *From Max Weber: Essays in Sociology,* ed. H. H. Gerth and C. Wright Mills (London: Routledge & Kegan Paul; 1961), p. 120.

[8] Ibid., p. 121.

order. As Weber concluded, "to rekindle the flame ever anew is
the purpose of his quite irrational deeds, judged in view of their
possible success. They are acts that can and shall have only
exemplary value." [9]

Weber's distinction between the "ethics of responsibility" and
the "ethics of conscience" is particularly relevant to all that has
been stressed here in connection with the ideological commitment and conduct of the Socialist and Communist parties in the
United States. As Daniel Bell has pointed out, only the "ethics of
responsibility" is applicable to politics. Politics is concerned with
listening to the many diverse and opposing groups in society,
conciliating them as far as possible, and giving them the freedom
and security to express their own interests so that they can each
contribute to the machinery of democratic decision-making. This
is the art and business of political rule, and one of its indispensable characteristics is that it does not proceed from a set of rigid
principles leading only to absolute goals. A major problem of the
Socialist and Communist parties in the United States was that
they could never adapt themselves to the "rules of the American
political game." They preferred to be "right" rather than popular, doctrinaire instead of flexible, intransigent rather than malleable. Tied to values and beliefs derived from a strict ideology,
the left-wing leaders were never able to free themselves so that
they could formulate political tactics that were better suited to
American conditions. Their ideological commitment, in short,
served to distort their perception of political reality in the United
States.

The role of the radical is not an enviable one. Like all
extremists who are at war with the major "rules" or premises of
the society in which they find themselves, they must make a
choice: they must decide whether they wish to adhere to the kind
of dogma and absolutes developed by small sects, parties, or

[9] Max Weber, loc. cit.

movements, or compromise.[1] To compromise is to recognize the need and accept the responsibility for developing a program and tactics which are culturally acceptable to at least half the population. This is the choice of democratic politics, and it will always be rejected by those who do not accept the basic precepts of the society within which they operate and make no attempt to work within the bounds of the existing social and political processes.[2]

[1] Seymour Martin Lipset has developed this argument in his *Agrarian Socialism* (Berkeley: Univ. of California Press; 1950).

[2] Daniel Bell has suggested an adaptation from Lutheran theological terminology that involves a threefold classification of political parties according to whether they are (a) movements which are in the world and of the world, i.e., accepting and working within the sociological, political, and economic "givens" of a nation; (b) movements which are in the world but not of the world, such as socialist political parties; and (c) movements completely outside the world and not of the world, e.g., communist parties.

In the writing of this chapter I owe a particular debt to Daniel Bell, whose articles and books have profited me in many ways.

CHAPTER FOUR

Politics and Religion:
The Quaker Commitment to
Eternal Truth

> *He who seeks the salvation of souls, his own as well as others, should not seek it along the avenue of politics.*
>
> MAX WEBER

1

The tension between church and state is as old as history itself. In the second half of the twentieth century men still debate, although perhaps in different terms, the degree to which their political loyalty should or should not be determined in the light of a higher duty to God. The early Christians, who believed that their own "outpost of heaven" was a society superior to any political order, are represented today by many voices in many lands also harboring strong hostilities to political life and political man.

Some contemporary spokesmen regard the political order as inferior to the "promised city" and necessarily condemned to rely on coercion rather than love. Their anti-politicism takes a variety of forms, but it rests on the fundamental belief that politics is evil in origin and purpose and will be dispensed with only at the end of history with the advent of the kingdom of God. From this belief, as Franz Neumann has observed, come two different and yet related attitudes: that of total conformism to political power on the one hand, and, on the other, that of total opposition. If politics is evil, withdrawal is mandatory. Both the forms of government and the objectives of political power become irrelevant. Salvation can be attained through faith, and the earthly life should be a mere preparation for it. But by the same token, as Professor Neumann points out, "the destruction of politics and the establishment of a Kingdom of God may equally be supported by the same premise. The Anabaptist movement was perhaps the most striking manifestation of the total rejection of society."[1] The Marxist rejection of capitalist society is another case in point, as we have already noted.

For nearly thirty centuries there has been general agreement about the ideal goal of human effort. In the Golden Age, to which all of the prophets (from Isaiah to Karl Marx) look forward, there will be liberty, peace, justice, and brotherly love. But unanimity gives way to confusion on which roads lead to that goal. Mahatma Gandhi, moved by the belief that religion must permeate all human activities to improve and ennoble them, was both a religious activist and an active religious politician.

To see the universal all pervading Spirit of Truth face to face one must be able to love the meanest creature as oneself. And a man who aspires after that cannot afford to keep out of any field of life. That is why my devotion to truth has drawn me into the field of politics; and I can say without the slightest hesitation and yet in all humility that those who say that religion has nothing to do with politics do not know what religion is.[2]

Sharing many of the same basic values of Gandhi, Dr. Henry T. Hodgkin, one of the founders of the Fellowship of Reconcil-

[1] Franz Neumann, "Approaches to the Study of Political Power," *Political Science Quarterly*, June 1950, p. 165.
[2] Mahatma Gandhi, *His Own Story*, ed. C. F. Andrews (London: Allen & Unwin). Quoted in F. W. Sollmann, *Religion and Politics*, Pendle Hill Pamphlet No. 14, Pendle Hill, Wallingford, Penn. (n.d.)

iation, nevertheless expresses his own conviction about religion and politics in a different way:

> With my conception of the Christian life I do not see that it would be possible for me to enter the world of politics as it is at present run. For example anyone who wants to make his influence felt must be allied to a party and accept many compromises. He must use methods current in politics but, to say the least, highly distasteful to a moral man. If he reaches office he becomes a partner in the machinery and so forth . . . a comedown from the highest level of Christian living.[3]

The Watchtower Society, in answering its own question, "Who Will Win the Struggle for World Domination?", provides yet another approach to religion and politics.

> Neither the East nor the West can create an adequate government. All men, regardless of political ideology, are born in sin. Although they now manufacture globe-circling satellites, they cannot produce a satisfactory government. Even their rockets repeatedly fail. "Who can produce someone clean out of someone unclean? There is not one." (Job 14:4) For adequate government man must look to God, of whom it is said: "There are new heavens and a new earth that we are awaiting according to his promise." (2 Pet. 3:13) The one he has enthroned as King is his loyal, integrity-keeping Son Christ Jesus. The Bible shows that Christ now rules as King in the heavens and soon will smash all the unrighteous oppressors of mankind and cause men on earth who exercise faith to enjoy to the full the blessings of his Kingdom rule.[4]

For the Quakers, to whom we will devote our attention in this chapter, their special dilemma is revealed in their own approach to the question of political obligation. Guided by a belief in the "spark of Divinity" within each private believer, the Quaker is

[3] Quoted in Sollmann, op. cit., pp. 5–6.
[4] "Who Will Win the Struggle for World Domination?" Leaflet of the Watchtower Society, 117 Adams St., Brooklyn 1, New York. (n.d.)

often morally conflicted when faced with situations which call for the use of political techniques of ruling, such as compromise, conciliation, and, most particularly, the application of power and force. His own preference is that of committing unmistakably his trust for moral victories to the armor of light and the sword of the spirit, to what Rufus Jones has called "the certainty of God's light and love in the individual's soul." In short, the Quaker response to politics is likely to be a reaffirmation of his own despair at the distance between the kingdom of God and the society of political man.

Few sensitive people can dispute the quiet courage and monumental patience of the Quakers, qualities all the more to be admired when it is remembered that theirs is a faith that has embraced men of widely different political persuasions, from George Fox to Whittaker Chambers, from William Penn to Richard Nixon. The central purpose here is to examine the nature of the Quaker commitment in order to bring to light some of the fundamental differences between politics and religion. There is no thought of questioning the sincerity of the Quakers' beliefs or doubting the depth of their convictions. Our basic interest and concern can be put in the form of a proposition: that "knowing" what the kingdom of heaven is like, and by working through channels of their own to bring parts of it to earth, the Quakers exhibit a philosophy of action which, were it to encompass the majority of the electorate, would have serious effects upon democratic political procedures.

〽〽〽〽〽〽 2

It is not a postulate within their philosophy, nor has it always been a fact, that the Quakers are committed to political action. In England and the United States they have gone through long periods of "quietism." That their principles, remaining relatively consistent throughout their history, have nonetheless brought them to certain forms of political action as a doctrine held by a majority of the members of the faith is a matter of interest in itself. A study of the range of conflicting attitudes which the Quakers bring to politics will help reveal not only their own long-standing dilemma over the role to be played in political affairs but some of the important consequences for a democratic state which are likely to result when politics is subordinated to religion.

It is necessary at the outset to understand the main principles of Quakerism.[5] First, and unquestionably of major importance, the Friend "declares that the Presence of God is felt in the apex of the human soul, and that man can therefore know or heed God directly, without any intermediary in the form of Church, priest, sacrament, or sacred book. God is for man both immanent and transcendent; immanent because He is not mechanically operating on man from without but sharing in his life; transcendent, for the Divine Life extends infinitely beyond or above all human life."[6] This so-called doctrine of "Inner Light," while not limited to Quakerism or even to Christianity, underpins a secondary doctrine which is peculiarly associated with the Society of Friends. This secondary doctrine is the application of the primary principle to worship and the conduct of Quaker business. In the meetings for worship and business "the individual

[5] I wish to express my thanks to a former student of mine, Betty Hershberger Zisk. Her B.A. thesis at Swarthmore College, in which she compared the Quaker and Mennonite views toward civil government, was extremely valuable in the writing of this section.

This fervent, semimystical religious group of the seventeenth century called themselves "Friends in the Truth" and their proper name today is The Society of Friends. But in 1650 an unfriendly judge scorned one of them as a "quaker" because his religion made him quiver and tremble. The name Quaker stuck.

[6] Howard H. Brinton, "The Nature of Quakerism" (Pendle Hill Pamphlet No. 47; 1949), p. 3.

experience of God's light and leading becomes a group experience by which the Divine Presence in the midst operates as a uniting or coordinating power." [7]

In the nonpastoral branches of the Society of Friends the meeting for worship is spoken of as a "silent meeting." It is a period of group meditation and waiting for the Presence of God to make itself felt and to speak through the individual. The silence is broken when a worshipper feels called upon to impart a message which he has received through this mystical mediation to the entire group. Some other worshipper may later continue the thought, thus making the period a profitable and productive one for all. It is in no sense a debate or discussion, but rather a statement followed by meditation and seeking for further insight.

The third group of doctrines of the Friends is the social message. Perhaps the most important of these is the belief in the value of the individual, implied in the doctrine of Inner Light and giving rise to two Friends' testimonies, among others: the peace testimony, which is the refusal to bear arms against one's fellow man, and the belief in the fundamental equality of all races and classes of man. Another social doctrine arising from this belief in the individual is the refusal to take an oath, on the ground that an individual's word should be taken as the truth. Another social doctrine of the Friends is that of the necessity for simplicity—in speech, dress, action, worship, in all of life. Thus one finds the "plain" garb, the "thee and thou," the austere meeting house, and the plain food and simple pleasures of the average Quaker family. Finally, there is the emphasis on the community approach—the interdependence of men and women and the need for harmony in all relationships. It is a spirit of love and brotherhood, with an emphasis on corporate action based in part on a theory of the community as an organic whole —as Brinton puts it, "a unified, closely integrated group of

[7] Ibid., p. 4.

persons which is not just a collection of separate individuals, but a living whole which is more than the sum of its parts." [8]

Individual conscience is the sole basis of all Quaker authority. Unlike the Mennonites, for whom nothing but the Bible can be relied upon as authority, the Quaker gives primary obedience to Divine Light. Walter Woodward, a modern Quaker writer, has expressed the attitude this way:

> When an issue of obedience to authority is raised, for the Friend it is not a choice to be made between one external authority, the State, and another external authority, the Church, or even the Book. His choice is between an outer, a human authority, and an inner and spiritual one. Given the Divine Light, as it illuminates life in general, and the question at issue in particular, he must give obedience to it above all else. [9]

While it may be improbable that a Quaker conscience would rule contrary to the teachings of the Bible, it is clear that the individual conscience is the supreme authority.

The Quaker method of conducting business meetings is thoroughly consistent with their high valuation of the individual. Furthermore, it provides some insight into the Quaker conception of the making of decisions. In addition to being a set of rules and procedures which are followed in conducting their own

---

[8] Ibid., p. 8.

[9] Walter Woodward, "The Individual and the State," in *Beyond Dilemmas*, ed. S. B. Laughlin (New York: Lippincott; 1937). It is worth noting that to the Mennonite theologian pacifism without the strong biblical foundation is regarded as weak and watered down, a belief which will flourish in peacetime but will crumble when it meets strong opposition. A man who believes he *must* obey God's commands, at all costs—called "biblical nonresistance" by the Mennonites—will be more steadfast than a man ruled by reason alone. When the early Mennonite occasionally engaged in debates and discussions (on doctrinal matters) with other churches, they refused to accept any argument, however logical it might be, which lacked the scriptural foundation. While this difference in basic outlook between the Mennonites and the Quakers is not our major concern here, it should be pointed out that it is clearly reflected in their respective attitudes toward civil government.

meetings, they also stand as the Quaker ideal of a governing process. Operating in small face-to-face groups wherever possible, the members constitute a closely knit community. The Quaker ethic has all but abolished self-interest, each member identifying instead with the larger group interest. No vote is ever taken—there are never any majorities or recalcitrant minorities. The chairman, in presiding over a meeting, attempts to ascertain the sense of the meeting. After a discussion period he will state what he feels that sense to be. If there is serious disagreement the discussion may be continued. The individuals present may search their own consciences to see whether they have really been adhering to that viewpoint which is best for all. It is expected that Quakers will not attend meetings with their minds already made up. They go to learn, "expecting the right solution to crystallize from the experience of all." If no agreement can be reached, the issue is shelved until a later meeting and then another attempt at coming to complete agreement is made.

Stuart Chase tells of an incident at a meeting that describes the Quaker method in action.

The Clerk proceeds to ask a member to give his ideas on the closed shop in union contracts. The others listen carefully; there is no discussion. Another member describes relief work in Greece, again without action by the group. These are apparently reports for information only. The agenda completed, the Clerk bows his head for a final period of silence, and the meeting is adjourned.

After the period of silence and adjournment, the Clerk told me that a really stirring issue divided the group, though no visitor could have guessed it. The issue was whether or not to build a meeting house. "We have had to ask for periods of silence when that comes up," he said. "Feelings are strong; but it will be settled right." "Unanimously?" I asked.

"Unanimously," he replied with utmost confidence.[1]

[1] Stuart Chase, "Roads to Agreement," quoted in *The Quaker Reader,* ed. Jessamyn West (New York: Viking Press; 1962), pp. 465–6.

To the Friend the making of decisions is an unhurried process. Yet there is surprising unanimity in reaching them, and feelings, in general, are spared. The mood and tempo of the Quaker meetings are in marked contrast to the charged political atmosphere of, say, a Senate committee investigating corruption in labor unions. This is to be expected, however, for the very cultural factors that shape the Friends' life stand in opposition to those that mold our complex, heterogeneous society.[2] The need for expediency in domestic as well as foreign policy matters, the continuous balancing of diverse forces which reflects both the conflictual and consensual elements in our country, the agreement on procedural but not substantive ingredients of policy— all these and more combine to make the method of Quaker decision-making an impractical instrument and guide in the rough and tumble of the political arena.

It is important to point out that the Quaker manner of conducting meetings follows in a tradition of political theory represented by Rousseau and the later Idealists. Rousseau and other organic thinkers who wished to see the individual "integrated" or molded into society believed in the existence of a general will made up of the "real wills" of the constituent members. For some who have turned this theory to their own purposes, an external authority, such as the state or the church, has been relied upon to discover this general will. For the Quakers, however, each individual must attempt to discover it for himself—through reason, insight, and the aid of the spirit. Only when there is general agreement—when the general will has been ascertained by all— will the decisions be regarded as having been reached properly and fairly.

[2] One study, Beatrice and Robert Pollard's *Democracy and the Quaker Method,* indicates that executive committees, boards of directors, and meetings under twenty persons with fairly constant membership are the most suitable gatherings for application of the Quaker method.

The principal concern of the Quakers has always been the constant danger of compromising entanglements. Many Friends have steadfastly insisted that government is a necessary evil, something to be endured simply because it cannot be avoided, but not to be embraced. The 1758 Quaker Yearly Meeting in Philadelphia told its adherents: ". . . beware of accepting of, or continuing in, the exercise of any office or station in civil society or government [that requires behavior in conflict with Quaker principles]." [3] But others have tried to refute this view by citing statements and actions of other Friends—Burroughs, Barclay, and Penn, to mention but a few. The impression one gets is that the Friends revere and *want* good government, but it is not clear whether it is felt they should seek political office and power themselves or leave this task to others. A statement by William Penn is cited with great approval: "Governments, like clocks, go from the motion men give them; and as governments are made and moved by men, so by them they are ruined too. Wherefore governments rather depend upon men, than men upon governments. Let men be good and the government cannot be bad; if it be ill, they will cure it." [4]

Yet the quietest attitude of aloofness and avoidance of political affairs is never without its outspoken adherents. "No art or contrivance of man or policy or wisdom of the creature will ever insure to us a divine blessing, or cause Zion to prosper or her borders enlarge; nothing short of individual and perfect obedience to the will of God, *inwardly revealed* and made manifest in man, can ever perform this, so desirable, an object." [5] Friends should wait for the spirit of God to come to them, meanwhile

[3] Frederick B. Tolles, *Quakers and the Atlantic Culture* (New York: Macmillan; 1960), p. 51.

[4] William Penn, *Frame of Government For Pennsylvania* (1682). From the Preface.

[5] *The Friend* (Philadelphia Orthodox), "Renunciation of the World," Nov. 18, 1854.

renouncing the world in pursuing individual salvation. The moral and political degeneration of the country is deplored by those who feel there is little to be gained from "mere political movements." The only means of reclamation is the upright, witnessing life.

The controversy over civic responsibility and the danger of compromising basic Quaker principles is an unending one. If one Friend urges a more active approach to civic affairs, another is almost certain to sound the grim note about compromise. Douglas Steere, in an editorial in *The Friends' Intelligencer,* praised the work of the American Friends Service Committee and laid particular stress on the fact that its activities in world affairs enabled the Friends to share civic responsibility without being entrapped in the snare of actual political life. In making his point about the corroding effects of political compromise, he said, "When you are 'one of the team,' when you 'belong,' it is easy to be so immersed in your valuable work, that a naval appropriations bill . . . or diplomatic blockage of a disarmaments conference may be overlooked." [6] James D. Hull, in an article on "Duties of Citizenship," also discussed the danger of compromise for the Friend in public life, but argued that "Friends should view the State as a potential source of action and not shy away from taking part in that activity." [7] The Discipline of 1911 of the London Yearly Meeting had made the same point with equal force:

The free institutions under which we live give many of our members a direct share in the responsibilities of government, and in forming the healthy public opinion that will lead to purity of administration and righteousness of policy. This responsibility belongs to them by virtue of their citizenship, and our members can no more rightly remain indifferent to it, than to the duties which they owe to their

---

[6] *The Friends' Intelligencer,* January 6, 1934, p. 6.
[7] Ibid., June 13, 1936, p. 389.

parents and near relatives. . . . In view of the opportunities for public service opened to Friends during the last half century, we desire to press upon them the duty of qualifying themselves, so that they may be "prepared unto every good work." [8]

The 1927 Philadelphia Yearly Meeting was even more definitive: ". . . the Kingdom of God on earth is advanced by those who devote themselves with unselfish public spirit to the building of a high national character, and to the shaping of a righteous policy of government both at home and abroad . . . be active in performance of all the duties of good citizenship." [9]

Yet, in 1937, in an article entitled "Is Compromise Of Quaker Pacifism 'Practical Politics'?" William I. Hull concluded that rather than risk compromise at all, it would be wiser to avoid politics altogether.[1] For other Friends the question is how *good* a compromise is being made between "idealism, realism, and capacity for sacrifice." The American Friends Service Committee has provided a concise statement of what may fairly be called the current popular view:

There are two views we may take of government. One that it is "our enemy," that it is organized for violence and that the pacifist cannot cooperate with it. The other view holds that the pacifist is not against government as such but against certain of its practices. In organizing conduct for an increasing area of life, government by the majority usually means a lag in moral conscience and, therefore, the minority has a responsibility for influencing government to take more advanced steps. The latter view would encourage the pacifist to take an active part in political action and refuse cooperation only when conscience or judgment forbade.[2]

Each Friend, receiving divine dictates through prayer and quest, must arrive at his own personal answer. Whatever that answer

[8] Quoted in Tolles, op. cit., p. 47.
[9] Ibid., p. 51.
[1] *The Friends' Intelligencer,* January 2, 1937.
[2] American Friends Service Committee, *Pacifist Living Today and Tomorrow* (Wallingford, Penn.; 1941), p. 30.

may be, the Quaker attitude toward government stems from the indisputable proposition that "ultimate values are incarnated in the individual human being, not in any institution or system." [3]

It is still a debatable point whether religion and politics are completely separable to the Quakers. For the Friend who joins them together he is constantly forced to measure the practices of politics against what Reinhold Niebuhr has called the "ethical utopianism" of the Quaker religion. "Be careful not to become entangled with the cares of this world," admonishes the *Friends Book of Discipline*, which is to say that the corrupting effects of political life will demean the will of God, "inwardly revealed." Through individual conscience the Friend knows and possesses the truth. If anything conflicts with his conscience, it is con- science alone to which he must adhere. Given this commitment it is not difficult to understand why there is no real practical conception in Quaker theology of a need for compromise in dealing with political matters. When one has found the truth, as in the Kingdom of Heaven, he does not compromise it. The truth is not negotiable. It is given. Man either lives by truth or untruth.

Yet in another sense politics and religion are not separable because to many Friends political matters are treated essentially as religious matters. Gandhi once remarked that the "best politics is right action." The Quakers have found their answer to the meaning of right action, and their "politics" is a direct function of this answer. The *Friends Book of Discipline*, dating from the Iowa Yearly Meeting of 1891, proclaims: ". . . this kind of conviction [is] not founded on minute reasoning, but [rests] chiefly on the practical and internal evidence of the truth." [4] For

---

[3] Theodore Paullin, ed., *Sourcebook on Peacetime Conscription*, American Friends Service Committee (Philadelphia; 1944), p. 4. The statement is that of A. J. Muste.

[4] *Friends Book of Discipline*, Iowa Yearly Meeting (Herald Print, Oskaloosa; 1891), p. 23.

the Quaker, individual conscience is held to be the core of society. A government is not viewed in terms of its theoretical foundations, its organization, its procedures, or any of the other traditional tools of political analysis. Government is viewed, rather, in terms of the spiritual nature of the individuals who compose it.

In a manner that was to lead to political action, the Quakers gradually broadened their outlook from the individual to the society. While they were never proselytizers—and are not now —they did come to feel a need to alleviate some of the problems of the society in which they lived. The Friend was still not militant in bringing the truth to others, but nevertheless attempted to apply it to more than the Quaker population. There came what Quaker Dorothy Hutchinson calls a "gradual development from general religious insights to specific convictions regarding Christian behavior and then from a personal testimony to a social testimony." [5] However, agreement on the social demands of Quaker belief has never been achieved among the believers. As Miss Hutchinson has put it, "Other Friends . . . tell us that we have no moral right to object to war as an institution in the present imperfect world and that our peace testimony must be, for the present, a personal testimony without social implications for a world which does not yet share our religious convictions." [6] There is firm agreement among the Quakers that their first commitment, an uncompromisable one, is to the Truth that is God's, as it has been shown to them. No matter what the social implications or political activity, action is upon a divinely based principle.

Aldous Huxley has provided some historical dimensions to this whole problem in a fascinating biography which deals with the

---

[5] Dorothy Hutchinson, *A Call to Peace Now* (Society of Friends, Philadelphia; 1953), p. 6.

[6] Ibid., p. 5.

·conflict between religious principle and political involvement.
The figure in whom this struggle takes on personal meaning is
Father Joseph, a dedicated servant of God who was diverted
from the road of mystical perfection by a set of temptations that
led him to undertake political work for his king and country.
Father Joseph joined the cause of God with the cause of France
in the first half of the seventeenth century by becoming the
political right-hand man to Cardinal Richelieu, whose two great
tasks were to unify France under an omnipotent monarchy and
exalt the Bourbons, once the power of the Hapsburgs had been
broken.[7]

There can be no mistaking the message of Huxley. In fact, it
is more than a message: it is a moral whose meaning cannot be
escaped by those who would learn the proper lessons from
Father Joseph's ill-begotten venture into politics. Huxley tells
the story of Father Joseph's mistaken belief that he could perform his higher duty to God by choosing a lower course of
political service to France. Personal ambition, the curse of all
politicians, is particularly dangerous when men of good will,
such as Father Joseph, succumb to its temptations. In his earlier
life of religious discipline Father Joseph had rid himself of the
passions of ambition. Now, as the devoted servant of a "provi-
dential France and a divinely appointed Louis XIII," he was able
to indulge the baser feelings which inevitably accompany a
political career. What is more, he did so with no sense of shame
or guilt. Father Joseph should have known better, for his reading
of the theocentric moralists had taught him long ago what the
relationship between man and God should be. As far as his
political career was concerned Huxley tells us that he could
always "annihilate" the questionable things he did for his coun-

[7] Aldous Huxley, *Grey Eminence* (New York: Harper; 1941). The
observations presented here are drawn largely from Huxley's account
and reflect his own commitment to many Quaker principles.

try by dedicating them all to God. It was his way of living and working, even at power politics, in a state of "holy indifference." On matters of domestic policy Father Joseph had always been in agreement with Cardinal Richelieu. By 1624, as Huxley says, "he was coming reluctantly to accept his foreign policy as well. . . . Within a short time the political conversion was complete; Father Joseph had become as determinedly an enemy of the Hapsburgs as Richelieu himself."[8] At still another point Huxley restates his major premise: "What happens when good men go into power politics in the hope of forcibly shoving humanity into the Kingdom of God? . . . Again and again ecclesiastics and pious laymen have become statesmen in the hope of raising politics to their own high moral level, and again and again politics have dragged them down to the low moral level upon which statesmen, in their political depravity, are compelled to live."[9]

Like many of the Quakers who wrestled with their own consciences as they confronted political conflicts in colonial Pennsylvania and finally withdrew from the political arena, Huxley rejects politics because it demands of man a loyalty to a cause inferior to the supreme good, a sacrifice of self undertaken in the name of something less than God. The particular tragedy of Father Joseph is that he was an "aspirant to sanctity," a man who had actually made some advance along the "way of perfection" toward union with God, but then was lured away. Huxley says it plainly: "He chose to go into politics."

Of the many features of politics which Huxley dislikes, one is of special interest because it serves to illustrate the despair of the moralist as he views the degrading qualities of political life. Politicians, Huxley says, are unable to foresee, for more than a very short time, the results of any course of large-scale political

[8] Ibid., pp. 181–2.
[9] Ibid., p. 221.

action. "If hell is paved with good intentions, it is, among other reasons, because of the impossibility of calculating consequences." [1] Why? Because actions undertaken by "ordinary unregenerate people, sunk in their selfhood and without spiritual insight, seldom do much good." It is in the nature of political action for the "ordinary run of average unregenerate men and women," as Huxley repeatedly terms them, to embark upon projects without having acquired through contemplation the power to act well and to give their souls completely to God. Even when it is well-intentioned, he writes, "political action is always foredoomed to a partial, sometimes even a complete, self-stultification. The intrinsic nature of the human instruments with which and human materials upon which, political action must be carried out, is a positive guarantee against the possibility that such action shall yield the results that were expected from it." [2]

Huxley has still more to say about what must take place, and take place on a large scale, if political action is ever to produce the beneficial results expected from it. There will be little general betterment in the world unless large numbers of individuals undertake the transformation of their personality by the only known method which really works—that of the contemplative.

For the radical and permanent transformation of personality only one effective method has been discovered—that of the mystics. It is a difficult method, demanding from those who undertake it a great deal more patience, resolution, self-abnegation and awareness than most people are prepared to give, except perhaps in times of crisis, when they are ready for a short while to make the most enormous sacrifices. . . . Because of the general reluctance to make such efforts during uncritical times, very few people are prepared, at any given moment of history, to undertake the method of the mystics. This being so, we shall be foolish if we expect any political action,

[1] Ibid., p. 274.
[2] Ibid., p. 305.

however well-intentioned and however nicely planned, to produce more than a fraction of the general betterment anticipated.[3]

It should be pointed out that Huxley's case against the debasing distractions of political activity is, on its own terms, self-confirming. His view of the world is from the elevated peak of a high morality, and it is little wonder that he has no use for the imperfect political instruments by which man is seeking to satisfy his immediate needs and wants in an imperfect world. Huxley's point is that man's political activities are doomed to failure because they almost wholly exclude God. Eric Hoffer once commented that those of the political left and right have at least one outlook in common: they both detest reality. It is easy for Huxley to be affronted by the mischiefs of the real world of man because, as a defender of God, he recognizes only an "ultimate reality," expressing itself in a "certain nature of things," whose harmony is violated by the crude excesses of man's political struggles, "with consequences more or less disastrous for all directly or indirectly concerned in the violation."[4] Thus to the question of "what the politicians can do for their fellows by actions within the political field," Huxley replies, "The answer would seem to be: not very much."

An important insight into Huxley's anti-politicism is provided by his own preference for the ethical standards within and between small groups of people, very much reminiscent of the Quaker feeling and attitude. Individuals and small groups do not always or inevitably behave well, but it is Huxley's contention that they *can* be moral and rational to a degree impossible in large groups. As numbers increase, personal contact and communication break down, with the result that behavior motivated by "personal affection and a spontaneous and unreflecting compassion" is replaced by behavior motivated by a reasoned and

[3] Ibid., pp. 306–7.
[4] Ibid., p. 305.

impersonal benevolence. In most men and women reason and the impersonal view of things are very slightly developed which, explains Huxley, is why the ethical standards of large organizations are lower than those in smaller groups. Therefore it is only a logical next step for Huxley to claim that "the poisons which society generates within itself by its political and economic activities" are the consequence of power politics, and the crime of power politics is that it sacrifices the ethical values which emerge only among individuals and small groups. Huxley's remedy is what he fittingly calls "goodness politics," although he is quick to recognize that it probably will not work:

Goodness politics have never been attempted in any large society, and it may be doubted whether such an attempt, if made, could achieve more than a partial success, so long as the majority of individuals concerned remain unable or unwilling to transform their personalities by the only method known to be effective. But though the attempt to substitute goodness politics for power politics may never be completely successful, it still remains true that the methods of goodness politics combined with individual training in theocentric theory and contemplative practice alone provide the means whereby human societies can become a little less unsatisfactory than they have been up to the present. So long as they are not adopted, we must expect to see an indefinite continuance of the dismally familiar alternations between extreme evil and a very imperfect, self-stultifying good, alternations which constitute the history of all civilized societies.[5]

Huxley is not alone in viewing with distaste what he calls "the brutal facts of political action." Like many others who prefer to seek inner peace through quiet contemplation or who rely on phrases of the Gospel as the only measure of what is right and good, Huxley dissociates himself from politics because it inevitably falls short of "ultimate reality." The fact that politics invariably deals with something short of the conditions prevail-

[5] Ibid., 312–13.

ing in the Kingdom of Heaven makes no difference. "Society," he says, "can never be greatly improved, until such time as most of its members choose to become theocentric saints." Father Joseph made his "gravest and most fatal mistake" when he went to work for Richelieu and thereby violated all of his religious principles and commitments. "Even if his mysticism had proved to be compatible with his power politics, which it did not, he would still have been wrong to accept the position of Richelieu's collaborator; for by accepting it he automatically deprived himself of the power to exercise a truly spiritual authority, he cut himself off from the very possibility of being the apostle of mysticism." [6]

It is altogether appropriate that Huxley should close his account of Father Joseph by turning briefly to another seventeenth-century figure, Quaker George Fox, who unlike Father Joseph remained true to his principles by never indulging himself in the sordid business of politics. Huxley's closing comments deserve to be read carefully, for they not only point up again his own view of political life but delineate sharply the anti-political posture of the Quakers.

Fanatically marginal—for when invited, he refused even to dine at Cromwell's table, for fear of being compromised—Fox was never corrupted by success, but remained to the end the apostle of the inner light. The society he founded [the Society of Friends] has had its ups and downs, its long seasons of spiritual torpor and stagnation, as well as its times of spiritual life; but always the Quakers have clung to Fox's intransigent theocentrism and, along with it, to his conviction that, if it is to remain at all pure and unmixed, good must be worked for upon the margin of society, by individuals and by organizations small enough to be capable of moral, rational and spiritual life.

Huxley then pays tribute again to the superior value of "intransigent theocentrism":

[6] Ibid., 314–15.

. . . the antidote has always been insufficient to offset more than a part of the poison injected into the body politic by the statesmen, financiers, industrialists, ecclesiastics and all the undistinguished millions who fill the lower ranks of the social hierarchy. But though not enough to counteract more than some of the effects of the poison, the leaven of theocentrism is the one thing which, hitherto, has saved the civilized world from total self-destruction.[7]

So long as the human instruments and material of political action remain untransformed, Huxley's place will be with the "antidotemakers," not with those who brew the poisons of politics.

There is no single Quaker attitude towards government and politics. Some Friends have never deviated from the view that compromise of one's ideals is under no circumstances allowable. Others have argued that "to achieve ultimate triumph one must risk his ideals to the tender mercies of a world not yet ripe for them." [8] In either case the Quaker's position is a tortured one. He may feel he can raise the level of political activity in his time, or maintain a comparatively happy and just and peaceful society, as the Quaker legislators of Pennsylvania did. But as Frederick Tolles has pointedly remarked, he can apparently do it only at a price—the price of compromise, of the partial betrayal of his ideals. "If, on the other hand, he decides to preserve his ideals intact, to maintain his religious testimonies unsullied and pure, he may be able to do that, but again at a price—the price of isolation, of withdrawal from the mainstream of life in his time, of renouncing the opportunity directly and immediately to influence history." [9]

The governmental process in a democratic state yields a politics of compromise arising from an implicit agreement among all

[7] Ibid., 320–1.
[8] Rufus Jones, quoted in Dorothy Hutchinson, op. cit., p. 25.
[9] Tolles, op. cit., pp. 52–3.

parties on its *procedural* nature. The *substantive* policies emerge from hard-headed bargaining between a myriad of groups and forces jockeying for political position and favor. The Quakers, however, have put themselves "one up" on a democratic polity. In "obedience to the soul's vision" they have long ago reached agreement on a number of fundamental questions from which there can be no dissent, thereby altering considerably the base upon which democratic decision-making operates. They speak as a group of believers whose agreed-upon "essentials" cover a much wider range than the accepted "fundamentals" of the democratic political process. When the Quaker speaks of give and take and of a "flexible attitude," he is leaving unpostulated a much smaller area than that left for most people. While he is prepared to give up "non-essentials" if he has to, he also believes that his "basic principles must not be compromised." [1]

It is important to point out that when religion takes precedence over politics, the mean-ends relationship necessary to effective majority rule is seriously jeopardized, if not made inoperative. Theological dogma, buttressed by a commitment to individual conscience as the sole measurement of what is right and wrong, disqualifies for many "believers," Quakers or otherwise, any action which falls short of the absolute ideal. Given the often cumbersome procedures of democratic decision-making, it is not reasonable for any one to expect to accomplish his goal right from the start in an uninterrupted straight-line way. Yet for the Quakers, politics as they would have it consists of a series of postulates which are accepted from the start as true and therefore uncompromisable. However, the realities of the political process demand something more along the lines of a syllogism, which is to say a step-by-step development of both the particular end in

---

[1] For a discussion of this point, see *Steps to Peace, A Quaker View of United States Foreign Policy,* American Friends Service Committee (Philadelphia; 1951), p. 33.

view and the multiple strategies appropriate to its realization, either in whole or in part.

Enough has already been said to show that the Quaker does not think very highly of practical politics. But in a special sense he also holds a different view of politics which leads in turn to a particular view he holds of himself. The Quaker does not accept "human nature" as it is, but rather takes it upon himself to bring about a change in the nature of man in society. In a curious way, the policies of the Friends are thereby believed to be more practicable as a result of the presence of "better" men. The Friend, it should not be forgotten, sees himself as the herald of a new and finer majority. He does not state that his principles are applicable for everyone under our present system. His commitment is not to the political process but to the hope of a change in the spiritual nature of man which at some point in the future will make the Quaker principles relevant and ultimately show the way to a new system.

The assurance of peace . . . lies in a radical transformation of the lives of men and nations through their acceptance of certain basic principles of human conduct. Since life is of one piece, these principles must apply to all areas of human relationships—spiritual, economic, social, political.

Whenever an apparent conflict exists between loyalty to family, state, class, race or other subdivisions of men, and loyalty to God and all mankind, we must hold to the higher allegiance.[2]

In the Quaker view one does not vote on or bargain about a truism because the "truth" is not open to political debate. As one Friend observed, "That which is morally and religiously wrong cannot be politically right."[3] The Quaker ethic is an ethic of perfectionism and by definition, therefore, is anti-political.

[2] *Looking Toward the Post War World,* Statement of the Friends Conference on Peace and Reconstruction at Wilmington, Ohio, American Friends Service Committee; 1942, p. 13.

[3] Hutchinson, op. cit., p. 9.

꧁꧂ 3

The conflict between the basic Quaker commitment to moral truth on the one hand and the difficult demands of democratic politics on the other is nowhere revealed more sharply than in the political trials and tribulations of the Friends in their governance of colonial Pennsylvania. Although they never constituted a majority of the population of Pennsylvania (except in the country districts until about 1740), they retained almost unopposed control of the legislature until 1756. For the last fifty years (1706–1756) the Executive was either a Friend or a man under the control of the Penn family of the legislature. Thus the record of William Penn's "Holy Experiment" is a reflection of the Quaker commitment in action.

Two schools of thought have largely dominated the discussion of pacifist action. The first urges political participation within the government structure itself, encouraging the participant to apply his principles as best he can and to work for legislation of social reform as well as for the outlawing of war and of the methods of power politics unacceptable to him. The belief is that only by reaching large groups of people through political action can pacifist principles hope to gain a footing in the world at large. For anyone who follows this view the stakes are high, for he must aim at large-scale social change. Thus his risks are great, and the greatest is his main pitfall: the danger of compromise. The second view asserts the position of nonparticipation. One should work outside the governmental structure, usually on the community level but in an individual, nonpolitical way. He may believe that legislation will accomplish very little in the world around him since those who agree with him are a small minority. Or he may believe that he is subjecting himself to the ever-present danger of compromise *if he participates*. From this standpoint the greatest service he can render to others is to remain a consistent, if less active, witness to his own ideals. His pitfall, however, is a direct result of his inaction: he is likely to be accused of being a parasite. The Quakers suffered the pains of both sides of the controversy in colonial Pennsylvania.

It must be remembered that Quaker political activity emerged only as restrictions on the Friends were lifted in seventeenth-century England. During the era of Cromwell a few Quakers began to voice their principles in political terms but were not engaged in much practical political action. George Fox, the founding Quaker who called himself the "son of God," once had a conversation with Cromwell in which he demanded that the military ruler reject all violence and instead rule through love. As Tolles has remarked, Fox was asking him to make England "a kind of pilot project for the Kingdom of Heaven." [4]

With the Affirmation Act of 1722 the Quakers were in effect enabled to hold office and receive full privileges of citizenship. Once the privileges were granted, however, they were not inclined to follow them. Their previous experiences had turned them against direct political action. Samuel Scott, whom Tolles calls a fairly typical "public Friend," stated in reference to the Parliamentary election of 1789:

The Parliament being dissolved, a general election is coming on; the devil cometh forth, and hell from beneath. . . . It becometh not the members of our Society to meddle much in those matters, or be active in political disquisitions. . . . In respect to elections we ought to go no farther than voting for the candidates we best approve, and declaring our preference of them, without endeavouring by any other means to influence others." [5]

Quaker Joseph Pease was the first to enter fully into the political process, as a member of Parliament. His accomplish-

---

[4] Tolles, op. cit., p. 38.
[5] Samuel Scott, *A Diary of Some Religious Exercises and Experience* (London; 1809), p. 12, quoted in Tolles, p. 45.

ments were not significant enough to merit analysis, but ten years later John Bright entered Parliament and led a full and active legislative career. He supported many successful causes, among them abolition of compulsory church tithes, repeal of the Corn Laws, extension of the franchise, emancipation of the Jews, abolition of capital punishment, and a protest against the bombarding of Alexandria in 1882, the issue which brought his resignation from Gladstone's Cabinet. As the first truly active Quaker legislator Bright was faced with the same dilemma which confronted William Penn: what should be the choice between effective responsibility on the one hand and consistency to principle on the other? Bright's contributions as a Quaker legislator were notable, but they were achieved at the sacrifice of consistency as a Quaker.[6]

Activity in England, while it poses many of the classic problems, is in no way as illuminating as that which took place in Quaker Pennsylvania. During the first half of the seventeenth century there were many English citizens who felt detached from the Anglican Church but who also disapproved of Calvinism and desired to revive an apostolic type of Christianity. Under the leadership of George Fox the new group (later to be called Quakers) departed for America, landed in Boston in 1656, only to suffer there further persecution at the hands of the Puritans. It was in 1682 that the Quakers finally achieved a semblance of security in the New World. William Penn was given the grant of the large province and set out to establish a government embodying all the Quaker recommendations and principles. There were many factors in favor of the success of such a government: the legislature was predominantly Quaker, the colonies were virtually untroubled by outside problems, and the overwhelming internal issue—Indian raids—did not become a serious one in Pennsylvania for many years. The colony was

[6] Quoted in Tolles, p. 47.

protected geographically. Penn was little hampered by the Crown; some historians believe he was given the grant in order to prevent him from causing political trouble in England. The society was simple and relatively self-sufficient. If a Quaker government could operate anywhere on earth, it was given every opportunity in Pennsylvania.[7]

Early in the governing experience the Quakers felt the pressure of their unyielding commitment to pacifism.[8] George Fox, who had gone to jail in England rather than take up arms in defense of the Crown, reminded his followers that the doctrine of Christ is to "love one another" and urged "the faith and patience of the saints, to bear and suffer all things." They had endured their lonely pacifism in England because, as a small minority, they were responsible only to themselves and the purity of their doctrine. In Pennsylvania, however, the Quakers had to assume the burdens and torments of rulership. No longer were they able simply to withdraw unto themselves in protest of the decisions of society: now they were charged with the responsibility of making decisions with far-reaching consequences for an entire colony. This was a different test of the dogma of pacifism. The Quakers had to demonstrate that they could practice in government what they preached in prayer.

[7] William Penn's province came to be the most consistently free colony in North America. The colony prospered to such an extent that its members were reluctant to join with the revolutionaries in 1775. One of the first blows to Penn and his followers was the apparent ungratefulness of the Quaker constituency. A people who had suffered for so long from persecution would seemingly have few reservations about accepting Penn's grant of a considerable measure of liberty and his presence as a "gracious and kindly feudal lord." Even though Penn was operating on purely Quaker principles and taking upon himself the preservation of them in the government, the spirit of the age demanded more democracy. Three parties formed in Quaker Pennsylvania and Penn pleaded "for the love of God, me, and the poor country" that they "be not so Governmentish."

[8] I have drawn heavily here on Daniel Boorstin's excellent account of the Quakers in Pennsylvania in his book *The Americans* (New York: Random House; 1958).

There were many problems to grapple with, and each one was a test of the essential issue of pacifism. Boorstin has pointed out that even in the earliest years the Quakers could govern only by compromising one principle after another. "Not only were they often driven to use fictions and evasions in defending the colony against external enemies, but in the domestic government of the colony also they had to come to terms with the non-Quaker ethic." [9] The controversy over oaths is just one of many issues which forced the Quakers to compromise their ideals in their exercise of political power. In this particular case the principle involved was capital punishment, a form of societal behavior to which the Friends had long been unalterably opposed. The Quaker legislature in Pennsylvania, under William Penn's personal leadership, had passed the Great Law of 1682 which was a radical departure from English criminal law on this very point. For thirty years the law remained untouched. But after a spectacular murder of a well-known citizen in Chester County, the issue of capital punishment rose to a fury at the same time that the recurrent threat came to a head to exclude Quakers from office altogether by insisting on the oath. The Quaker legislators, now frightened, became receptive to the suggestion that if they would give in on their stand on capital punishment they might be able to elicit a compromise on the matter of the oath. The situation could be resolved quite easily: all they had to do was adopt the criminal laws of England, a move that would automatically make many additional crimes punishable by death. The compromise was adopted. The Act of 1718 permitted the assumption of office without an oath and combined the capital laws of England with those of Quaker Pennsylvania. Boorstin provides a telling footnote to the bargain:

Thus, to remain "pure" in the matter of oaths, the Quakers bargained the lives of all those men and women who might be convicted of any one of a dozen miscellaneous crimes. The episode was not

[9] Ibid., p. 43.

merely a testimony against absolutes as guides to political behavior. It showed how zealous men might sacrifice the welfare and even the lives of their fellowmen to the overweening purity of their own consciences.[1]

The doctrine of Quaker pacifism was put to its sternest test over the issue of colonial defense. Specifically, government provisions for defense in a land beset by frontier raids were a life-and-death matter to the backwoods settlers at the mercy of the Indians and the French. In England the Quakers were free to protest violence and go to jail for their beliefs; as an act of civil disobedience it was solely a question for individual decision. In colonial Pennsylvania, however, they were responsible for the protection of many thousands of lives.

The Quakers avoided decision on the matter, and indirectly acknowledged the impossibility of an uncompromisable moral approach to political decision-making by making the deputy-governor at all times a non-Quaker and turning a good number of executive powers over to him.

It was the plain duty of government to protect the people; no private religious scruple could relieve a legislator of that duty. Franklin urged the Quaker legislators "that if on account of their religious Scruples, they themselves could do no Act for our Defense, yet they might retire; relinquish their Power for a Season, quit the Helm to Freer Hands during the present Tempest." The public funds raised from all the people had been spent by the Quakers to secure the enjoyment of their own religion, to oppose anti-Quaker petitions, and to put themselves in a favorable light at the English court. How could they justify their refusal to use these funds for the benefit and defense of all? [2]

---

[1] Ibid., p. 48.

[2] Ibid., p. 53. The defense problem, the most serious faced by the Friends, epitomizes in many ways the problem of regarding politics as religion and merits analysis in light of the contemporary Quaker impetus to the peace movement.

In 1748 the Quakers refused to vote money for the defense of Pennsylvania. In keeping with their doctrine of love, they instead gave 500 pounds to be used to supply Indians "with necessaries towards acquiring a livelihood and cultivate the friendship between us and not to encourage their entering into a war." A good part of the money was used by the Indians to buy supplies of war. By 1756 Indian raids on the backwoodsmen were so frequent and so serious that further action could not be forestalled. The Quaker legislature replied to the raids by enforcing fair price for trade with Indians and guaranteeing good treatment of them. Backwoods homes still burned; frontier scalps were still lost.

The Quakers could not hide from themselves the possibility that they were failing in their duties. In 1702 James Logan had said to Penn that governing was "ill-fitted to their principles." There was no denying that the events at hand highlighted the dichotomy between responsible governance and adherence to religious principle. Both, apparently, could not be sustained simultaneously.

The Quaker stand forced action to be taken outside the government. Benjamin Franklin conceived a plan "to try what might be done by a voluntary association of people"[3] and outlined it in a pamphlet entitled *Plain Truth*. As the organization was not approved by the assembly, it had no constitutional status. "Here then an army of considerable size had been raised without action by the rightfully constituted authorities. The members were not paid, their claims for injuries, pensions and the like would have no legal foundation, and their officers did not receive commissions from the Crown."[4]

The Quakers could not deny events after the fact and were not

---

[3] Quoted in Robert L. D. Davidson, *War Comes to Quaker Pennsylvania* (New York: Columbia Univ. Press; 1957), p. 50.

[4] Ibid., p. 53.

violently opposed to the association. Some even believed in the defense of the country, provided they were not a part of it. London Quakers began to encourage Penn to give up rule as quickly as possible so that part of the blame for the bloody events could fall upon someone else. They made a bargain with the president of the privy council, Lord Granville: they would persuade the Friends in Pennsylvania to resign if he would see that they were not flatly disqualified from holding office. Pennsylvania Governor Morris realized a declaration of war was unavoidable, but he also knew that it would meet strong opposition. "Strict and reputable" Quaker Israel Pemberton led the movement to discourage Friends from any compromise that would bring about the passage of war measures. A return to the principles of religious faith over political expedience was encouraged.

The French and Indians Wars proved the end of Penn's Holy Experiment in the Delaware Valley. In mid-1756 war was declared against the Delaware and Shawnee Indians by the governor and the council. On the same day six Quaker leaders resigned their positions in the assembly, offering the following statement:

. . . as many of our Constituents seem of Opinion that the present situation of Public Affairs calls upon us for Services in a military Way, which, from a Conviction of Judgment, after mature Deliberation, we cannot comply with, we conclude it most conducive to the Peace of our own Minds, and the Reputation of our religious Profession, to permit in our Resolutions of resigning our Seats, which we accordingly do; and request these our Reasons may be entered on the Minutes of the House.[5]

Rule by the Friends, who had said government was "a part of religion itself, a thing sacred in its institution and end," [6] was over.

---

[5] Quoted in Boorstin, *The Americans*, p. 60.
[6] Ibid., p. 61.

After the abdication of political power by the Philadelphia Yearly Meeting, the Quakers turned to a purification of their sect. Quakers did not run for office and many did not vote. Still, there remained a vague hope that someday they might return to power, if only they did not have to compromise their principles. But as Boorstin has commented, that day was never to come.

. . . the reins of government cannot be picked up and laid aside at will. The Quaker abdication, with its avowal of the inconsistency between their principles and the responsibilities of governments, was perhaps the greatest evidence of practical sense they were ever to give. But their secret hope of returning to power with the peace of the 1760's showed their fundamental failure to understand society and its problems.[7]

The major reason for the failure of the Friends in their governing of colonial Pennsylvania can be stated quite simply: their religious dedication to the purity of dogma and conscience was incompatible with the trials and responsibilities of political rule. "Let's do our duty," William Penn remarked in 1701, "and leave the rest with God." But what is left to God is often precisely what must be shouldered by political man. The American Revolution was fought by men who believed the cause was right and just. God's will could be invoked in prayer, but it was the will of many thousands of Americans that led to the severance of ties with England. And so it is with governments. They are instituted and run by men who learn quickly that political rulership can have little success if it is ever put in bondage to

[7] Ibid., p. 61. The Quaker "ethic of perfectionism" became an additional curse when the American Revolution was upon them. Their hostility to killing and war led them to oppose the struggle for independence, demonstrating once again that they were more concerned with keeping their consciences pure than with the compelling complex questions of government. They refused to pay taxes and fines levied by the American government and, for their actions, were labeled as Tories. As Boorstin has pointed out, to the earlier charge of fanaticism was now added the greater odium of treason.

moral absolutes. For the Quakers, however, resignation to the will of God coupled with a dogmatic insistence on pursuing the purity of their own principles could never be sacrificed to considerations of government necessity. Thomas Jefferson called them "a religious sect . . . acting with one mind, and that directed by the mother society in England. Dispersed, as the Jews, they still form, as those do, one nation, foreign to the land they live in. They are Protestant Jesuits, implicitly devoted to the will of their superior, and forgetting all duties to their country in the execution of the policy of their order."[8]

Boorstin is even more harsh in his judgment of the Friends. Preoccupied with his rites of self-purification, the Quaker, he observes, preserved his dogma from the most corrosive of all tests, the acid of everyday experience. But the Friends, he points out in a final comment, also made a dogma of the absence of dogma.

It was a primary article of their creed that a true Christian could have no creed. This deprived the Quaker of that theological security which had enabled the Puritan gradually to adapt Calvinism to American life. The Quaker was haunted by fear that every compromise was a defeat, that to modify anything might be to lose everything. Because his doctrine was suffused with the haze of mystical enthusiasm, he could not discern clearly which were the foundations and buttresses of his cathedral and which the ornamental gargoyles.[9]

ΙΙΙΙΙΙΙΙΙ 4

It would be unfair to judge the political ramifications of the Quaker commitment to conscience and moral truth solely on the basis of the failure of the Holy Experiment. The Quaker-sup-

[8] Ibid., pp. 64–5.
[9] Ibid., p. 67.

ported (and greatly Quaker-inspired) contemporary movement that has put the Friends in close proximity to the give and take of contemporary political disputes is the so-called "peace movement." An examination of this movement will further illuminate the political difficulties in being guided rigidly by absolute moral principles.

Anyone who has ever attended a peace meeting will perhaps understand what is meant when it is said that the atmosphere is in many ways close to that of a small-town prayer meeting. The informality, the coffee-cookies-and-punch, the intensity—they are the regular accompaniment to a meeting of serious and dedicated people who have found their answers to the problems of a prodigal world. Large gatherings of peace-group members, along with the peace rallies and marches, exhibit the fervor of evangelism, an evangelism that is directed to people who already believe and revel in their own reinforcement. A verbal or graphic view of the blood, gore, and death of war is found as repulsive and motivating as would be a Cotton Mather description of Sodom. And the logic of the prayer meeting and the peace meeting is on the same basis: for the religious zealot nothing is worth sinning for because sin is the destroyer of humanity; for the peace fanatic nothing is worth warring for because war is the undoing of mankind.

There is nothing here that is open to compromise. To be "politic" in these matters is to be immoral. Impatience, often bordering on contempt, is felt for those who fall short of the absolute; at best, there is the grudging indulgence one has for the heathen. The process of politics is not only unwanted but unnecessary. For this type of movement the focus is on the individual. The fundamental appeal is to love, brotherhood, and the undeniable verity that war is evil. Through petitions with 50,000 names, rosters of one hundred thousand, student picket marches, vigils, and extra-governmental contact with "the people" of all the nations of the world, the call of Truth will be heralded over the heads of the slow-moving politicians and statesmen.[1]

While the pacifists account for a large number of the active members of the peace movement, there are many non-Quakers who also support organizations which deal specifically with world peace through law, or unilateral disarmament, or a variety of other proposals. For all of the differences between the disciples of Gandhian nonviolence and those who were merely seeking a cessation of atmospheric testing, there is a certain bond of approach and commitment.[2] The essence of the peace movement stand on war is simple: war is wrong. There is little interest in

[1] It is notable that religious groups are most attracted to absolutist politics. The many tracts going through the mails on both anticommunism and peace exhibit a high percentage of religious sponsorship. Both right- and left-wing absolutes have much of the same approach, e.g., concentration on the individual and extragovernmental action. Both sides have extensive resources for pamphlets, tracts, film strips, and movies featuring top names: Roy Rogers for anticommunism, Steve Allen for peace. There is an appeal to the expert: signed petitions of university professors, top-level scientists, and former government officials are but a few of the more popular devices. The extragovernmental approach of both the "right" and "left" absolutist was demonstrated at a foreign policy conference held on the campus of a leading university. A small group of campus peace-group members left the auditorium before the closing of an address by former Secretary of State Christian Herter. Not too long after the departure of the peace-group members, several followers of the local right-wing Young Americans for Freedom left the hall. Both sides were "disgusted" by the "weaseling" of the former Secretary of State on the question of disarmament. Even this demonstration does not fully illustrate the prevalent attitude of these groups, for a substantial number of both declined to attend such a conference in the first place. In the words of a member of the "Forum for the Discussion of Nonviolent Alternatives to War," "Why bother to go? All they're having there is a bunch of politicians."

[2] It should be made clear that my major concern here is not with the merits of the various policies or stands, or even in citing them. I am more interested in trying to describe the commitment of the majority of those who are active in the peace movement. The essential questions I am raising are: (a) What is the general philosophy of the active peace-group member? (b) What does he conceive his role to be in the political process? (c) What are the methods used by these groups?

scientific or military arguments that are limited to pointing out the impossibility of "conventional" warfare in our time or the futility of the "no cities" doctrine or even the biological and physical effects which will accrue from a nuclear war. These are in no way as arresting as the simple axiom that in the nature of war there is a definite evil. The Quakers are the most vociferous in stating what they believe to be the relationship of "common sense" and scientific reasoning to the question of war:

We have tried to face the hard facts; to put the case for non-violence in terms of common sense. Yet, we are aware that the man who chooses in these terms alone cannot sustain himself against the mass pressures of an age of violence. If ever truth reaches power, if ever it speaks to the individual citizen, it will not be the argument that convinces. Rather, it will be his own inner sense of integrity that impels him to say, "Here I stand. Regardless of relevance or consequence, I can do no other." [3]

The basis of the Quaker stand is an absolute: ". . . in like accordance with his command to love one's enemies, and not to return evil for evil, they believed all war was unlawful to the Christian." [4] The essential denial is not that all ends sought through war are wrong, but that war cannot achieve any good ends.

Some ends may be served by war but they are not moral ends. If men fight to maintain the political status quo, or to change the boundaries of nations, or to eliminate a hated group of their fellow men, they may succeed but these are not the men whose motives we respect or whose ends we feel any wish to encourage.

The men whom we feel bound to respect are those who are fighting for the Four Freedoms, international justice, and the eventual establishment of the Kingdom of God on earth. But these are fighting for moral goods which cannot be won by war and they are bound to be completely disillusioned, as they were after the First

[3] *Speak Truth to Power,* p. 68.
[4] *Friends Book of Discipline,* p. 19.

World War, by the results of military victory. It is to these we must say that good ends cannot be attained by bad means because the end is inherent in the means.[5]

The absolutist stand on war is combined with the frank admission of an anti-political outlook. Politicians are compromisers. They are regarded as men of little principle. The individual removes any guilt he personally feels for the state of society by expressing his faith in the nature of individual man, at the same time noting that he has been betrayed and is ill-represented.

Once one is aware of the absolutist commitment of the peace-movement follower, it is essential to note the follower's own conception of his role in the political process. Despite all the demands and strivings for united action, the members of the peace movement—much like the Quaker ancestors who had plans for a better world but did not feel they should administer them—do not wish to assume political rule and responsibility. In coining the phrase "moral elite," Albert Einstein offered an insightful statement of the place of these people, by their own feelings, in a democratic pluralist society:

The War Resisters League is important because, by union, it relieves courageous and resolute individuals of the paralysing feeling of isolation and loneliness, and in this way gives them moral support in the fulfillment of what they consider their duty. The existence of such a moral elite is indispensable for the preparation of a fundamental change in public opinion, a change which, under present-day circumstances, is absolutely necessary if humanity is to survive.[6]

The religiously dedicated members of the peace movement see a definite dichotomy between politics and their own action. They are in no way claiming that their stands, methods, and views are those which can be used to run the country today. They are more concerned with keeping their views uncompromised and doing

[5] Hutchinson, op. cit., p. 13.
[6] Albert Einstein, Address at Princeton, N.J., Aug. 10, 1953.

their best to change human nature. They will be among the first to admit that their commitment to peace greatly overshadows their commitment to democratic political processes. Their concern is with something that is not politics, despite the fact that they must use political action. To tell them they are playing politics is to insult them, to accuse them of not working for their basic purpose—the creation of a new man and a new world.

Religious pacifism . . . is not antigovernment in the sense that it does not believe in government, but it looks upon government as an imperfect attempt to conduct human life, and it believes that unwillingness to conform may sometimes be the highest loyalty to a better way of conducting human affairs in the future. The pacifist is not afraid to be in a minority, because he feels that he is a trustee to truth which he wants the majority to hold and believe in.[7]

His "truth" is that "deterioration of the moral fiber of a nation is a greater disaster than armed attack."[8]

We Quakers are perfectionists who strive to accept no compromise with evil in our personal lives and to hold up perfectionist ideals before the world. We believe in the irresistible power of good will and we do not like the sound of "bargained peace."[9]

We shall of course encourage our statesmen to do everything humanly possible to secure a reasonable and workable scheme for the international control of atomic weapons, and to be unwearied even in the face of apparently endless disappointment. At the same time we shall remember that what statesmen can do is limited by the outlook and character of their peoples. Peace between nations is only possible if the peoples genuinely seek that which makes for peace. Every aggressive, self-centered and self-righteous temper, even in

[7] *What About the Conscientious Objector? A Supplement to the Pacifist Handbook,* Joint Committee on Peace and Freedom of the American Friends Service Committee and the Women's International League for Peace and Freedom, Philadelphia, 1940, p. 15.

[8] Harvey Seifert, "A Christian Reappraisal of Realism in Foreign Policy," in Keys, op. cit., p. 90.

[9] Hutchinson, op. cit., p. 24.

small matters, helps to generate a similar temper in the nation as a whole. On the other hand, humility, thought for others and a forgiving spirit generate in the nation as a whole a temper which makes peace possible.[1]

The members of the peace movement regard themselves as either a permanent minority or prophets of a future day, but never as a possible majority in the present world. They themselves admit that their principles and stands can only be adapted to minority action.

(On the Political Relevance of a Minority:)

Further implications for the state will appear as the minority of its citizens who resolve to practice peace begins to grow. The larger the minority, and the less self-centered and self-righteous it is, the greater the impact and the greater the accommodation that will be made to it. A government which reflects the will of the people must modify and adjust its policies in accord with the growth of opinion, and this is precisely the reason why a minority view has political relevance. Indeed, the presence of vigorous, pioneering minorities has been generally recognized as essential to a healthy democracy. In the First World War the United States government originally made no provisions for the rights of conscience, but the fact that it was confronted with a minority that refused military service was a political reality that could not be ignored. As a result, some recognition of conscience was embodied in executive regulations, and conscience was recognized explicitly by Congress in World War II. The act of conscientious objection in 1917 was, in fact, politically relevant. Or, to cite a current example, we point to the political impact of extremist leadership in the fields of anti-communism and Asian intervention. Although it seems clear that senatorial spokesmen in these areas represent no more than a small minority of viewpoints, their poisitions actually set the poles and pull the whole range of public discussion toward them. In short, we believe the vocal minority has an important polarizing effect that makes it politically relevant in a very practical way.[2]

[1] Leslie Newbigin, "The Gift of Peace," in Keys, op. cit., p. 106.
[2] *Speak Truth to Power,* p. 60.

In their own words the members of the peace movement exercise a polarizing effect on the political dialogue of our time. This approach was illustrated in a candid manner by H. Stuart Hughes, Harvard professor of history and a candidate in 1962 for the United States Senate on a disarmament platform with peace-group backing. "I contend that getting elected is not the main point," Hughes stated during his campaign in Massachusetts. "The main point is to make a dent in the American political consensus by taking a strong stand on the decisive issues of war and peace and locating the public backing that exists for this stand." [3]

Hughes, who claims that he is "not a pacifist but a historian," sees the role of the permanent minority as voicing an extreme opinion to widen the gap between the poles that determine the locus of the political mainstream. He sees the polar view as not the business of the politician but of the intellectual, the writer, the teacher. Hughes, like many of the followers of the peace movement, reveals subtly that his ringing statements are actually more extreme than would be his own personal actions were he in a position of political responsibility, but that the voicing of these views is necessary.

I have a sense of attempting *in extremis* to give voice to the common interests of a humanity transcending the barriers drawn by the cold war, before the blight of national and ideological hatred descends on us once again.[4]

In running on an independent peace platform Hughes was acting outside the political mainstream. He hoped, by raising the extreme position, to force his prominent opponents of the Democratic and Republican parties to answer his challenge. He had no

[3] H. Stuart Hughes, personal letter to author's research assistant, Ilene Strelitz.

[4] H. Stuart Hughes, *An Approach to Peace and Other Essays* (New York: Atheneum Press; 1962), preface.

intention, however, of becoming the senator from Massachusetts.

I think it is impossible to speak in terms of maximum and minimum aims. Anything more than 5,000 votes in November [1962] would represent progress over the present state of the peace movement. A balance of power position swinging the election to one major party candidate or the other would represent a real triumph.[5]

Hughes's position was representative of many nonpacifist followers of the peace movement. In their view there is a responsibility which must be assumed by a vigilant few whose primary duty is to make absolutely clear that any compromise position is just that—a compromise. The absolute position must be kept firmly in mind to prevent the lowering of the common denominator of compromise or the treatment of compromise as the ideal.

There are two types of commitment involved in the peace movement. One is basically political, accounting, for example, for the not unusual phenomenon of a paid political statement on disarmament or nuclear testing that is signed by prominent political figures whose own voting records fall considerably short of that stand. The other involves an ethic which is anti-political: it is a religious commitment, of which social action is a function rather than the independent result of what Eric Goldman has called "hammering out the compromises." It becomes a form of moral liberation whereby the individual who "practices peace" frees himself from the demands and responsibilities, political and otherwise, of complex decisions. He has released himself, as it were, "to burst the bonds of practical politics" and to add his weight to a "positive attack on the causes of violence."[6] *The "How-To" Handbook, A Tool Kit for Christian Social Action,* explains the need for social action this way:

---

[5] Hughes, personal letter, op. cit.
[6] *Speak Truth to Power,* pp. 57–9.

Why Act?

1. Social action is the will of God. God wants all men to have the fullest opportunity to use the resources of His creation for spiritual growth. He wants no man exploited or murdered or suppressed. We should be concerned about everything. . . .

2. Our religion ought to change every part of our lives. If God is the Lord of all of life, we ought to offer to him our economic attitudes and political activity as well as our prayer, life and tithe money. Part-time or part-way Christians are not real Christians. . . .

. . . . .

5. Such action is necessary for the life of the church. The Church exists to do the work of Christ. Evangelism is harder when social conditions blight man. Religious education is incomplete without acts which express commitment. Missions may become impossible unless social action stops the spread of totalitarianism in other lands. Pastoral care can pick up the pieces. Social action may prevent the breakage.

Is not social action necessary for all the rest of the church's program? [7]

The moral philosophy expressed in this view not only results in action which goes out of the range of politics, but is so broad that its adherents encounter difficulty in interpreting it. "There is no perfect answer, no completely consistent stand which fits every pacifist," say the American Friends. "Many occupations and investments help feed and service the war machine. Even watches may be used to time bombs and potatoes to feed soldiers. The ultimate decision always lies with the individual." [8] Another pacifist voice has said:

It is not a political formula, a diplomatic theory, a gospel of economics or a master plan for world government, but something which, on the one hand, reaches far beyond them all and, on the

[7] Harvey Seifert, *The "How-To" Handbook, A Tool Kit for Christian Social Action,* Public Affairs Commission of the Church Federation of Los Angeles, p. 2. (n.d.)

[8] *Pacifist Living Today and Tomorrow,* p. 57.

other hand, is their foundation, the only real hope for their fulfillment. It goes to the root of them all.[9]

In a popular peace film entitled *Does Disarmament Make
Sense?* Raymond Massey states, "Peace is more than the absence
of war. . . . [It is] the presence of justice . . . in short, the
presence of God." One active pacifist and peace-movement organizer in northern California, whose activities and vigils
brought him a prison sentence, was described as follows in a
local newspaper:

He speaks glowingly of "love," "truth" and "nonviolent action" and
enunciates these words like an incantation.
    Amplifying them, he explains: "Love is everything that promotes,
enhances, and develops life. Truth is found in all great religious
tradition."
    "Nonviolence," he continues, "is the political expression of
love." [1]

The lack of commitment to the democratic political process on
the part of the peace groups is revealed in their methods of
action. Their main guide, as we have already seen, is the individual and his conscience. The major concentration is not directed to
alternative steps which might lead to political effectiveness in
resolving disputes, but upon enabling the individual to keep
pure his principles.

One of the great concerns of the dedicated pacifist is that in a
period of crisis men will not rouse themselves to the monumental efforts needed to usher in a radically new way of life. What
he finds equally disappointing is that the Christian churches and
religious teachers are not proclaiming the great hope which will
summon men to revolutionary action. A. J. Muste, in expressing
his own religious pacifist principles, has commented that "Yester-
day it was the liberals in the churches and the Socialists, in and

---

[9] Samuel H. Drensner, "Man, God, and Atomic War," in Keys, op.
cit., p. 132.
[1] Palo Alto *Times,* June 12, 1962.

out of the churches, who offered that hope. Today it is the Communists." Whatever the errors of the Communists may be, it is not "in holding before men the vision and hope of a liberated and redeemed humanity." [2] For the pacifist it has always been necessary to perpetuate the vision of a "redeemed humanity," and it is in its name that he can reject all politics as being antihuman. He seeks a "politics of the future," and it is his hope that he will one day find the ultimate fusion of personal responsibility and social action. Meanwhile, in concentrating on individual action and looking to the world that is to come, he has sought to escape a world he is powerless to change.

Bertrand Russell, the aged philosopher who at one time was spokesman of the British unilateralist movement, has raised his voice in behalf of a pacifist-neutralism designed to bring about England's withdrawal from the harsh world of military alliances and power politics. In his many pronouncements one finds both the sense of frustration and the cry of anguish that is often the tormented expression of moral indignation.

We used to call Hitler wicked for killing off the Jews, but Kennedy and Macmillan are much more wicked than Hitler. The idea of weapons of mass extermination is utterly horrible and is something which no one with one spark of humanity can tolerate.

I will not pretend to obey a Government which is organizing mass massacres of mankind. I will do everything I can to oppose the Government in any way which I think can be fruitful and I exhort you to do the same.

We cannot obey these murderers. They are wicked. They are abominable. They are the wickedest people who ever lived in the history of man and it is our duty to do what we can against them.[3]

---

[2] A. J. Muste, *Pacifism and Perfectionism,* undated pamphlet reprinted from *Fellowship,* the monthly journal of The Fellowship of Reconciliation, pp. 17–18.

[3] Address delivered by Lord Bertrand Russell to the Midland Members of the Youth Campaign for Nuclear Disarmament at Birmingham on April 16, 1961.

These comments of Lord Russell do little to illuminate the complexities of international affairs in an imperfect and troubled world. They are, rather, assertions reflecting his deep sense of moral outrage. In assuming almost personal responsibility for the saving of mankind, Lord Russell has gone far beyond the bounds of political and diplomatic communication and has resorted instead to impugning the sincerity and sanity of those who hold positions of power:

There are supposed to be two sides, each professing to stand for a great cause. This is a delusion. Kennedy, Khrushchev, Adenauer, De Gaulle, Macmillan and Gaitskell are pursuing a common aim: the ending of all human rights. You, your families, your friends, and your countries are to be exterminated by a common decision of a few brutal but powerful men. To please these men, all private affections, all public hopes, all that has been achieved in art and knowledge and thought . . . are to be wiped out forever.[4]

This outburst by Lord Russell is eloquent testimony to his determination to reduce the world's problems to what he conceives to be their moral elements. His feelings are frequently voiced in high-pitched anger, and it is the anger of someone who is unable to believe that others cannot grasp the point he is trying to make—that peace is good and war is horrible, and that everybody else is out of step. The difficulty is that it is not the only point that needs to be made. The isolation of moral principles from all others is a dubious enterprise at best, but in the international arena of power politics it is clearly impossible. Rarely are the alternatives only two in number—"red or dead," love or hate, peace or war. The pacifists and unilateral disarmers do their thinking in the oversimple categories of either an arms race leading to a nuclear holocaust or the destruction of all weapons which will lead to peace. Given these two polarized

[4] Quoted in H. A. De Weerd, "British Unilateralism: A Critical View," *The Yale Review,* Summer 1962, p. 586.

choices, Lord Russell's other proposal, advanced in the years immediately after the Second World War, becomes more understandable though hardly more respectable. During this period, when the United States enjoyed a monopoly in nuclear weapons, Lord Russell thought it would be "worth while" to threaten preventive war against the Soviet Union in order to achieve implementation of the Baruch plan internationalizing nuclear energy. As one student of military affairs commented:

> Since responsible statesmen cannot make threats of this kind without being prepared to carry them out, we must assume that Russell would have been willing to use nuclear weapons against the Russian people if this demand was not met. We must also assume that he would have been willing to undermine if not destroy the United Nations, which would have had to oppose such an action. Since Western Europe was practically undefended at the time he proposed a preventive war against Russia, Russell would have to risk the possibility of its being overrun by the Red Army.[5]

Lord Russell has stated that his proposal in those years was put forward to save the world from war. Although the world situation and his point of view have both changed since the late forties, it is worth noting that each of Lord Russell's drastic proposals—preventive war earlier and unilateral disarmament later—represented the most extreme and opposite forms of possible action, both pronounced in the name of peace. His suggestions, while unquestionably springing from the highest of motives, reflect nonetheless the limitations of moral absolutes as a guide to public policy. Apart from "witnessing for human values" and "arousing the conscience of mankind," the general tone and thrust of most pacifist avowals amount to a declaration that the end or goal which the pacifist designates to be supreme is alone sufficient to justify whatever means he deems to be necessary. But the means themselves are given secondary importance

[5] Ibid., p. 580.

because the pacifist, focusing as he does on the moral imperative that peace is desirable and war is evil (with which no one disagrees), is unable to bring to bear the temperament and judgment necessary to help in evaluating alternative courses of action which might lead to the desired goal. And it is precisely on the subject of what means (policies) should be adopted that there is intense disagreement. To borrow a phrase from Professor Stanley Hoffmann, the question is not "the bliss in the millennium," but how one gets there. The fervor in the heart of the pacifist for world peace as the ultimate goal mirrors his deep moral concern for what is right and even righteous, but politics deals with something far short of the ultimate condition.

A major difficulty for the pacifist in his religious dedication to peace is his inability to recognize that serious conflict remains at the heart of the world's problems. In his preaching of "love" he often is unable to admit that his wish for "a simple harmony of men of good will" is in conflict with the brute realities and struggles of our time. William Lee Miller makes the important point that the proponents of harmony and tolerance are not inevitably or necessarily serving "the larger value."

They may be sacrificing truth to harmony, encouraging a sleepy acquiescence in whatever happens. . . . "Love" does not mean that we refrain from opposing and resisting our opponents. We need to know what, and who, should be opposed. Don't try to deny that conflict exists. Admit it. Then try to make it serve useful purposes.[6]

During the anxious days of the Cuban crisis in the fall of 1962 one strain of pacifist thought was given forceful expression in the exchange which appears below. This particular woman, long dedicated to peace, announced she had just sent a telegram to President Kennedy indicating her strong disagreement with his quarantine policy and urging him to call a halt to his "threatening moves toward Cuba."

[6] William Lee Miller, *The Protestant and Politics* (Philadelphia: The Westminster Press; n.d.), p. 47.

"What would you do about the building of missile bases in Cuba?" she was asked. "Or would you do nothing?"

"Those bases are not a threat to us. The Russians don't want a war. They want peace."

"How do you know that?"

"Well, I don't *know* it, of course, but I really believe the Russians want peace."

"But if you were President of the United States and therefore responsible for the defense and protection of the country, what would you do if you suddenly learned that offensive missile sites were being erected in Cuba and that the weapons to be launched from them were already at hand? Or would you do anything?"

"I would send a protest to the United Nations," she replied.

"But protests, and meetings to discuss protests, take days and sometimes weeks. Meanwhile the missile bases are finished and Russia has accomplished her goal. What then?"

"It is inconceivable to me that those bases in Cuba could ever be used against us," she said.

"Suppose for a moment that they were used. Suppose, for example, that one landed some place on the East Coast—say, Miami or New York. Given your own views about war, wouldn't you still maintain, even under those drastic conditions, that the United States should not take any military action of any kind?"

She paused. "I don't want a nuclear war. I don't like to think about it."

"But isn't it your position that you would always rather surrender than take any steps which might entail some risk?"

"Yes," she answered. "I would surrender. That would be better than war."

"But in terms of deciding what is the best policy, which is what the President must deal with—"

"My position, I admit, is completely emotional," she interrupted. "It has nothing to do with policy. I don't know what the

President's policy should be. My telegram to the President just expressed my own personal feelings. I just don't want a war."

Her position has the merit of being consistent and clear. It is not necessarily representative of all pacifists, but it puts into sharp relief the deep dilemma of having to face hard political facts with the visceral weaponry of emotion. In her case there must either be peace or surrender, and if the former is threatened the latter is required. The vast gulf of "in-between" is too difficult and risky to contemplate. To state it another way, her position is one that lacks completely any theory of limits. There are no lines to be drawn which could serve as useful guides to the consideration of policy proposals. Instead there are two categories—peace or surrender—from which all choices, if not blessings, flow. Whatever personal and emotional comfort may be derived from such reductionism, it has nothing to do with political alternatives or the processes by which difficult decisions are made.

The American pacifist frequently suffers from an inability to remember that the arms race is not an isolated problem, but exists as an integral part of our whole foreign policy and the factors that motivate that policy. He has failed repeatedly to make real contact with the general public because in any discussion of the arms race he has often been unable or unwilling to answer the one question that is always asked: "What about the Soviet Union?" As a result he insulates himself from the complex problems that are constantly in flux and chooses instead to de-emphasize the justified concern of the American people regarding Soviet expansion, and attempts to override it with an emotional preoccupation with the horrors of war. Thus in many quarters the peace movement has become identified with the slogan "Better Red than Dead," and those who point with pride to their stout-hearted preference seem completely undisturbed by the knowledge that in doing so they have made communication with the general public impossible.

The peace movement in the United States has failed to gain any substantial following among the American people not because it alone awards the highest priority to peace, but because for too long it has misperceived reality both at home and abroad. It is not enough to acknowledge the well-meaning intentions of those who are "for peace"; a person's motives should not be confused with his ability to make reasoned judgments based on the world as it is. A great number of the peace activists have constantly leveled their strongest attack on many significant groups in the United States which, in their view, have wanted war. They have charged that the State Department, whether it was headed by Acheson, Dulles, or Rusk, has intensified tension in the world rather than worked for its reduction. They have viewed American society as being manipulated by certain powerful elites whose actions and policies have undermined the universal desire for peace. They have consistently maintained that since the end of the Second World War the United States has been equally responsible with the Soviet Union for the dangerous impasse between East and West. If one asks why the peace movement has steadfastly maintained these erroneous impressions in the face of accumulated evidence to the contrary, he will be led to answer that it is these very misperceptions themselves that have constituted the necessary justification for the present posture of the peace activists. By explaining the global conflict in terms of a small but powerful minority of individuals who are operating in the United States to subvert the quest for peace, they have provided the rationale they need to justify and sustain their self-appointed mission to save the world for mankind. The pity is that the efforts of the peace movement will continue to be ineffective and will go largely unrewarded until both the leaders and followers are prompted to rid themselves of their particular form of political and ideological myopia.

It cannot be denied that the widespread fear of a nuclear holocaust has contributed to the growth of the peace movement.

However, the atmosphere which generally accompanies this approach does not facilitate full and open political discussion of all the important issues involved. The survivalist position is built around vivid descriptions of what the ashen world will look like after the bombs have fallen, culminating in a great emphasis on the urgent necessity of achieving peace. Thus once more the problem rather than its solution is restated in the tendency to be sordid and graphic about the horrors of war. Those who constantly approach the difficult problems of international politics by dwelling on the possible destruction of the world in two (or five or ten) years are likely to make a number of intellectual concessions regarding the role that the Communists have played in the arms race in order to devise a seemingly reasonable way of avoiding world catastrophe. For example, on the premise that the only real hope for disarmament rests in negotiations, they are quick to argue that Russia is fully prepared to negotiate and wants disarmament or anything else, for that matter, that may be necessary and convenient to fit the pacifist's desire for an immediate negotiated agreement. There is a real tendency to apply a double standard to the United States and to the Soviet Union. Some survivalists are more than willing to criticize the faults of the American system or point out errors in our own position but are reluctant to do the same with Russia. Because of the emotional attitude that peace cannot wait and that something must be done immediately, the survivalist must convince himself and others that immediate disarmament is possible even though negotiations, summit meetings, and the like are failing. If he attaches more blame to the United States than to Russia he will tell you it is because he supposedly can have some effect on America's foreign policy. To admit that a sizable responsibility for the problems standing in the way of a real peace lies somewhere else—with the Soviet Union, for example—where he can have no appreciable effect is, for the survivalist, a frustrating admission because it is tantamount to giving up any hope that anything can be accomplished. It is in the face of such frustration that one often hears the pacifist claim that the real struggle today is not between two powerful nations or opposing ways of life but rather is "the struggle of man for peace." Only the pacifist, however, really believes it.[7]

The person who claims a love of peace should not be led to presume that his is a monopoly. Nor should his passion for peace encourage him to believe that repeated and fervent declarations in its behalf, no matter how genuine the motivations from which they spring, thereby endow him with special insights into how it can be achieved. As we have already suggested, the reverse in many cases is more likely to hold true. The "passionate state of mind" of the peace activist is often a barrier to his understanding that peace can neither be pronounced from on high nor wished into being, but must be forged out of difficult and complex political decisions based on a recognition of the need to use both persuasion and power. Peace, if it is to have any concrete meaning at all, must be based on something more than motives and abstract principles. Facts, conditions, possibilities—these are what deserve serious attention. A "moral crusade" for peace is easy; so are a good man's motives. The real challenge lies in the continuing interplay of the intellectual, moral, and practical problems of the political world.

[7] *The Nation* magazine, in discussing the lack of interest in governmental policy on the part of the Committee for Nonviolent Action, offered a sober observation: "Had the American peace movement been better informed it would have been able to participate effectively in the test ban debate in the context in which the decisions were made, that is, in terms of national security as seen by the policy makers rather than in terms of fallout hysteria and of claims to moral superiority. Fallout dangers are apparent to most . . . but these factors are simply not decisive with those who are presently responsible for big-power policies in matters of war and peace. "An Alternative to Slogans," *The Nation,* March 24, 1962, p. 250.

In a statement that is remarkable for its insight into the dilemma which confronts most pacifists, a Quaker publication offered the following comments:

We hesitate to declare for an immediate peace not because we are afraid of expressing political opinions as such but because we are afraid of political power; afraid of prostituting our religious insights by the use of the pragmatic argument; and afraid of compromising our perfectionist ideas by supporting an imperfect political program. . . .

If we offered leadership to the thousands of our fellow citizens who are groping desperately for a way out of this hell of war and they accepted our leadership, would the cowards and the violent among them flock to our banner and jeopardize the whole program? Would we find ourselves involved with people whose actions we could not sponsor because their political views would not have the same religious basis as ours? . . . If we stress the sacrificial nature of our program for a just peace, it is safe to assume that only men of good will can be attracted by it. . . .

Our fear of stooping to the pragmatic argument in urging political action arises from our natural desire to keep the whole matter on a religious plane—to preach from the Sermon on the Mount. . . .[8]

5

The extremely cogent and often profound Quaker arguments about politics frequently have the effect of obscuring the fact that they are, fundamentally, a religious group. At the end of almost every major book on Quakerism one finally arrives at a statement of pure faith:

Man plays with the politics of time, thinking to be master of his own destiny. But God is not mocked; His politics still govern. . . . Men strive for security in a world where security cannot exist. . . . To risk all may be to gain all . . . to put into action the laws of the Kingdom before the Kingdom has really come . . . [but] it [will]

[8] Hutchinson, op. cit., pp. 22–3.

never come until somebody [believes] in its principles enough to try them in actual operation. . . .[9]

Everyone has different views on the validity of religious "truths" and a wide range of feelings about the strengths or weaknesses supporting any policy based on faith. This is merely another complicating factor in trying to assess the Quaker views on individual conscience, foreign policy, nonviolence, and the like. It is no real circumvention of the question of whether God exists or not to ask simply: are religious "truths" useful? What is regarded as useful will vary, depending upon whether or not it is believed that Christianity and God are true. For the moment, however, it is only necessary to point out that the substratum underlying the Quaker's ethical, psychological, historical, and sociological arguments in defense of his position is in reality his faith in God.

The politics of eternity works not by might but by spirit; a Spirit whose redemptive power is released among men through suffering endured on behalf of the evil doer . . . such love suffers long, is always kind, never fails. . . .
. . . there must be renewed in a disintegrating society the sense of community . . . such community is built on trust and confidence, which some will say is not possible now because the Communists cannot be trusted. The politics of eternity does not require that we trust [the Communists]. They require us to love [them] and to trust in God.[1]

As we have already seen, there are both liberals and conservatives in the Quaker ranks. I have tried to indicate the variety of opinions that can be found in their writings as well as some of the major points around which there is general agreement. But it should be kept in mind that the Quakers are not just a package of principles which can be dissected like frogs. Quakers are living, learning, maturing people, and anyone who has ever

[9] *Speak Truth to Power,* pp. 69–70.
[1] Ibid., p. 69.

worked with them knows that they are warm and generous human beings. More and more the Quakers are insisting upon the validation of their "inner light" by the "facts of experience," asking if what they believe to be right fits the hopes and aspirations of the times. There should be no misunderstanding about their place in our society: they are immensely valuable to us. They are among the few "inner-directed" groups still among us. They are extraordinarily socially conscious and desirous of doing well toward their fellow men. In their relief work, their charities, their missions with the American Indians and with refugees abroad they have demonstrated a depth of good will and sacrifice not easily to be found in modern life. They also fulfill the necessary minority function of setting the extreme poles of political discussion, bringing to practical politics the kind of idealism, optimism, and farsightedness that might otherwise be lacking.

My concern in this chapter has been directed to a different problem. In talking about the anti-political tendencies in the Quaker position and philosophy I have sought to show that those who are faithful to their expressed principles are likely to be more concerned with their own ends than with the preservation of democratic politics as a method and procedure. The Quaker who refuses to pay his income taxes or sails into nuclear testing zones or refuses to vote or will have nothing to do with politics or government because it is "evil" is explicitly denying the power of a state built on democratic principles and is refusing to make the kind of compromise that is at the root of all democratic politics. Those Quakers who argue that "militarism and modern democracy are incompatible" may strike a sympathetic chord in all of us who lament the psychological effects that are the result of a continuing cold war. But they are advancing what many regard as a fallacious proposition. It is not necessarily (as many Quakers suggest) a matter of either/or: *either* we give up our guns *or* we give up our democracy. It may very well be that *if* we gave up our guns we would *lose* our democracy, militarized as it is, morally debased as it may be. The point is that the Quakers are giving their total commitment to the particular end *they* consider worth preserving, namely, the almost total freedom of action and conscience. Others might argue that for the purposes of survival these facets of democracy might necessarily be temporarily suspended. But some Quakers are unwilling to make this compromise.

It is only a step or two from this Quaker attitude to accept the proposition that we are all "better off Red than dead." The argument is familiar: that under even the most severe conditions there will linger in the breast of man a spark of freedom, of free will and liberty of thought and conscience. This is precisely the belief of the man who goes to jail because of an act of civil disobedience; like Thoreau, he believes that true freedom is within the jail, not outside it. In addition, the Quakers also believe in God, a God whose "politics of eternity" promises eventual justice for the righteous no matter how atrocious man's temporal conditions.

The combination of the above attitudes would, I suspect, produce a Quaker argument that ran something like this: The arms race means eventual, and mutual, suicide. Furthermore, our military strength is corrupting our morals and depriving individuals of their freedom. We must unilaterally disarm. (We do.) Now, if by some quirk the Russians are really so callous and immoral as everybody says, they will invade us. It is unlikely, but they may. But surely they will prove incapable of slaughtering all of us, and so we will have adequate time and opportunity to win them over by demonstrating how happy we are and how well democracy works. But they may slaughter us. It is unlikely, but they may. In that case, God will see that justice is done in the end. At any rate, each of us will have done the only thing his conscience would allow him to do, and we shall be rewarded, if not in heaven, then at least by our own sense of having done the right thing.

Here is the heart of the matter. *If* one does *not* believe in a just God and the "politics of eternity," this is dangerous antipolitical thinking. *If* one believes that man, though perhaps essentially good, *is* too often quite corruptible and made callous and indifferent to the conscientious claims and rational arguments of unarmed people, then again one must declare that this is dangerous anti-political thinking. *If* one believes that between "guns" *or* "democracy," "guns" *and* "democracy," faith and/or facts, deadness and/or Redness, that between the Scylla and Charybdis of "individual conscience" and/or "civil obedience," there lies a land of workable, achievable compromise, then one is exercising the kind of thought that democratic politics thrives upon, and one must therefore regard the Quaker position as a conscious or unconscious willingness to sacrifice democratic politics to private ends.

It would be a difficult matter to run a democracy in which each individual's duty of civil obedience ended at the point where it conflicted with what he felt to be the "conscientious" course of action. It would be a most unstable democracy wherein each citizen could decide for himself whether or not or when he would pay his taxes, serve in the armed forces, or take action into his own hands when political means did not give satisfaction to his own desires. There is no such thing (and many Quakers are fully aware of this) as "absolute freedom." All human activity is based on the existence of limitations; true freedom implies a recognition of those limits which do exist. Politics, too, as an expression of freedom in a democratic society, requires the recognition of limits—the limits of what an individual can do for himself as well as the limits of what an individual or faction should be allowed to do according to a system of justice which the majority has agreed to enforce and abide by.

The pacifist approach to politics—what some have called "the love ethic of the New Testament"—has been seriously limited in

its operational value by its general abhorrence of the realities of
political power. As defenders of the *ideal form* of political life,
the pacifists have devoted so much of their energy and dedication to the "city of God" that much of their doctrine and many of
their beliefs, when confronted by the awesome problems of our
times, have been rendered largely inoperative in the "city of
man." In their revulsion to war they have frequently overlooked
or minimized the inhumanity inherent in the forces of tyranny
and oppression. In proclaiming steadfastly their opposition to
war and the militarists who feed on its spoils, they have been
unable to see that their repeated rejection of military strength as
a defensive measure might well lead to the aggrandizement of
power by autocratic regimes for tyrannical purposes and perhaps
even to war itself.

In the Holy Experiment of colonial Pennsylvania the pacifists
held to the same principle which serves today as a basic tenet of
their faith: that reason can be freed from power and can act
without the implementation of force. It is only a short step to the
principle of nonresistance taught in the Sermon on the Mount,
and for the Quaker it leads to the ultimate realization of divine
love on earth. But the problem is much deeper than this. In
implying that suffering love can conquer the difficulties of this
world and create a balance of power that will make force no
longer necessary, pacifism is engaging in what Reinhold Niebuhr
has called a utopian illusion. If acted upon, he says, it would
cause its proponents to fall a complete prey to the sinful
proclivities of human nature.[2] The pacifist approach is to identify
the use of physical force with evil. Yet it is perfectly plain that
all acts of physical force do not necessarily constitute "violence
against personality." To make evil coterminous with violence is

[2] See Reinhold Niebuhr, *Beyond Tragedy: Essays on the Christian
Interpretation of History* (New York: Scribner's; 1937), especially
Ch. 9.

one thing; to identify violence with physical force and all physical force with violence is something entirely different. Furthermore, as Niebuhr points out, "spiritual" force can be just as self-centered, as egoistic, and therefore as violent, as physical force.[3] The point to be made is that there is no hope for a just political system if one insists that the use of physical force as such is the equivalent of injustice and that the use of spiritual or moral power will automatically result in justice.

The fault in the pacifist theory of politics lies in its particular brand of religiosity. As a religion it fails to understand that politics does not concern itself merely with ideals, pure or otherwise. A religious humanitarianism which focuses its attention on the divine aspirations of man may offer great hope to those who are comforted either by the words of Jesus or by their own moral conscience, but it will be of little value to those who are responsible for the judicious exercise of power in the actual political contest. To view politics in this religious light is to miss the central point about politics—namely, that it is related directly to policy, to its formulation and promulgation in the less than ideal attempt for an accommodation of many diverse interests. Politics is the art of the possible, which is to say that it is a constant process of trying to relate particular objectives to other objectives. To insist that all political issues—civil rights, disarmament, and so on—must be treated as moral issues may have "the ironic result of relieving, rather than increasing, moral tension," but it also obscures the realities of power, minimizes the democratic necessity of competing interests, and gives little attention to the burdens of political responsibility.[4]

---

[3] Niebuhr, *The Nature and Destiny of Man* (New York: Scribner's; 1941 & 1943), Vol. II, p. 261. For an excellent analysis of these criticisms by a leading pacifist and scholar, see Mulford Sibley, *The Political Theories of Modern Pacifism,* The Pacifist Research Bureau, Philadelphia, Series V: No. 1, July 1944.

[4] William Lee Miller has made an astute observation on this point: "The whole idea of the 'moral issue' is dangerous because it tends to

"Our success or failure," a leading Quaker has written, "will depend upon whether we put our trust completely on the spiritual side and refuse to compromise with violence. The people who base their power completely on the spirit, and have nothing else to lose, cannot be finally crushed or destroyed."[5] Perhaps not. But to put one's trust "completely on the spiritual side," or to base one's argument solely on conscience or personal morality, is to refuse any responsibility for the consequences. To take this position is to adopt the ethic of the Sermon on the Mount, an ethic which only a person who lived like Jesus could be expected to adopt. For the apostles, St. Francis, or the Quakers themselves perhaps there is no higher law than that which commands, "Resist not him that is evil with force." But as Max Weber has pointed out, for the politician the reverse proposition holds true: thou *shalt* resist evil by force, or else you are responsible for the evil winning out. Only an ethic of moral truth, of individual conscience as the sole guide, of personal certitude—clearly an absolute ethic—can afford the sanctitude which permits a person to be unconcerned with consequences. It is an ethic which a man in politics should adopt only if he is eager to be returned to private life.

---

lead toward a small, select, rather stereotyped and often even trivial set of problems. It implies that 'bingo' is a moral issue—and public housing is not; that 'liquor' is a moral issue—but Federal aid to education is not; that grain for India is a moral issue—but the depletion allowance of oil is not; that economic aid abroad is 'moral'—but military aid is not. All political issues are, in a sense, moral issues; it is not helpful to select items for emphasis on the basis of which can be called 'moral'; often that leads away from the more difficult and important problems to the edges and corners." Miller, op. cit., p. 38.

[5] *Pacifist Living Today and Tomorrow,* p. 38.

CHAPTER FIVE

Politics and Psychology:
The Limitations of
Psychological Determinism

> *It is not too farfetched to say that everyone is born a politician, and most of us outgrow it.*
>
> HAROLD D. LASSWELL

〰〰〰〰〰 1

We live in what has been called the Age of Analysis. It might just as easily be termed the age of disclosure, since some of the predominant forces of our time have, as one of their chief purposes, the self-assigned task of unmasking the false and revealing the "truth." The original prophets of disclosure—I am thinking particularly of Marx and Freud—turned their intellectual efforts toward an enriched understanding of the human and social condition, but many of their present-day disciples, as is so often the case, have vulgarized their masters by transforming important insights into the foundations of individual and social behavior into blunt instruments of distortion. At its worst, it is a game of parlor psychology that anyone can play.

Nothing is immune from this kind of psychological reductionism. In an article entitled "The Sexual Symbolism of Christmas," an "expert in applied psychology," D. J. Bennett, explained the subconscious meaning of the virgin birth, the upright

Christmas tree, and Santa's coming down the chimney.[1] I have no particular fondness for Christmas, knowing full well that it is a holiday essentially for children and the national economy. But I am prepared to accept it for what it is—an annual ordeal that, as *The New Yorker* once put it, "is at our throats again." Like many other forms of pain, it comes, it is endured, and it passes. But apparently I have not really understood what Christmas is all about and, more important, what it represents. For one thing, the "good will" that is generated at Christmas is merely a rationalization. "Our good behavior at Christmas," says Dr. Bennett, "is dictated by the fact that the nativity is the Christian embodiment of the Oedipus fantasy, the most violent and most feared of all our wish-fantasies. As we approach the celebration, the acute effect of the fantasy on our psyche triggers our subconscious guilt, and embroils us in an orgy of atonement." I cannot comment on Dr. Bennett's Christmas, but either I have repressed everything, or Christmas was never like that in our house.

But there is more that I have not considered. The whole structure of the Santa Claus fabrication is strikingly sexual, according to Dr. Bennett. "Santa, driven by the virile, horned reindeer, brings a gift through the chimney and deposits it in a stocking." In fact, according to Richard Sterba, a psychiatrist, "The fireplace and chimney signify vulva and vagina in the unconscious mind, and Santa's gift is symbolic of the ultimate gift to man—a child." [2] For that matter, adds Dr. Bennett, "much of the secrecy, anxiety, and mystery that surround the preparation of Christmas gifts in the home is reminiscent of the excited anticipation of childbirth. This activity can be explained when one recognizes that Santa, who ultimately brings the gift, is

---

[1] D. J. Bennett, "The Sexual Symbolism of Christmas," *Fact*, January–February 1964, pp. 61–4.

[2] Richard Sterba, "On Christmas," *Psychoanalytic Review* (1944) quoted in *Fact*.

subconsciously regarded as a father bringing a child." How did Father Santa get into the picture in the first place? He is part of the reaction to "the mother-goddess worship of the Mediterranean countries, an attempt to upgrade the father in the celebration of the nativity. But the way this father-substitute has entered American lore has made it a source of bewilderment and disturbance to the child. While the child may believe in a mythical gift-bearer who, like God, cannot be seen, he can hardly be expected to place any faith in a visible person masquerading in an undignified manner, of whom he sees countless facsimiles throughout the Christmas season."

Eric Hoffer once commented that considering how light-hearted we feel when we do not take ourselves seriously, it is surprising how difficult the attainment of this sensible and practical attitude seems to be. "It is apparently much easier to be serious than frivolous." [3] Dr. Bennett is deadly serious about Santa Claus as father-substitute, the oedipal implications of the Christmas season, and the "generative power of the human male, the phallus," which is represented by the Christmas tree. But above all, he takes himself very seriously, which is why there is no room for frivolity in his attitude toward Christmas. How can there be when he explains (in all seriousness) the lasting popularity of Christmas by saying that "in our subconscious we are attracted to the sexual meanings of the ceremonies even if we do not quite understand them"? Once again psychological analysis has probed beneath the surface of "reality"—in this case Christmas—and stripped away its various disguises. Christmas is a façade, and all the candles, colored papers, ribbons, and mistletoe are merely contrivances to conceal what is "real" underneath. Besides, all explanations that rest on "surface phenomena" are suspect. Reality is never what it appears to be.

[3] Eric Hoffer, *The Passionate State of Mind* (New York: Harper; 1954), p. 61.

It is not surprising, then, that politics has succumbed to the same abuse and in the process been reduced to nonpolitical terms. More specifically, politics is often reduced to psychological terms so that what are considered "ultimate" political realities can be made to reveal themselves. Seen in this light, an interest in politics has been called a surface manifestation of realities underneath, perhaps an escape from a domineering father or a search for political utopia as a result of a disappointing childhood. The range of such explanations is endless.

However, politics, far from being illuminated or understood, is vulgarized and distorted. The man who could write that "Preoccupation with international rights and wrongs is a useful substitute activity, a vicarious discharge of emotional tension, the original source of which is infantile sadism," has no use for politics.[4] He has neither the desire nor the capacity to treat it as something important.

The issues here are certainly more profound and serious than the facile example of Santa Claus would suggest. In its broadest context the basic problem is the tension between those who look upon man as endowed with reason and the capacity to express ideas, on the one hand, and on the other those who seek to reduce man's reason either to his sociological moorings or his subconscious makeup. There is a considerable history dealing with these two perspectives on man and society which cannot be reviewed here. However, the vulgarizers of Marx, in reducing the notion of self-interest to class interest, insist that a person's ideas cannot be understood apart from his class or group affiliations. A man's beliefs and values have only superficial meaning because the "real" meaning of his ideas emerges only when we discover the groups to which he belongs. What a man says or believes is no longer judged at the level of ideas, but as Reinhard Bendix has

[4] Quoted in Norman Jacobson, "The Unity of Political Theory: A Case for Commitment," op. cit.

said, "in terms of who his friends are and how his ideas might be used to further their cause." Thus we are led to think not of individual man but of group man. Similarly the vulgarizers of Freud have discredited rational motivation in man by pointing to the "inner man" and his unconscious motivations. Ideas are not to be taken seriously because they are "emotionally biased." A person's political expressions are seen as reflections of irrational desires and, if the "truth" could be known, they are not what he "really" has on his mind anyway. The truth does not lie in what a man says, but in why he said it. Thus, Bendix points out, "only a man who can keep a straight face while telling an outrageous lie has a chance of escaping this inquisition into his motives." But assume a man whose emotions are deeply involved with the ideas he expresses; that man's motives, and hence his ideas, are suspect. What a man says is, therefore, regarded as merely a "surface manifestation" of his ego.[5] Reason, and all efforts at reason, are thereby easily and quickly depreciated.

It is but a short step from these vulgarizations of Marx and Freud to the view that politics can only be understood by stripping away its superficial appearances and unmasking the forces at work beneath the surface. For example, political institutions are frequently categorized as "formalistic" and as such cannot be expected to lead to the discovery of reality, which is never formal. The American Constitution is a case in point. The so-called "realist" school, of which Charles Beard was one of the charter members, has made it clear that what took place when

[5] Reinhard Bendix, "Social Science and the Distrust of Reason," University of California Publications in Sociology and Social Institutions, Univ. California Press, April 1951, pp. 19–20. Professor Bendix makes it clear that "Freud's theory of personality held that man's consciousness does not reveal what really motivates him to act as he does. This approach implied an assessment of conscious ideas in terms of what they reveal about an individual's unconscious motivation. But it did this in the context of a theory of personality, and it did *not* imply an evaluation of these ideas themselves."

the Founding Fathers convened in Philadelphia in 1787 reflected their economic position and stake in society. It is considered naïve and unrealistic to examine the interchange and impact of the various political theories of these learned men or the fascinating debates on the different strands of federalism which they ultimately pulled together to form the structure of the new government. The "realist" evaluation, as Beard has made clear, is that the drawing up of the Constitution was obviously the result of compromise dictated by the economic holdings of the delegates themselves. Any thought that the whole question of federalism might have raised some crucial issues of political and legal philosophy is felt to be unworthy of the serious attention of busy men. The ideas, much less the ideals, of Adams, Madison, Hamilton, and all the others only camouflage the hard realities of money and property. Politics mirrors economics, and only the latter is "real." [6]

Our concern in this chapter, however, is with the role of psychology in the analysis of politics. In the determination to get at "inner realities," modern psychology has heavily infiltrated the vast realm of political life. More important, the penetration of psychology has often led to a reckless treatment of politics. In rejecting the rational and voluntary model of political man, contemporary psychology has frequently been led to magnify the irrational and involuntary side of man. It is one thing to recognize the relationship between politics and psychology. But if and when politics gives way to psychology—or, for that matter, to sociology, theology, morality, or anything else—it runs the risk of being distorted beyond recognition. The psychological assaults on politics have been so ubiquitous that politics itself has been

[6] Norman Jacobson has touched on these points more fully in "American Institutions in the Age of Analysis: The Descent into Reality," a paper prepared for the Panel on Federalism and Local Government, Annual Meeting of the American Political Science Association, Washington, D.C., September 6, 1956.

corrupted to the point where it is treated as an epiphenomenon. Just as men's ideas and actions are thought (by many Marxists) to be determined in the long run by the changing organization of production, so politics has been reduced to the emotional components of man's personality. But it has been our central contention throughout this book that politics is a legitimate enterprise and activity because political decisions, rather than being the conditioned reflex of a society's economic structure or the ego defenses of the human personality, are the end-product of the conflicts, tactics, and strategies which are characteristic of political life in democratic societies. This proposition is denied, however, when politics is reduced to some form of psychological determinism. The school of psychological environmentalism, for example, identified with John B. Watson and B. F. Skinner, comes close to rejecting the voluntary, rational, and conscious character of human behavior. Politics cannot help but be given short shrift because of the pervasive assumptions of determinism.

But more significant here is the Freudian connection between psychology and politics. Little needs to be said about Freud's immeasurable contributions, but the impact of Freudianism on the analysis of political behavior merits attention. Nor will much be said here about the therapeutic features of Freudian doctrine, except to point out that what may prove to be useful techniques in the treatment of individual disorders may have little application in analyzing political activities. There have been too many instances where a clinical familiarity with what goes on in an individual's mind has been presumed, by analogy, to be relevant to what takes place in social and political life. Psychological modes of analysis, while they may provide the psychologist or psychiatrist with a necessary frame of reference for asking questions which will help the patient unravel the meaning of disturbing symptoms in his life, cannot be similarly used to interpret political phenomena. What is useful in studying and leading to the cure of individual problems does not automatically lead to an understanding of the complexities of politics.

The focus in this chapter, then, will be on the anti-political temper of Freudian psychology. The variations on this theme are many and diverse, only some of which will be dealt with here. The dominant note, however, is by now familiar—namely, the rejection of politics as an independent activity, the denial of its autonomous meaning, and the devaluation of its democratic premises.

〰〰〰 2

The specific features of Freudian psychology which have had profound implications for politics are considerably diverse. The first and most critical is the fundamental notion that the unconscious represents the true psychic reality of man. Conditions and events taking place on the conscious level are looked upon as overt manifestations of hidden motives. The basic character structure of an individual takes its essential shape from the psycho-biological dynamics that occur during one's infantile family experiences. Thus the Oedipus complex is central. Responding to the unconscious, man is driven by instincts which result from an interplay of the libido and his fears of death. In fact, in his *Civilization and Its Discontents* [7] Freud described the fate of man and his whole culture in terms of this struggle. Freud went on to say that civilization or society is possible only at the price of instinctual frustration. Since society frustrates and stifles instincts, man inevitably experiences anxiety as a member of society. Put another way, individual and cultural development constantly oppose each other, from which the resulting frustration may be transformed into aggression.

[7] Sigmund Freud, *Civilization and Its Discontents* (London: Hogarth Press; 1953).

In explaining the stability of society, Freud pointed to the relationship between the leader and the led. After the primal father was killed, men wanted to atone and reinstate him in the form of the leader. Consequently, as Read Bain has observed, culture can be regarded as a product of a mythical Oedipus murder.[8] In *Totem and Taboo*,[9] Freud elaborated on this theme, claiming that a social contract as an expression of feelings of "murder guilt" preceded political society. More important, he developed all of the themes of coercion and submission that were to preoccupy him throughout his life. The leadership is self-sufficient and has authoritarian overtones. Society is characterized by dominant personality types resulting from infantile sexual-biological configurations. These dominant personality types, in turn, determine the nature of society—a capitalist society, for example, develops where the "anal character" predominates.

It is neither necessary nor possible to examine in any depth the above aspects of Freudian psychology, presented here in gross and incomplete form. What should be underscored in passing is that the Freudian perspective is in direct conflict with the Marxist attack on psychology. The antipsychological position of Marxism maintains that specific social organizations require certain personality types, rejecting the opposite notion that personality types demand specific social organizations: Marxism is the antonym of Freudianism.[1] Paradoxically, Marx and Freud represent two exclusive varieties of determinism, namely, economic and psychological, each of which is a systematic attempt to deduce from its basic premises a range of facts and, from these facts, to draw conclusions. Thus for contemporary Marxists, as we have

[8] Read Bain, "Sociology and Psychoanalysis," *American Sociological Review*, April 1936, p. 206.

[9] Sigmund Freud, *Totem and Taboo* (New York: New Republic, Inc.; 1918).

[1] Philip Rieff, "History, Psychoanalysis at the Social Sciences," *Ethics*, January 1953, p. 107.

seen in a previous chapter, politics is determined by class interests and the class organization of society. For the Freudians politics is a repercussion of emotions.

Perhaps the most cynical psychogenetic devaluation of politics is the notion that all public political behavior is the response of unconscious and irrational psychic mechanisms. In discussing Freud's disparagement of political life, Philip Rieff remarks that "by his anatomy of the familial sources of group coercion, of the inner compulsion that gathers membership into chance crowds, churches, states, by his sinister evocations of the guilt from which obedience springs, Freud absorbed the study of society into a medical science—but one in which any thought of a complete cure had become a rationalist piety." [2] Politics had no independent meaning to Freud because it was just another form of man's nature writ large. He never concerned himself with the busy world of everyday government, if for no other reason than his strong belief that man's human nature cannot be elevated by government since the state itself epitomizes the worst elements of human desire. Carried to extremes, the orthodox genetic and biological school of psychiatry stresses the invariant psychological impact that infantile suckling as well as excretory and genital functions have on the adult personality. Adult political behavior is interpreted as, in part, the acting out of infantile striving which has either been interfered with or not sufficiently gratified.[3] The cultural and social context of political behavior is dismissed as superficial and is assimilated by unconscious motivation. A person's political conduct or principles "are merely ways of regarding the world and . . . are determined and directed by a man's inward make-up," by those deeply rooted factors "which

[2] Philip Rieff, "Psychology and Politics," *World Politics,* January 1955, p. 299.

[3] See Nathan Leites, "Psycho-cultural Hypotheses About Political Acts," *World Politics,* January 1948, p. 116.

are governed neither by logic nor by intellectual considerations."[4] What is objective and social is regarded as subjective and individual. Thus it is not difficult to discover the implicit suggestion that "participation in politics is incoherent, emotional, and utterly capricious. In short, it is irrational."[5]

Neither Freud's geneticist overstatements, however, nor the importance attached to motives buried deep in a person's childhood are sufficient orientations for considering the impact of Freudian thought on the contemporary study of political behavior. A number of general theories of personality types have been regularly invoked to explain everything from who participates in politics and why, to the makeup of our political leaders and the nature of public leadership itself. Our own interest is with those particular theories of political behavior which lay claim to a "political personality."

Harold D. Lasswell was a pioneer in relating personality to political behavior, suggesting that the foundation of politics lies in emotional instability. In some of his earliest works he developed the notions of displacement and rationalization as the major devices whereby private motives and repressed feelings are transformed into political activity. Private motives, Lasswell maintains, are displaced onto public objects. A more orthodox psychogenetic approach to politics would assert that members of a political party decide to join "not out of any balanced consideration or deliberate intellectual decision following a considered analysis of existing conditions, but . . . as a result of unconscious factors and qualities which are integrated within them from the days of their childhood, and of which intellectual judgment and consideration are merely a rationalization to ex-

---

[4] M. Brachyahu, "A Contribution Towards the Psychology of the Parties," *Psychoanalytic Review,* 36 (1949), p. 429.

[5] Floyd W. Matson, *The Broken Image* (New York: Braziller; 1964), p. 87.

plain to the individual why he should attach himself to any viewpoint." [6]

According to Lasswell, the essence of politics revolves around the shaping and sharing of power, and the political personality type "accentuates" the value of getting and using power. The person who seeks political power has an unsatisfied craving for deference, a craving whose emotional roots go back to ungratified needs when he was a child. In trying to satisfy the urgent need for deference, he seeks attention and even adulation in the political arena. To complete the circle, the individual then rationalizes his displacement of private feelings by insisting that he is fulfilling his role as a democratic citizen working in behalf of the public interest.

The basic personality type that Lasswell is describing is one who turns to politics to compensate for inner misgivings, doubts, or fears. Power, he is saying, is a defense, and individuals turn to it in the hope of overcoming low estimates they have of themselves. Lasswell advances a general proposition that "the accent on power rather than some other value in the social process has come because limitations upon access to other values have been overcome by the use of power." When nonpower values fail to remove deficiencies, hope is focused on power. "And when the expectation is accepted that other values depend on power, the pursuit of power looms larger in the personality system. When we try to account for the component of the self on whose behalf power is sought (and especially the primary ego), one general proposition appears to be that extreme egocentric fixation reflects an environment that provides meagre emotional support during the early years." [7]

[6] Brachyahu, op. cit., p. 430.
[7] Harold Lasswell, "The Selective Effect of Personality on Political Participation," in *Studies in the Scope and Method of "The Authoritarian Personality,"* ed. Richard Christie and Marie Jahoda (Glencoe, Ill.: Free Press; 1954), pp. 206–7.

The idea that political leadership reflects a "displacement of private motives" is abundantly provided with ambiguities and other difficulties. I remember a heated dinner-table discussion several months after the election of President Kennedy in which the argument was being made that Kennedy had not only fulfilled his father's hopes for his son but, in getting into politics in the first place, was acting out his childhood identification with his father. It was one of those arguments that had no end because there was no way of offering proof or disproof. But the assumption was that Kennedy was a hostage to his early fixation on his father, who had predetermined his political career. One can easily grant that all of the Kennedy children grew up in a political family charged with political discussion and debate and that this experience may clearly have whetted their appetites for political careers. But for how long through a man's life must it be said that he is still "working out" his attachment to his father? It seems reasonable to believe that President Kennedy's political career can be accepted and evaluated outside the narrow framework of a father-son relationship. In the three years that Kennedy occupied the White House he developed a political style and manner all his own. It was clear to everyone that this was a man who loved the excitement of public life and warmed to its every challenge. Whatever the relationship with his father, the President went his own way when it came to making political decisions that affected the nation and the world. In fact, it was no secret that the President and his father had parted company when it came to matters of public policy. To explain the President's flair for politics or his ascent to high political office as representing a "displacement of private motives" is to reduce what is political to a kind of psychological irrationalism. Instead of discussing Kennedy's commitment to American politics in the context of his own interest and accomplishments, we end up evaluating the man by presuming to examine his motives. The results are dubious at best. "If political psychologists would make a sharper distinction between infantilism and motivation that is strictly contemporary and of age, most of the debunking theory of political leadership which has appeared—wrongly—as Freud's chief contribution to political science would be obviated." [8]

The notion that men engage in political behavior in order to relieve personal psychic disorders has received wide currency. After all, there is a simplistic logic in the belief that politics is really just a form of vicarious pleasure or escape for those whose lives are in some form of emotional disarray. This must certainly be true of many people, just as it is unquestionably true that all of us do a lot of things throughout our lives that are really forms of compensation. But this does not tell us much that we do not already know. However, the more serious implications of the psychogenetic approach to politics are less easily passed over. For example, one of the major premises of a democratic political system is that man's reason, supported and disciplined by the web of constitutional and institutional arrangements in society, is a positive force leading to the peaceful resolution of difficult and divisive issues. But the instinctual determinism that animates so much of the psychological perspective exhibits little more than a disregard for the political process, since politics is looked upon essentially as the mirror of irrational conflicts. Men are not held together by rational bonds but by myths grounded in emotions. The only way to mitigate these conflicts is to bring the irrational to the level of consciousness.[9] For some the only solution is the

---

[8] Rieff, "Psychology and Politics," op. cit., p. 301. It should perhaps be pointed out that the notion that personality syndromes are established in the first years of life involves the obvious fallacious assumption that personality does not change in response to post-infantile experience or cultural influences. This amounts to a mechanistic determinism which basically fails to consider the human personality as a socio-cultural product as well as a culture producer.

[9] For a discussion of this general point of view and a synopsis of Lasswell's orientation, see M. Mark, "What Image of Man for Political Science?" *Western Political Quarterly,* November 1962, pp. 593–604.

application to politics of the therapeutic insights of psychoanalysis. Thus we are admonished that "perhaps a great deal of
spiritual energy, so precious for the good of society, could be
saved, were the spokesmen of [political] parties to agree to be
psychoanalysed, a process which is so important for anyone who
works in the education of individuals, or masses." [1] Any public
discussion aimed at ameliorating a political or social problem
becomes tenuous and irrelevant. Man's rationality is a prisoner of
his psyche, an assumption that subverts the very basis of political
communication in a democratic society. In the words of one
psychogenetically inspired commentator, "When you have analyzed to its roots the meaning of the mechanisms which are the
dominant motive forces of the psyche, you feel all the useless-
ness of heated discussions and of the desire to convince an
opponent of the truth. . . ." [2] In short, political action is a
symptom of inadequate adjustment and political participation is
the clearest form of irrational expression.

The psychological current that has stressed the role of personality factors in political behavior has taken many forms. The
most noteworthy is the framework that has developed in connection with the study of the "authoritarian personality," to which
we shall return presently. This general orientation has produced
a number of investigations of the personality traits of individuals
in society who are either active or inactive politically. I mention
a few here because they point up again the difficulties in using
personality typologies and characteristics to evaluate political
behavior in general and political leadership in particular. The
major problem is that there is no firm empirical evidence to
support the wide range of theories and speculations. The personality approach to politics suffers from the same embarrassment
that has handicapped other approaches examining the motives of
participation in political affairs: it explains both too much and

[1] Brachyahu, op. cit., p. 438.
[2] Ibid., p. 430.

too little. For example, Janowitz and Marvick found in their national samples that "authoritarianism" was significantly and directly related to feelings of political ineffectiveness.[3] People who scored high on the authoritarianism scale tended to feel that it was impossible to influence governmental actions, while those with low authoritarian scores tended to feel that they could influence government. In addition, individuals with high authoritarian scores, when compared to the rest of the population, were significantly less likely to vote in the 1948 elections. On the other hand and contrary to these findings, Robert Lane found that authoritarians and equalitarians did not differ with respect to whether or not they voted.[4] Other differences appeared. The voting of equalitarians was found to be motivated by such considerations as "a sense of civic duty" and "conscience." Authoritarians were more likely to vote as a result of pressures from the social groups to "act conventionally" and from a desire to exercise even a small amount of political power. But if these findings are accurate, what of Lasswell's contention that his political type, which he connects with the authoritarian personality, tends to rationalize his political behavior in terms of the public interest? If Lasswell is right, then authoritarians should show a tendency to give "a sense of civic duty" as a reason for political action. But Lane finds that authoritarians are less likely than equalitarians to give such a reason. It is clear that more research is needed. It is also clear that the general personality approach to politics is encumbered with enormous difficulties.[5]

Much of the work of political psychologists has contributed

[3] Morris Janowitz and Dwaine Marvick, "Authoritarianism and Political Behavior," *Public Opinion Quarterly,* Summer 1953, pp. 185–201.

[4] Robert Lane, "Political Personality and Electoral Choice," *American Political Science Review,* March 1955, pp. 173–90.

[5] I want to acknowledge the ample use I have made here of Wendell Bell, Richard J. Hill, and Charles R. Wright, *Public Leadership* (San Francisco: Chandler Publishing Co.; 1961), especially pp. 161–8. This is an excellent review of the literature of public leadership.

valuable speculation at the level of broad generalizations. The trouble is that the generalizations often break down when they are applied to specific cases. This is especially true when individualistically oriented theories of political motivation are used to explain different forms of political activity. While Lasswell's writings are the modern seminal source, others have followed in his trials and have sought to provide some data to support the Freudian presuppositions about political behavior. It is one thing to understand the motivation of behavior in general; it is something else, however, to understand the motivation of political behavior. This is where various broad theories suffer from a lack of specificity, resulting in serious limitations. For example, Robert Lane has spent a good deal of time and effort in constructing what he calls a "grammar of motives." Political activity, according to Lane, serves a number of basic human "needs." Men go into politics to satisfy their needs for friendship, or to seek power over others (because they have doubts about themselves), or to defend and improve their self-esteem. Men seek to relieve intrapsychic tensions, chiefly those arising from aggressive and sexual impulses, by immersing themselves in politics. As others have pointed out, there are many difficulties and ambiguities in Lane's position. Consider the following:

We have suggested that such social adjustment needs may lead people to join political parties—although they may also lead them to avoid joining where this might antagonize others who are important.[6]

If the intra-psychic tension does, in fact, find political expression, how does this come about? Two means are particularly relevant: first, the use of political participation as a means of blocking out the tension, distracting the individual from his personal troubles, and, second, the use of political participation as a means of expressing the

[6] Robert Lane, *Political Life* (Glencoe, Ill.: Free Press; 1959), p. 110.

troublesome impulse, or as a means of rationalizing the resolution of the conflict in socially acceptable terms.[7]

But as Bell, Hill, and Wright pointedly ask, under precisely what conditions, then, will "social adjustment needs" result in political behavior? When is political behavior to be viewed as "blocking out" the "intra-psychic" tension, and when must it be interpreted as "expressing the troublesome impulse?" As they are presently formulated, these "needs" of man "can be invoked to 'explain' any general behavior, be it political, economic, scientific, familial, criminal, or athletic. In other words, while it is possible to view political behavior as the expression of general needs, such a view does not 'explain' the very thing we are seeking to understand."[8]

The paramount issue here, above and beyond the various attempts to understand political life in terms of man's needs or his irrational unconscious motives, is the fundamental assumption that psychiatric modes of analysis are useful and applicable in explaining political behavior. Our own contention is that psychological interpretations of politics are not so much fallacious as they are ambiguous and incomplete. In his well-known book *Childhood and Society* Erik Erikson talks of the ethic of competition in American life in terms of the cultural determination of child-rearing. American mothers encourage their sons to accept and live by this competitive spirit, Erikson says, because self-reliance was the essential condition of survival in the westward-moving days of the frontier. Erikson's explanation is

[7] Ibid., p. 118.

[8] Bell, Hill, and Wright, op. cit., p. 167. The authors underscore a point that also is pertinent to everything that is being said in this chapter—namely, that "the above criticism is not to be interpreted as a denial of the importance of personality factors in political behavior. The refusal to recognize the importance of such variables would be naive and contrary to research evidence. The above criticism is intended to point out certain inadequacies in existing personality-based theories of political behavior, nothing more."

not wrong, but it is also not complete. The pervasive competitiveness in American life cannot be explained in terms of any single cause or factor.

So it is with many of the attempts to explain political behavior by pointing to psychological origins or individual symptoms. To state the point in still another way, psychological traits cannot be substituted for political symbols. When a man joins the right-wing John Birch Society, we are immediately prone to believe that his behavior springs from a character structure which we go on to describe in terms of a host of compulsive personality traits familiar to anyone who has perused the psychoanalytic literature. The John Birch Society appeals to him with its extremist slogans and propaganda, and we "explain" those who accept these symbols by insisting that people with compulsive personality traits respond more readily to the kind of appeals that play up such traits than people who do not have them. The result is a self-confirming circularity. The point being emphasized here is a limited but important one: that people respond to symbols (including right-wing propaganda) for many reasons other than their character structure. Consider what happens when we turn the proposition into a question and ask whether it has any predictive value. Could we predict the political conduct and behavior of people whose personality traits presumably predispose them to act in a certain way? Or, to ask the same question differently, has the John Birch Society emerged in this country because of the existence of "authoritarian personalities"? The complex answer is that people respond to symbols out of fear, ignorance, apathy, outrage, and for many other reasons "in spite of, as well as because of, their psychological disposition." [9] By itself, the psychological analysis simply explains too much.

It was not too many years ago when it was the fashion to

[9] Reinhard Bendix, "Compliant Behavior and Individual Personality," *American Journal of Sociology,* November 1952, p. 297.

employ a psychological analysis to explain the rise of German fascism. Professor Lasswell, writing as early as 1933 about the "psychology of Hitlerism," discussed the special appeal of Nazi propaganda for the masses of Germany. "The psychological impoverishment of the lower middle class precipitated emotional insecurities within the personalities of its members, thus fertilizing the ground for the various movements of mass protest through which the middle classes might revenge themselves." [1] In analyzing Hitler's public role among middle-class conservatives, he commented that "there is a profound sense in which Hitler himself plays a maternal role for certain classes in German society. His incessant moralizing is that of the anxious mother who is totally preoccupied with the physical, intellectual and ethical development of her children." In still another way Hitler performed a "maternal function in German life." The disaster of the 1918 defeat, Lasswell pointed out, left the middle classes in Germany shocked and humiliated. The "we" symbol which meant so much was damaged, and they were left shorn of means of revenging themselves upon their enemies.

When an individual is suddenly deprived of his customary mode of externalizing loves and aggressions, the resulting emotional crisis is severe. In extreme cases, the aggressive impulses which were formerly directed against the outside world are turned back against the personality itself, and suicide, melancholia, and other mental disorders ensue. Most thwarted people are protected from such extreme reactions by finding new objects of devotion and self-assertion. [2]

Emotional insecurities are reduced by hating scapegoats, such as the Jews, and adoring heroes, like Hitler. Thus, Lasswell observed, "in so far as politics provides the formulae and the

---

[1] Harold Lasswell, "The Psychology of Hitlerism as a Response of the Lower Middle Classes to Continuing Insecurity," reprinted in his *The Analysis of Political Behavior* (London: Routledge & Kegan Paul; 1949), pp. 235–45.

[2] Ibid., p. 241.

activities which satisfy these requirements, politics is a form of social therapy for potential suicides." In general, Lasswell concluded, while the acts of Hitlerism lowered the labor costs of the upper bourgeoisie, "the symbols of Hitlerism have assuaged the emotional conflicts of the lower bourgeoisie." [3]

The attendant difficulties in this kind of psychological analysis arise from a confusion over the relevancy of different but equally important perspectives. We have already cautioned against the misleading use of analogies that are derived from the study of individual cases but then invoked to interpret political movements or behavior. Homosexuality in a man may be traced to the overprotectiveness of his mother, but it cannot always be said that it stems from this same source. As a matter of fact, maternal overprotection does not always result in homosexuality. Thus it is not really possible to talk in terms of psychiatric propositions because the aim of therapy is to cure the individual patient, not to establish valid generalizations. A psychiatrist may treat a homosexual and discover, through therapy, the source of his problem, but even successful treatment in a given case does not provide a reliable basis for generalization. This is what Bendix means when he states that "psychiatric generalizations based on retrospective interpretations of individual case-histories are fallacious because they state in effect that the difficulties which have created neurotic symptoms in the one case, will do the same in all cases. In fact, we know that they will not." [4] It is even more precarious, therefore, to proclaim broad psychiatric propositions that are supposed to be true for whole classes of people in complex societies that number in the millions.

Recognition of the purposes of psychotherapy should lend support to our contention that the concept of authoritarianism has limited utility when it comes to explaining and understand-

[3] Ibid., p. 245.
[4] Bendix, "Compliant Behavior . . . ," op. cit., p. 296.

ing political phenomena. Assume for the moment that there is agreement about the "authoritarian character" of the German lower middle class in the period around 1930. The shopkeepers, craftsmen, teachers and the rest were beset by concealed hostilities that expressed themselves in a deep distrust of everything and everyone around them. They were rigid in their adherence to conventional morals. They were suspicious of alien groups and punitive in their attitude toward outsiders. The list of psychological particulars is familiar and needs no extension here. But once again we come up against a major difficulty in political analysis. There is no doubt about the existence and composition of the Nazi totalitarian movement. The question is whether the prevalence of "authoritarian character traits" can be cited as a major cause for the success of Hitlerism. Professor Bendix does not believe it can.

First, the fallacy of retrospective determinism applies here also: we study a group whose support swept a totalitarian movement into power, we find that it is authoritarian, and we infer that the second fact caused the first (among many others, to be sure). But ethnocentric people were always authoritarian, long before they became supporters of a movement. . . . The issue is not whether people of an authoritarian bent will support a totalitarian regime more wholeheartedly than others, once it is in power, though even this may be doubtful, since authoritarianism can take many forms. The question is rather whether, under trying circumstances, people of such character will jump on the band wagon, as well as despair, earlier than people of a more permissive disposition. I believe that we lack the necessary comparative evidence to answer this question properly.[5]

Reducing politics to characterological problems can take a variety of forms. However, the limitations are equally severe no matter what the direction. Descriptions of the "authoritarian personality" are matched by those of the "democratic personal-

[5] Reinhard Bendix, "Social Stratification and Political Power," *American Political Science Review,* June 1952, p. 375.

ity." Again it is Harold Lasswell who has focused on "democratic attitudes" which, as he says, develop in individuals who, from their earliest days as infants in society, received "enough positive indulgence from the human environment to enable [them] to be indulgent toward [themselves] and others." [6] The "democratic" personality is presumed to have been nurtured from early childhood with freedom and affection, in contrast to the "authoritarian" personality who has been reared in the strictest pattern of obedience and discipline. It is difficult to estimate the value of these different sketches in depth psychology for either predicting political behavior or, without falling into the trap of retrospective determinism, reconstructing past political activity. But one thing is certain. If the authority of government is looked upon as nothing more than the enlargement of parental authority, then it will follow as a matter of course that politics will be viewed as essentially the reflection of psychology. The Freudian conceptual apparatus of repressions, projections, and displacements has much that is valuable to tell us about the origin and meaning of private emotions and motives. But it is a distortion of the grossest form to look upon politics as merely the superstructure of emotions and political behavior as the "petty displacements of private motives." There are those who claim President Johnson's vigorous stand in behalf of civil rights does not reflect what he *really* believes in the privacy of his closest friends. His compassion for the plight of the American Negro, they maintain, comes not from his heart but from a keen sense of politics. They fail to understand that this is exactly as it should be. It is perhaps interesting to speculate on what the President may say to his wife on a wide range of public issues when they are alone, but the only thing that is important while he is President is what he has to say publicly and what he tries to get

    [6] Harold D. Lasswell, *Power and Personality* (New York: Norton; 1948), pp. 162–3.

done. For the President knows, as does anybody else who has ever given any thought to it, that in politics it is results, not motives, that count.

〰〰〰 3

What is usually missing in the emphasis on personality factors as a way of explaining political behavior is the element of politics. This was true of Freud himself, who talked about the difficulties and problems of cure not in terms of changing political and social conditions but of adjusting to them. There was no *political* conception in Freud because his primary interest was in helping his patient to live with reality which, in essence, was identified with a person's childhood experiences. His concern was more with the past than with the present. Many of today's social Freudians, such as Erich Fromm, part company with Freud on precisely this point because of their reformist, if not revolutionary, stress on not only up-to-date realities but on rooting out the very conditions in society that are causing the individual's sickness. Thus Fromm, unlike Freud, has spent a good part of his life as a social critic deeply immersed in the political problems of his time.[7]

Any discussion of the role of personality in influencing, much less determining, political attitudes must turn to one of the modern classics dealing with the psychological aspects of politi-

[7] However, Fromm himself has little interest in the democratic politics of change as we have been discussing it because he, too, has no clear conception of the political. To put this another way, he has gone beyond the boundaries of the political by reducing politics to nature and society which, in effect, is tantamount to destroying politics itself. For an excellent analysis of Fromm's social and political perspectives as they are derived from his basic psychological orientation, see John H. Schaar, *Escape From Authority* (New York: Basic Books; 1961).

cal behavior, *The Authoritarian Personality*.[8] What began as a study of anti-Semitism developed into a wide-ranging exploration of the relation between personality, social discrimination, and political ideology. The substantive themes themselves were not new, but the theoretical system of psychoanalysis which permeated every chapter represented an important change in focus and interpretation.[9] Our concern is not so much with the psychological outlines of the "fascist-type personality" which emerged from the study (although we will have something to say about this, too) as with the general theory which guided the over-all research. As stated by the authors on the opening page, the basic thesis is that "the political, economic, and social convictions of an individual often form a broad and coherent pattern, as if bound together by a 'mentality' or 'spirit,' and that this pattern is an expression of deep-lying trends in the personality."[1] What may seem at first glance to be simply a reasonable and acceptable comment is, in fact, the theoretical frame of reference for the entire study which has far-reaching implications for the analysis of political behavior.

The basic premise is that those who are anti-Semitic are also antagonistic to Negroes, Puerto Ricans, and every other minority in American society, while at the same time "potentially fascist" in their political and economic views. These attitudes in combination were said to be consistent with the basic feelings of hostility the subjects had toward themselves which, in turn, arose from a particular pattern of events in early childhood. At the end of their study the authors maintained they had demonstrated

[8] T. W. Adorno, Else Frenkel-Brunswik, D. J. Levinson, and R. N. Sanford, *The Authoritarian Personality* (New York: Harper; 1950).

[9] For the most perceptive analysis and constructive criticism of *The Authoritarian Personality*, see *Studies in the Scope and Method of "The Authoritarian Personality,"* ed. Richard Christie and Marie Jahoda, (Glencoe, Ill.: Free Press; 1954).

[1] Adorno and co-authors., op. cit., p. 1.

that

. . . a basically hierarchical, authoritarian, exploitative parent-child
relationship is apt to carry over into a power-oriented, exploitatively
dependent attitude toward one's sex pattern and one's God and may
well culminate in a political philosophy and social outlook which has
no room for anything but a desperate clinging to what appears to be
strong and a disdainful rejection of whatever is relegated to the
bottom. The inherent dramatization likewise extends from the parent-child dichotomy to the dichotomous conception of sex roles and
of moral values, as well as to a dichotomous handling of social
relations as manifested especially in the formation of stereotypes and
of ingroup-outgroup cleavages. Conventionality, rigidity, repressive
denial, and the ensuing break-through of one's weakness, fear and
dependency are but other aspects of the same fundamental personality pattern, and they can be observed in personal life as well as in
attitudes toward religion and social issues.[2]

It bears repeating that the quarrel here is not with the proposition that those who hate Jews also hate Negroes and other
minority groups. Nor is there any reason to question the notion
of "authoritarianism" as applied to the personality types who
were interviewed and studied. Our point of departure is with the
basic assumption, reaffirmed in a hundred different ways in *The
Authoritarian Personality* as well as in other studies which have
followed in its path, that the social structure of society produces a
personality structure in individuals that ultimately modifies a
person's feelings about politics. It is this overly simplistic causal
process that relegates politics to the determinist trap. Within this
framework there is no way of recognizing that an individual's
political beliefs could come from his own interest and involvement in public affairs. There is no acknowledgment that the political process itself can give shape and substance to a person's
political values. Like so many others who have based their

2 Ibid., p. 971.

political interpretations on the Freudian instinct theory, the authors of *The Authoritarian Personality,* in their close attention to psychoanalytical theory, have overlooked the importance of "non-personality" factors in their approach to politics.

What is open to serious question in all of the researches of this kind is the implicit premise that there is a close correspondence between an individual's personality and his political outlook. One does not have to deny the role of psychology to show that political attitudes need not be the consequence of basic personality characteristics. Gabriel Almond has pointed out that what is vulnerable is not the assumption of the importance of personality factors, "but the assumption of congruity between personality and political orientation and role. And this assumption of congruity was the consequence of the neglect in the Freudian school of the role of cognition in psychological motivation, a neglect only now being remedied by the newer emphasis on ego psychology." [3] People's ideas about political affairs derive from a multitude of sources and experiences and cannot be reduced to any single component, psychological or otherwise.

Take the whole question of prejudice. Those who follow the psychological current are quick to maintain that prejudice is a form of extreme irrationality nurtured perhaps by fear or repressed hostility or some other variation of the psychodynamic process. The theme has a familiar ring to it and may not be very far from the truth. But when it comes to assessing political behavior it is neither the whole truth nor the most pertinent. Those who are prejudiced toward Negroes, for example, are likely to be low on the educational ladder in this country, rural rather than urban in their place of residence, and poor. (While

[3] Gabriel A. Almond, "The Appeals of Communism and Fascism," an informal essay circulated to the students enrolled in Political Science 166b at Stanford University in the spring quarter of 1962. I am indebted to Professor Almond for a number of important insights he developed in this paper.

this is not a definitive portrait, it is at least a plausible composite.) The point is that the ethnocentric person can be explained in a variety of ways without resorting to psychological determinants. When it comes to his political alternatives, other explanations must be given equal weight.

It must not be forgotten that politics, whatever else may be said about it, is a process of choosing. Inasmuch as there is no clear and undisputed data explaining how an individual makes up his political mind, it is understandable that a wide variety of theories would be advanced to fill the void. What is really needed is a theory of political choice that will embrace the individual's interests and personality in the context of the political process. The theory followed in *The Authoritarian Personality* distorts the political process by assuming that psychodynamic factors are at its base. The depth perceptions of psychology, intuitive as they are, may in fact be far from the mark, much less the last word, when it comes to explaining a person's political behavior.

Consider again the conservative who is a member of the John Birch Society. There are those who would try to explain his political affiliation by associating the right-wing extremism of the Birchers with some form of psychological disorder in the individual. He is a Bircher, they would say, because of deep personality tendencies. The difficulty with this kind of explanation is that there is really no reliable way for most of us to know if it is, in fact, the explanation. It corresponds, of course, to the stereotype of the political authoritarian, and thus it is easy enough to fit the individual into the mold. But this can hardly be equated with evidence. It is far more likely that he belongs to the John Birch Society because he has been exposed to its literature and doctrine and accepts its program as the only way of meeting the political and social problems of our time. His right-wing orientation is a response to the contemporary political situation of which he strongly disapproves. His political choice, as Professor Almond was suggesting earlier, is a reflection of his own cognitive equipment. His attitudes serve the purpose of a limited but necessary "problem solving" at the political level where "deeper personality tendencies" are not particularly engaged.

One can extend still further the categorization of political attitudes which need not be reduced to characterological problems. The man who is a right-winger may have adopted the outlook of the John Birch Society because its extremist attitudes primarily have a socially adjustive purpose. Many attitudes fall into this category, where the substance or content of the attitude is less important than the function of social conformity. For this type of attitude there is no need to search for a deep-seated personality problem or probe the individual's unconscious. In this kind of situation the person's attitudes can be seen as fulfilling the function of social adjustment. It is not necessary to go to the great length of discovering that in his childhood he had a highly ambivalent relationship with a domineering father which he resolved by "identifying" with the authoritarian John Birch Society.

Is there no reason at all, then, to talk of a person's attitudes in the context of unconscious personality tendencies? On the contrary. There are many attitudes which cannot be understood apart from one's emotional history dating back to childhood experiences. The great value of *The Authoritarian Personality* is that our knowledge of the way a particular class of attitudes is influenced by psychodynamic factors has been deepened by the important findings of this imaginative study. But just as the complicated problem of war cannot be reduced to explanations which turn on the "death instinct," so every effort to understand the function of different attitudes in people's lives need not begin and end with a psychological plunger.

Those who have turned to psychological theory to explain the "authoritarian type" in politics have engaged in still another oversimplification by focusing almost exclusively on the kinds of personality characteristics that are presumed to be correlated with the extremist attitudes of the right wing or, in the case of *The Authoritarian Personality*, "potential fascism." [4] The profile of the "anti-democrat" or "fascist type" is familiar. He is anti-Semitic, ethnocentric, and economically conservative. He is rigid in his beliefs, makes frequent use of stereotypes in his political perceptions and judgments, sympathizes with the use of violence against his enemies, and distinguishes sharply between his "in-group" and the "outgroups" which he sees as menacing his security. More specifically, he shares the most commonplace of the vulgar clichés about Jews, foreigners, reformers, homosexuals, and intellectuals, while admiring strong men, businessmen, successful men, manly men who have no tender side or who allow it no play in their lives.[5] At the other extreme is the "complete democrat" who rejects every tenet of the authoritarian's faith. He is distrustful of the motives and practices of businessmen and supports strong government control over the

[4] Professor Almond has concluded that "the collaborators in the *Authoritarian Personality* study would have been better advised if they had proceeded on the basis of a psychological typology of potential fascism rather than on the basis of a linear pattern of causality in which psychogenetic patterns are shown to produce personality characteristics, and these in turn are shown to be related to political attitudes. They should have sought for other types of causal sequences than the one stressed if they were to satisfy the claims as to the relevance of their findings to the understanding of fascism." He goes on to suggest that there are "cognitive fascists," "conformity fascists," and "projective fascists." "Cognitive fascists would be those whose attitudes were adopted as a way of assimilating to a social milieu in which such attitudes were influential. Projective fascists would be those whose ethnocentric and authoritarian attitudes were related to personality tendencies of the type made familiar in the 'Authoritarian Personality' research." Ibid., p. 5.

[5] Edward A. Shils, "Authoritarianism: 'Right' and 'Left,'" in Christie and Jahoda, op. cit., pp. 28–9.

American economy. For those who like to think in terms of villains and heroes, this is a ready-made formula. But apart from the obvious fact that our politics, like our milk, is now homogenized, the political "right" and "left" today share many important features and are no longer worlds apart. More important for present purposes, the kinds of personality characteristics described as being specific to "potential fascists" are also to be found among many Communists, liberals, and conservatives.

There are individuals of left-wing persuasion, of both the Communist and non-Communist variety, whose intensity of feelings and rigidity of outlook have their counterpart in the repressed hostility of the right-winger. It is only the *content* of their attitudes—and I do not mean to underplay its importance —that distinguishes them. I know a woman who considers herself a liberal in the best international sense of that term, a socialist in her economic views, and a pacifist. The substance of her views are hard-core convictions around which she builds her life and picks her friends. She lives in a passionate state of political involvement. But she is not a tolerant person. She is all for civil liberties for those whose causes she supports, but silent when it comes to the defense of the same liberties for those she despises. And her emotions run very deep. She likes all Negroes and hates all policemen, and is never uncertain who is right and wrong when the two confront each other. The United States is blamed for every foreign policy decision, while Russia is defended at every turn. She espouses the principle of pacifism when dealing with the Chinese Communists, but would clap her hands in unrestrained joy if a "white bastard" were shot in Georgia. If the right-wing authoritarian is correctly described as "intolerant of ambiguity," she in her leftist authoritarianism can similarly never permit herself to confront an ambiguous situation. She is always ready with a clear and unequivocal prescription for every problem that arises because there are no subtleties in her distinctions, no qualifications in her beliefs, and no doubts in her mind.

One does not have to deny that the opinions of the right wing and left wing are significantly different in their content to show that there is nonetheless an authoritarianism of impressive proportions among both right-wingers and left-wingers. If one insists on talking about personality tendencies commonly met in emotionally disturbed persons as being peculiar only to fascism, he is overlooking the same kinds of characteristics frequently encountered among the "neurotic Communists" in Professor Almond's *The Appeals of Communism.*[6] The deeper cognitive and emotional dispositions of "authoritarian personalities" are traceable to the extremes of both right and left. Thus we unearth a serious distortion in the psychological approach to politics which insists on relating political attitudes to personality tendencies. If, as the evidence shows, the same basic personality tendencies can be related to fascist attitudes, communist attitudes, liberal attitudes, and even to those who hold no political attitudes at all, the whole theory of the relationship between personality

[6] Gabriel A. Almond, *The Appeals of Communism* (Princeton, N.J.: Princeton Univ. Press; 1954). Professor Almond points out that the emotionally maladjusted American Communist has on the whole similar characteristics to the emotionally maladjusted American ethnocentric. The personality tendencies and family background related to neurotic ethnocentricism and authoritariansim are substantially the same as those related to the neurotic appeal of communism. The one significant exception is the dimension of conformity. But even this, Almond says, is a surface difference, for both types appear to be badly adjusted to authority and convention, although they solve the problem differently. The ethnocentric solves his basic feelings of isolation, vulnerability, and antagonism by *overconforming* or by *anticonforming*. The neurotic ethnocentric represses his antagonistic impulses and projects them on outgroups who are pictured as immoral, unclean, and generally threatening. The neurotic Communist, repressing his own antagonistic impulses, projects them on the dominant groups in society (e.g., capitalists, the FBI, and so on) and expresses his deep-lying personality needs for order, authority, and submissiveness by affiliating himself with the rigidly authoritarian Communist party.

and political orientation on which *The Authoritarian Personality* is based must be thoroughly restated. Further reflection and study has demonstrated that personality characteristics affect political choices in a variety of ways, and that the assumption of a close correspondence between types of personality and types of political attitudes is an untenable one.

It is perfectly clear that the extremists of the right and of the left, while differing in their ideological commitments and political prescriptions, share many of the same personality maladjustments commonly found among neurotics. But what is missing in the whole concept of political personality is a soundly conceived theory of politics. It is one thing to maintain that neurotic personalities will be attracted to extremist political movements such as the fascists and the Communists. What is not explained, however, is why some neurotics turn to extremist political movements for solution to their inner conflicts while others take to drink, sexual promiscuity, the divorce circuit, or still other forms of personal escape. It overshoots the mark to talk about "underlying antagonistic needs" or some other variation of personal neurosis to explain, much less predict, the many different roads a person can travel in seeking relief from his own storehouse of tensions. Those who believe that political behavior is a function of deeper personality characteristics make no allowance for the accidental but nonetheless real factors of experience, learning, and social situation. Monistic psychological explanations by their very nature fail to bring out the complexity and variety of political phenomena. Furthermore, there is no type of personality that can be exclusively identified with a specific kind of politics. The same personality tendencies may be related to ideologies of the far left or the far right, and may also coexist with a moderate democratic ideology. "All that one can say," observes Professor Almond, "is that there is a certain tendency for deviant personalities to select deviant political ideologies, while normal or modal personalities tend to select normal or modal ideologies. The factors which influence these specific political choices are the social and intellectual characteristics of the individual, and the objective political exposures with which he is confronted." [7]

Nothing that has been said here should be interpreted to mean that political psychology has nothing to contribute to the understanding of political behavior. Our criticism has been directed to the distortions of politics that come to the surface in the form of a politicized psychiatry that reduces the complexities of political choice to deep-rooted personality characteristics. This overemphasis on the unconscious, beginning with Freud but carried on in many unanticipated ways by his followers, has led to a new alchemical interpretation that set out to "wipe away the appearance of gold and reveal the real dross beneath." As Philip Rieff has commented, we can only distrust the "masochistic rush to psychology" if all it has to teach us, "redressed in the modern consciousness of the unconsciousness," is the superficiality of politics. "Plunging below war, psychology turns up varieties of 'aggression' as if these somehow subsume diplomatic history and the development of modern weapons. Exploring behind the offices of institutional authority, psychology revives the classical analogue of state and family. Burrowing under creeds, aspirations, altruisms, psychology uncovers the petty displacements of private motives." [8]

It would be foolish to reject the influence of personality factors on political behavior. But *influence* does not translate out into *determinative*. It is both too much and too little to say that a person goes into politics because his emotions, rooted in childhood frustrations, are attracted to power. This is a narrow con-

---

[7] Almond, "The Appeals of Communism and Fascism," op. cit.
[8] Rieff, "Psychology and Politics," op. cit., pp. 304–5.

cept of political man which has the additional limitation of treating politics itself as though it was primarily understandable in terms of unconscious tendencies and psychological mechanisms—as "compensation for," "projection of," "reaction-formation to," or "displacement of" libidinal fixations of one kind or another.[9] This goes to the root of our concern and is the basis of our objection to reducing political phenomena to unconscious motivation.

[9] Almond, "The Appeals of Communism and Fascism," op. cit.

CHAPTER SIX

The Elimination of Politics:
The Utopian Distortion of
Freedom

> *Men commit the error of not knowing*
> *when to limit their hopes.*
>
> MACHIAVELLI

1

Politics is essential to freedom. Indeed, it has been one of our central themes that in a free society politics is unavoidable. The point is obvious only to those who understand a fundamental principle: that politics is the activity by which democratic government is made possible when differing interests in society need to be conciliated. This is an axiom of political science that goes back to Aristotle's criticism of Plato's *Republic,* wherein he pointed out that Plato erred in trying to reduce everything in his ideal political state to "mere unison." The truth is, he said, that the *polis* is an aggregate of many members which will lose its essence if it sacrifices the parts for the whole, if it loses diversity in its quest for total unity.

Politics arises when different interests vying with each other under a common rule are given a share in political power commensurate with their importance to the general welfare. Tyranny, of course, is one solution to the problem of political order—one man ruling over the rest of the community in his own interest. Politics, however, provides a different response. The political method of rule grants in actual practice what all tyrannical regimes have never even been able to acknowledge in theory: that free government is possible and best conducted where rival interests are permitted and encouraged to sell their wares in the open market of free debate. There is no politics under totalitarian rule precisely because it is politics which represents a tolerance of different truths. It is only in this light that we really can understand Fidel Castro when he says: "We are not politicians. We made our revolution to get the politicians out. We are social people. This is a social revolution." The Cuban "leader" is not the first and he will not be the last to declare his intention to protect "the people" from the evils of politics and politicians. What Castro does not understand is that politics arises from diversity, permits various types of power in society to compete for support, and provides an effective and democratic way by which the many antagonistic interests "can discover that level of compromise best suited to their common interest in survival." [1]

Freedom is the key. But freedom, like time, is elusive: we all know what it is until someone asks us.[2] It will be sufficient for our purposes to define freedom as the widest possible range of choice for each individual through each moment of time. Like all definitions, however, this one does not settle but merely restates the problem. Yet it has the merit of making clear that without freedom an orderly society can be stagnant, unanimous and, as an end in itself, futile. In another vein, there are those who claim that peace, not freedom, is the ultimate aim of Ameri-

[1] Bernard Crick, *In Defense of Politics* (Chicago: Univ. of Chicago Press; 1962), p. 25.
[2] Robert Bierstedt, I believe, made the same point about the ambiguous concept of power.

can policy. It is not true, although there is enough truth to it to comfort those who prefer to believe that peace should be purchased even at the cost of freedom. It is not my intention here to play with words or to manipulate symbols. I am only suggesting that anyone can have peace by simply surrendering whatever is demanded in its name. The difficulty with freedom is that it is not cost-free.

Perhaps the highest price that a democratic society must pay for its freedom is conflict. In fact, without conflict freedom is robbed of any substantive meaning. The hallmark of a free society is the toleration of political opposition, and politics is a way of arriving at public decisions within the boundaries of free and vigorous dissent, without serious violence. Yet voices of disillusion and despair have been raised in the tumult of the hour, as have the voices of the prophet and the reformer. Those who have written and dreamed of utopian societies as worlds by themselves have not attempted to conceal their feelings that the price of conflict is too high. Their chimerical plans deserve the attention of all those who at one time or another have wanted to exchange the sordidness of the democratic political process for the beautiful dreams of peace and happiness that lie just beyond man's outstretched grasp. But the elimination of politics in the universe of utopias comes at a high price too.

The utopians share the common premise that conflict in human society, and particularly political conflict, is a symptom of social disease. It shatters security and threatens stability. They are unsparing in their criticism of efforts to achieve equality through political action. They hold out no hope that man can attain justice through political means. Organized society itself is upbraided for its absence of social harmony, for its being split into quarreling classes, factions, and parties. In democratic politics, as we have seen, these factions and parties constitute the moving forces that generate progress. In a separate reality of utopias they are to be extirpated. This is one of the major reasons why the utopian schemes can be classified as anti-political in their philosophy. In analyzing the aims, goals, and *raison d'être* of a number of utopias, along with the principles upon which they are based, we will discover that the price of unity in the perfectly planned society is the loss of individual choice and action. That the utopians have diluted the concept of freedom and rejected the meaning and importance of politics will be one of our principal concerns.

⩘⩘⩘⩘⩘ 2

In the realm of their imaginations men have postulated social organizations almost since the beginning of time, either as pictures of the past or views of the future, in an attempt to correct, curb, or direct forces and tendencies they see around them. More recently, the numerous failures in community experiments, the disillusion with the Leninist-Stalinist experience of Soviet Russia, and the genuine quest for a sense of community in modern technological life have reawakened an interest in utopian thought. Cogent and clear criticisms of our world and society, projections of ideal forms of government, extended powers of the community, faith in the power of mankind to work out its own salvation—all these abound in the world of utopias as they seek to offer solutions to the complexities of the present period.

It is worth noting that a number of utopian communities have arisen in the United States at one time or another, each of them in its own way aiming bravely at the good life and blaming the organization of society for the troubles of the world and, more specifically, of American culture. One thinks immediately of Brook Farm in Massachusetts, which was a limited though generous effort to realize a new social order. Springing from the New

England transcendental movement, Brook Farm was founded by a young Unitarian minister and lasted from 1841 to 1846. Its organization was based on some very general and simple intuitions which were not clearly elaborated and lacked that definite form which comes from careful analytic thought.[3] While poverty and fire were the direct causes of the dissolution of Brook Farm, the basic cause was deeper.

The organization was not adopted to the natural and manifold wants of its members: the legitimate aspirations and ambitions of the individual found there no satisfying field of action. . . . It was inevitable, finally, that individual members, perceiving that there existed outside of their little community a field of action more in harmony with personal requirements and ambitions, should turn their backs on the ideals of youth to mingle again with the outside world in broader and more complex spheres of action.[4]

Another utopian community was founded in 1842 in Amana, Iowa, by a society of religious people who had emigrated from Germany. Organized as a rural cooperative, Amana was still another attempt at escaping from the tensions and strife of the outside world. The political ideal of the Amana community was a strong central authority wisely administered and implicitly obeyed. A board of trustees, consisting of thirteen members elected annually by a vote of a whole Number of Elders, conducted all affairs, spiritual and temporal. It was felt that politics and the whole American two-party system was not beneficial because conflict arose between factions seeking diverse selfish ends. Amana, seeking to avoid any form of friction, had but one major goal: living as good followers of Christ. Religious sentiment existed against allowing personal ambition to play any part in the government of the community. Their idea of government

[3] Redelia Brisbane, *Albert Brisbane* (Boston: Arena Publishing Co.; 1893), p. 216.
[4] Ibid., p. 218.

was to perfect the machinery and allow a few smart men to run it. Their belief was that if men would only work together with good will, there would be more than enough of God's pleasures for all. Their basic assumption was that man is fundamentally good, that his selfish instincts can be subordinated, and that somehow or other any economic or political development may be rationalized into a blessing.[5]

In general, the utopian builders in America have rejected politics as a means toward their ends. Concerned with designing the features of a better world, few of them have bothered to work out careful plans. They have not been afraid of innovation or sweeping change. They have not been averse to saying that the American system was decaying; they have been willing to propose socialistic, communistic, or even totalitarian solutions. No American institution has been held sacred—the family, the church, the government have all been attacked. Whether they are denouncing an institution or heralding some reform, they are intensely serious of purpose. Reform is taken zealously, and the reformers do not intend to fail from lack of zeal. Whereas there is a commitment to the political process in democratic societies, in the idealized world of the utopians there is no time for it. Men with a vision are in too much of a hurry.[6]

[5] Vernon Louis Parrington, Jr., *American Dreams* (Providence: Brown Univ. Press; 1947), p. 217.

[6] Many of the utopias combine the community life, which is their own universal creed, with a highly centralized sovereignty. "The combination has much to recommend it. The democratic process is a sop to equity. The autocrat is a device for efficiency." Frances Thereas Russell, *Touring Utopia* (New York: Dial; 1932), p. 61. Another advantage of the efficient regime is its trim and tidy neatness. Utopian government may then assume jurisdiction over all life. It may decide whether someone shall be born, when and how he shall be educated, how hard he will work and for what wages, how he should be clothed, and what kind of a funeral he is to have. The extent to which the utopias reject the basic premises of the democratic political process is manifested once again. "The right of the common people to be well governed did not imply the right to govern themselves." Ibid., p. 63.

In spite of the carping of cynics, the utopias have made important contributions to man's material and spiritual progress, ranging from an emphasis on the environment as a decisive factor in shaping the life of both individual and society to support for the social theory of property, pleas for racial and religious tolerance, and advocacy of equality of the sexes. Many practical programs, too, have stemmed from the utopian movements, including systems of universal and compulsory education, plans for industrial reorganization, and various proposals for the avoidance of conflict between classes and nations. Yet utopian views have been generally rejected because man, preferring mere palliatives and tentative measures to thoroughgoing reforms, has felt he must first contend with the exigencies of the here and now.

Beginning with the assumption that the perfect state is conflictless, the utopian writers attempt to fashion in an institutional ordering of society a substitute for what they regard as the inherent and unhealthy conflict of politics. Saint-Simon and later Aldous Huxley develop the utopian view based on the logic of hierarchical organization in contrast to the democratic claims of equality. Saint-Simon's society promised the rule of scientific laws rather than of men, the administrative leadership deriving from the social functions of production itself, and the eventual disappearance of the political in favor of a "science of production." [7] In viewing reality as socioeconomic in nature, Saint-Simon saw a need for social cooperation rather than the competition and conflict that are the reason and justification for politics. To him, the divisions of public opinion in society arise from the fact that each man has too narrow a view of life and does not dare to free himself from the restrictions of his economic position. Marx said much the same thing, arguing that this tendency to see the world

[7] Martin Buber, *Paths in Utopia* (Boston: Beacon Press; 1960), p. 17.

from one's fixed class position would persist until the equality of economic status destroyed the conflict it produced.

Aldous Huxley's "utopia" is the classic satire on the prevailing thought that a proper arranging of institutions as well as economic production and distribution is the cure-all of human society. In *Brave New World* he assumes that six hundred years from now (the book was published in 1932) mass production methods of material goods will have been perfected, Freudian psychology will have triumphed, and biological experimentation will have borne fruit. The result will be an efficient totalitarian state in which the all-powerful administrative bosses and their army of managers will control a population of slaves who will not have to be coerced because they will love their status. Huxley postulates an established hierarchy which would be accepted by the members and which would eliminate conflict. The urge to order is carried to extreme limits; scientific progress has dehumanized humanity—babies are incubated in bottles, and strictly scientific conditioning insures that each individual will perform automatically his allotted social function. In *Brave New World* an attempt is made to iron out all differences, to create a standardized human product within each of the five defined social strata, not sustained by means of terror but by manipulation of the mind, by pharmacological methods, and by physical, psychological, and genetic modification. Horrified by the spectacle of mechanization, its effects on life, and the resultant loss of individuality, Huxley accuses society of desiring security and stability and yearning for a state of nonconflict that will do away with the development of free and independent individuals. Thus Huxley claims that in spite of protestations that their dream societies are for the benefit of the individual, the basic assumption underlying the increasing organization designed by the utopians is a return to the organic conception that the social whole is of greater worth and significance than its individual parts.

However sincerely and loudly individual values of freedom are proclaimed, social analysis and experiment both attest to the abridgment, if not the elimination, of individual values. This is necessary in order to achieve the degree of order in economic production and distribution which the utopists present as the prerequisite of the ideal society.[8]

In contrast to the liberal-democratic belief in the value of the individual, there is in utopian thought no regard for the idea of man except as he is related to the all-embracing state. Freedom means the absorption of the individual into the larger social unit, since it is the collective which is felt to be more real and worthwhile. The requirement of total self-identification with the customary and institutional life of the greater whole is found in all utopian plans. In Zamiatin's words:

Here we have our scale: on the one side an ounce, on the other a ton. On the one side "I," on the other "we," the united state . . . To asume that "I" have any right as far as the State is concerned is like assuming that an ounce may equilibrate a ton in the scale! . . . And the natural road from nothingness to greatness is to forget that one is an ounce and to feel that one is one-millionth of a ton.[9]

The world of *We* is governed by the principle that freedom and unhappiness are incompatible. In attempting to show the insidious pressures for conformity arising at least in part from the 1917 revolution in Russia, Zamiatin satirizes the Marxist conviction that the state is a precondition to man's achieving his

[8] Glenn Negley and J. Max Patrick, *The Quest for Utopia* (New York: Schuman; 1952), p. 17.

[9] Eugene Zamiatin, *We* (New York: Dutton; 1952), p. 109. Zamiatin was a Russian writer of the 1920's, the founder of the "Serapion Brethren," an independent writers' association which affirmed the freedom of artistic expression and refused to accept political dictation. Since the 1920's saw the first major effort of the Communist party to control literature, it is not surprising that the organization did not survive. Marc Slonim, *An Outline of Russian Literature* (New York: New American Library; 1959).

rational—and in many cases, predetermined—ends. Marx had insisted on the elimination of all social sources of differences as the only true solution to the antagonism between man and nature and man and man. The ruling principle of Zamiatin's utopia is based on the premise that men are incapable of using their freedom for individually or socially constructive ends and merely make themselves miserable by their abuse of it. They yearn instead for a materialistic happiness and are eager "to surrender their troublesome freedom and be reduced to the status of lotus-eaters."[1]

In creating a social structure the utopist exalts the values of peace, order and unity, to be controlled by various degrees of power and psychology. With the educational and propaganda instruments at its disposal the State can produce a standardized man who has willingly exchanged civic liberty and humanist culture for security, collectivist pride—and orthodoxy. "Orthodoxy," wrote George Orwell in *1984*, "means not thinking—not needing to think. Orthodoxy is unconsciousness."[2] The utopias of Plato, Zamiatin, and Huxley inculcate a specific world view in their subjects designed to have them accept unquestioningly the outlook of the leadership. Winston, the rebel in Orwell's Oceania, believed that reality is something external, objective, existing in its own right, that imagination is primarily the capacity for apprehending reality, for seeing clearly and deeply whatever it is that exists. O'Brien, the spokesman for the party, says that only an unimaginative, disciplined mind can see reality because reality exists only in the human mind. As Thrasymachus in Plato's *Republic* had said that justice was the imposed will of

[1] Zamiatin, op. cit., Introduction. The philosophy of *We* is the guiding light of Dostoevski's Grand Inquisitor, who promised to make men happy in exchange for the terrible burden of freedom to choose on the basis of conscience.

[2] George Orwell, *1984* (New York: The New American Library; 1948), p. 47.

the strong, O'Brien claims that reality is the imposed vision of the strong, nothing more. "Whatever the Party holds to be truth *is* truth. It is impossible to see reality except by looking through the eyes of the Party." [3] In creating this dependency tie, the party is able to maintain not only its own position but the stability of the entire system. The antithesis to the politics of a democratic society is complete.

Two alternative ways of approaching freedom emerge as a result of the totalitarian quality of utopian thought. The concept of freedom can be viewed from the standpoint that freedom is knowledge or wisdom, which also contains the assumption of an understanding of what freedom is for. Or freedom can be viewed as individual will or volition, implying a belief that man realizes himself only through exerting himself, that man's freedom must be obtained through his own efforts. The first implies an elitist doctrine, derived ultimately from Plato but running through Marxist doctrine—the presumption that society cannot be permitted to run itself through the democratic avenues of individual political choice, but must have an elite to organize and a mass to submit. Right is seen as the function of might, and might encompasses superiority of both power and knowledge. The democratic view of freedom is based on a concept of developing personality and possible self-realization for each individual through his unique combination of choices. Choice means opportunity, and opportunity means a society that is not organized to avoid conflict and differentiation. The safety of no conflict guaranteed by well-functioning mechanisms for the technical control of nature, the psychological control of man and the organizational control of society is bought at a high cost: man, for whom all this has been invented as a means, becomes a means himself.

One of the requirements of utopian rule, according to Orwell, is an inaccessible elite and an available population. A society

[3] Ibid., p. 205.

organized to avoid conflict, tension, and insecurity must relinquish all the attachments that would tend to create them. Thus
the people remain interconnected only by virtue of their ties to
national centers, thereby lacking any sort of insulatory grouping.
In destroying the autonomy of social groups, the utopian systems
fill the void with a highly coordinated and centrally managed set
of institutions. Utopian systems such as *Brave New World* and
1984 facilitate the achievement of perfect order and unity by
having the government control every act and every interest of
every individual or group in order to enhance the strength and
prestige of the system. The government is not only absolute in its
exercise but unlimited in its application. There is no area of
privacy that an individual can call his own; there is no aspect of
social life that is not subject to absolute control. In free societies
the open contest of political groupings and factions mortgages
the power of the government to the consent of the governed.
This, after all, is one of the principle features of democratic
politics. But in the world of Utopia there is no need for political
expression because the conception of man as an independent
thinker simply does not apply. There is no politics in *Brave New
World.* Instead, the concentration is on happiness, manifesting
itself in manifold ways of fun, relaxation, and togetherness
which practice the destruction of privacy, the inability to tolerate
silence, and the proud exhibition of cruelty and brutality.

The question Huxley and other utopian writers are asking is
an old one: would men find a state of perfect happiness and
contentment desirable or even endurable? In attempting to ban-
ish conflict, the society Huxley "predicts" has eliminated the
political in favor of the psychological and the mechanical. The
drive for security, perfection, and certitude is admittedly a basic
fact of human nature, but as Huxley points out it becomes
destructive if the risks are totally avoided. A society which
replaces poverty, misery, and conflict by varying degrees of

security in return for social servility and political discipline can no longer lay claim to being free. For the comfort of happiness as the Sovereign Good, the people of the Brave New World must surrender the hope of individual consciousness. Art, science, and religion are viewed as destructive to utopian stability and are carefully regulated. "That's the price we have to pay for stability. You've got to choose between happiness and what people used to call high art. We've sacrificed the high art. We have the feelies and the scent organ instead." [4] The Brave New World civilization has no need of artistic nobility or heroism of any kind. "These things are symptoms of political inefficiency. In a properly organized society like ours, nobody has any opportunities or desire for being noble or heroic." [5]

In a democratic society, as we have repeatedly said, politics is the handmaiden of freedom. Man, for all of his contradictions and imperfections, is deemed able to determine his own self interest and to give expression to his political needs and beliefs through political action. In the Brave New World, where politics has been eliminated and decisions are administered from above, freedom is regarded as freedom from the tyranny of emotion. The derivative of this theory is the source of the right of authority to "force men to be free," to create a unity and order under an efficient monopolization of power. The harmony thus attained is seen to represent "right reason," rational rules for planning society discoverable from the observation of the Hobbesian will-to-security in human nature. No matter that this is only a partial truth concerning man: the ideology claims that production and consumption reproduce and justify domination. The repressiveness of the whole lies to a high degree in the reality of its benefits: it enhances the scope of material progress, facilitates the procurement of the necessities of life, makes com-

---

[4] Aldous Huxley, *Brave New World* (New York: Modern Library; 1932), p. 264.   [5] Ibid., p. 284.

fort and luxury cheaper, and draws ever-larger areas into the realm of industry while sustaining toil and retaining destruction in an integrated system. But the individual pays by sacrificing his time, his consciousness, and his dreams. The society pays by sacrificing its own promises of liberty and justice for all.

Claims for freedom—in the arts, in the sciences, in government and politics—spring from the desire of men to give expression to their individuality. They are rooted in man's wish to be a self, a center of activity, response, and purpose reflecting a nature that is his own and at least partially of his own making. It is the threat of the loss of individuality—the right of self-affirmation —which has prompted Huxley, Zamiatin, Orwell, and others to launch their attacks. With the rise of technical civilization they see an alarming process in which people are transformed into pieces of reality that pure science can calculate and technical science can control. They recognize also the temptation of democratic man to systematize, to manipulate, to control. It is here, of course, that some of the similarities between totalitarian and democratic conformity are found. But for the utopian writers man's freedom is partly the discontent and occasional misery that keeps him from being totally submerged in the group, yet allows him to remain courageously involved within it. Without this relationship to himself or to his world, man is only an object among objects. He ceases to be a person and becomes instead a process and a function, without meaning for himself and unable to find meaning in his world. For self-affirmation implies the acceptance of want, toil, insecurity, pain—and possible destruction. These are among the high costs of individuality and freedom which a democratic society must pay.

In 1948 Professor B. F. Skinner, a psychologist teaching at Harvard, developed his own scientific philosophy which gave a higher order of preference to the cultural group rather than the individual in what might be termed "the last of the utopias,"

Walden Two.[6] Based on the premise that human behavior is lawful and determined and can therefore be controlled for the greatest good of the community, Skinner replaces the traditional democratic primacy of the individual with adjustment, adaptation, teamwork, group living, and group thinking. It represents a powerful attack on democratic assumptions, proceeding from Skinner's conviction that the problems of man and society can be solved with the available principles of behavioral engineering. Rather than Orwell's assumption that human nature is infinitely controllable, Skinner regards human nature as infinitely malleable, a conception "not taken from theology but from a scientific examination of man himself."[7] Placing a heavy emphasis on control of the social environment as a way to the internalized control of behavior, Skinner finds it necessary to change from the traditional western philosophy which gives ethical priority not to the group or culture but to the individual. One can understand, therefore, why Skinner is moved to observe early in this account of a utopia with a contemporary American setting that "political action was of no use in building a better world, and men of good will had better turn to other measures as soon as possible."[8] Like all the utopists, Skinner has little use for politics because it reflects the conflicts of individual and group interests in society. In the idealized world of *Walden Two,* the root causes of these differences leading to individual political expression and activity will be removed when science and the products of science gain a more complete understanding and control of human behavior.

Walden Two is the realization and combination of Skinner's idea of a rational community founded on psychological precepts. The story is of a visit paid by a professor named Burris to an experimental community that has been founded by Frazier, one

---

[6] B. F. Skinner, *Walden Two* (New York: Macmillan; 1948).
[7] Ibid., p. 165.   [8] Ibid., p. 9.

of his former students. The problem is whether and how men can live in freedom and peace. Skinner sets out to build a social structure which will satisfy the needs of everyone and in which everyone will want to observe the prevailing and supporting philosophy. The Good Life, as seen by Frazier, consists first of health, then a minimum of unpleasant labor, a chance to exercise talents and abilities, intimate and satisfying personal contacts, and, finally, relaxation and rest. By emphasizing cooperation to the exclusion of competition, *Walden Two* establishes a high standard of living with a low consumption of goods. A productive working day of about four hours per person provides time for leisure; the basic theory is that a man's work should not tax his strength and thereby threaten his happiness. More important, the community does away with the pressures and the "meaner and more annoying" emotions that breed unhappiness in a society of competitive consumption. Instead, there is a world in which conflict occurs as seldom as possible and, with luck, not at all. "Most people live from day to day. . . . What they ask is merely some assurance that they will be decently provided for. The rest is a day-to-day enjoyment of life." [9]

In Walden Two, an efficient society is created by the technique of "positive reinforcement," [1] a social engineering practice which starts by controlling the environment at earliest infancy to shape the behavior of the members of the group so that they will function smoothly for the benefit of all. Two major questions are raised: what is the best behavior for the individual so far as the group is concerned, and can the individual be induced to behave in that way? Frazier concludes that the best behavior for the individual is that which promotes the "good life" of the group. To induce this behavior it is necessary to use and perfect psycho-

[9] Ibid., p. 138.

[1] "If it's in our power to create any of the situations which a person likes or to remove any situation he doesn't like, we can control his behavior. When he behaves as we want him to behave, we simply create a situation he likes or remove one he doesn't like. . . ." Ibid., p. 216.

logical techniques and practices which will shape the behavior of members of the group. "It requires all the techniques of applied psychology, from the various ways of keeping in touch with opinions and attitudes to the educational and persuasive practices which shape the individual from the cubical to the grave." [2]

Although Walden Two has an established code of behavior, it is clear that all problems cannot be answered by code. Therefore it is necessary to set up certain behavioral processes which will lead the individual to design his own good behavior when the time comes. This is what results from scientific study and the consequent use of "positive reinforcement." Any condition or event which can be shown to have an effect upon behavior must be taken into account. Once they are discovered and analyzed behavior can be predicted and, to the extent that conditions and events can be manipulated, behavior can be controlled. In this way Frazier manages to allow a peculiar kind of freedom, a control under which those being controlled, though they are performing in a predetermined way, nevertheless *feel free*. "By a careful cultural design we control not the final behavior, but the inclination to behave—the motives, the desires, the wishes. . . . They are doing what they want to do, not what they are forced to do. . . . It's not control that's lacking when one feels free, but the objectionable control of force." [3] The controlling principle of Frazier's plan is to keep intelligence on the right track, which is to say for the good of the society rather than the intelligent individual. By making the individual aware of his personal stake in the welfare of the group, he is made to see that he is better off and happier when the group as a whole is happier.

It is important not to lose sight of what has happened in Skinner's fictional community. [4] His ideal state is based on the

[2] Ibid., p. 145.   [3] Ibid., p. 218.

[4] See Spencer Klaw, "Harvard's Skinner: The Last of the Utopians," *Harper's*, April 1963, for a commentary on his plans to establish the community.

collectivist impulse and on what he believes are the universal goals of men. In claiming that men are wholly products of their environment, he takes steps to eliminate all forms of external conflict which culminate in the manipulatable harmonizing of individual interests and differences for the good of the group. The democratic notion that conflict is a positive force in a society of free men is obliterated. Frazier's criticism of democracy is that it is based on a scientifically invalid conception of man and fails to take into account the fact that ultimately "man is determined by the state."[5] He builds his state not on the reason which animates liberal democracy, but on habit and reflex, a premise pervasive in Marx and other determinists. *Walden Two* asks men to be less than human, to be controlled by set reactions to established situational stimuli. "And while I recognize that that's [Walden Two] a form of despotism, we must use it temporarily to achieve a better government for all."[6] It is a familiar argument, used by countless elitists who have felt impelled to destroy the fabric of political and social freedom in their determination to reconstruct society on their own terms and, to get the consent of all, maintain the acquiescence of those whom they control.

Political democracy, too, rests on consent. But what sets the totalitarianism of utopias apart from democracy is the manner in which the government attains the consent of the governed.

Totalitarianism creates that consent through the monopolistic manipulation of the mass media of communication; the consent of the people does not set limits of the government, but is a function of it. In a genuine democracy, on the other hand, the consent of the governed is the temporary result of the free interplay of antagonistic forces, competing freely with each other for popular support.[7]

[5] Skinner, *Walden Two*, p. 227.   [6] Ibid., p. 193.
[7] Hans Morgenthau, "The Dilemmas of Freedom," in *The Essentials of Freedom*, A Conference at Kenyon College, ed. Raymond English (Gambier, Ohio; 1962), p. 132.

In a democracy government by consent means more than the passive acquiescence in the existing regime, such as that symbolized by the Day of Unanimity, the annual re-election of the Well-Doer in the single state of *We*. The government and politics of democracy also mean more than turning the entire process over to an elite group, as in *Walden Two*. "Most of the people in Walden Two take no active part in running the government. And they don't want an active part. . . . The only thing that matters is one's day-to-day happiness and a secure future." [8] In denying the democratic premise of self-determination of the individual, the utopists have replaced the function of politics by the superior knowledge of an elite. The commitment to democratic politics implies the acceptance of the conflict between loyalty to society and loyalty to one's inner necessity as a free and human being. In doing away with conflict the utopian planners have eliminated the political in favor of the psychological and the mechanical.

3

In examining some of the grand designs of the utopians, I have wanted to show that in the societies they have created they have left no room for politics. Their overriding desire to control the discoverable "laws" which govern both man and society has led to a rejection of the theory and practice of democratic political action. But the utopians are not alone in their discarding of politics, and in a more important sense I have focused on their principles and plans because they provide a helpful backdrop against which more immediate and earthly anti-political tendencies can be revealed and observed.

There are many men of influence today—spokesmen for busi-

[8] Skinner, op. cit., p. 223.

ness, leaders in government, academicians of high intellect— who would reduce politics to an impersonal body of principles or who would prefer to see a government not of men but of scientific truths. They look upon politics not as an art or a strategem but as a science. Just as the utopian thinkers have banished politics from their ideal societies, they, too, would turn for guidance and direction to other and more reliable forms of leadership rather than to the uncertainties of political action. Long ago Engels had predicted that the state would one day wither away, to be replaced by the "administration of things." In a paradoxical sense these current voices are the present-day echoes of that prediction. They are responding to the rapid pace of technological change and high social mobility in our industrial time that have created a deep sense of loneliness and bewilderment for contemporary man. Whether they are psychologists or corporate managerialists, in looking at the symptoms of personal demoralization, many of them have concluded that modern man needs to belong. Only by being integrated into a group that will provide him with a definite role and assured expectations, they feel, will he be able to identify and realize himself. In all of this there is a mood of impatience to transcend the political.[9]

Every age has its form of elitism. Ours, being the age of organization, is characterized in part by the ethic of manipulation. In a democratic society manipulation is an evil-sounding word, and so the manipulators do not think and talk of themselves in precisely these terms. At the very most they regard themselves as benevolent social engineers who believe that modern society can be held together only by intelligent social cooperation. They believe that politics is a futile activity because they are firmly convinced that the realities of our technological age

[9] For an excellent discussion in depth of this particular theme, see Sheldon S. Wolin, *Politics And Vision* (Boston: Little, Brown; 1960), esp. pp. 352–434.

cannot be grasped within the framework of political action. What is urgently needed in society is creative direction, and this, they affirm, cannot be supplied by politics. We live in a time of crisis, and the need is for social cooperation and solidarity if society is to survive. Politics, however, means conflict, and conflict must be replaced by the judicious exercise of social skills and expertise in the hands of knowledgeable and enlightened elites of the present and future.

I would be the first to caution against an overestimation of this trend. But there is no doubt about the trend itself. In its most representative form it is found in the managerial collectivism of many large-scale business organizations in the United States. The challenge: "to recapture something of the sense of human solidarity" by restoring the meaning of community in the industrial age. The function of the corporate managers is no longer administration but social integration. In a word, the managerial elite must define and perceive the "true interests" of the workers. It is their social responsibility to get behind the thoughts and beliefs of the workers in order to determine what is in their best interest. "At the same time that the worker's economic grievances are being sublimated by social therapy, the ancient ethic of the business manager is being similarly diverted from such purely economic goals as profit and production. Thus along the line there is the call to transcend despicable material interests for the preservation of the social group: what the workers really want is *camaraderie;* what the managerial elite must give is social integration." [1]

The writings of Elton Mayo on the problems of industrial society in particular and modern life in general offer a basic argument for the need to promote the values of social stability and cohesion. His "human relations approach" to worker-management relations represents a sizable contribution to the

[1] Ibid., pp. 406–7.

study of employee morale as well as to the personnel practices of factory managers. But it is Mayo's strong dislike of conflict in society, a unifying theme running through all of his major works, that is of special interest to us here.

Mayo is troubled by what he regards as the plight of the industrial man. The society in which man lives today is characterized by the growth of hostility on all sides, whether it be the conflict of group against group or nation against nation. The latent cause is conflict within the individual, who is seen as basically isolated, lonely, unhappy. The root of our difficulty, Mayo tells us, is that we have lost the art of "social skills," which in its simplest terms is the ability to foster cooperation. But social cooperation is not easily achieved, and those who would believe that it can be attained by political means or with the help of the government are dangerously misled. Party politics and other forms of democratic action serve only to aggravate the forces which lead to social chaos. For that matter, Mayo does not look upon political involvement and activity as a sign of social health. At one time he wrote:

Revolution or civil war is the only outcome of the present irreconcilable attitude of Australian political parties. The methods of "democracy," far from providing a means of solving the industrial problem, have proved entirely inadequate to the task. Political organization has been mistaken for political education; the party system has accentuated and added to our industrial difficulties. Democracy has done nothing to help society to unanimity, nothing to aid the individual to a sense of social function. Under its tutelage, social development has achieved a condition which democracy as such can apparently do little or nothing to cure.[2]

Mayo's first principle, it must be kept in mind, is that cooperation, not conflict, is the mark of social health. He repeatedly

[2] Elton Mayo, *Democracy and Freedom* (New York: Macmillan; 1919), p. 44.

emphasizes the need for what he calls the "spontaneous growth of human cooperation," a point of considerable importance in his analysis because it allows him to claim that politics, "political nostrums," and other similar "ad hoc remedies" are only "artificial substitutes." As Bendix and Fisher have observed, "It is difficult to understand Mayo's work unless one realizes he abhors conflict, competition, or disagreement. . . . He deplores competition as well as class struggle, politicians as well as election campaigns, economic self-interest as well as interest in political affairs. He deplores them all because they do not contribute to 'spontaneous cooperation.' "[3]

There is in all of Mayo's publications an expressed fondness for the healthy social organism found in the Middle Ages. The reason is clear: here was the ideal organic community where each individual had a sense of social function and responsibility and where cooperation was assured because the purposes of each were the purposes of all. For Mayo it is this basic unanimity that is the social foundation of all human collaboration, the very condition which he finds so lacking in the social institutions of modern society. In much the same way that the utopians projected their communities on a basic identity of purpose, Mayo looks to the rooting out of conflict in our modern social order by the deliberate planning of cooperation on the part of administrative elites within the private and, more particularly, the industrial organizations of society.

The world over we are greatly in need of an administrative elite, who can assess and handle the concrete difficulties of human collaboration. . . . If at all the critical posts in communal activity we had intelligent persons capable of analyzing an individual or group

[3] Reinhard Bendix and Lloyd Fisher, "The Perspectives of Elton Mayo," *Review of Economics and Statistics,* Vol. 31, No. 4 (1949) p. 314. This particular article is one of the few to analyze Mayo's writings in the context of the larger themes of political theory, which is why I have found it especially helpful here.

attitude in terms of . . . the irrational exasperation symptomatic of
conflict and baffled effort; if we had an elite capable of such analysis,
very many of our difficulties would dwindle to a vanishing point.[4]

As Bendix and Fisher point out, Mayo's quest is an ancient one.
"It started with Plato's unsuccessful attempt to persuade the
tyrant Dionysius of the virtues of philosophy. It ends—for the
time being—with the attempt to persuade businessmen that they
are able and ought to be willing to rescue our civilization." [5]

It is in this context that Mayo's anti-political orientation and
perspective should be seen. One cannot quarrel with his desire to
infuse intelligence and understanding into the admittedly serious
problems of modern industrialism. The studies to which he has
devoted so much of his professional life are without question
significant contributions to the realization that the relationships
between management and labor cannot be resolved without a
sympathetic concern for human relations. But in attempting to
mitigate the harshness of industrial conflict, he has minimized if
not downgraded the importance of the very *freedom* to have
conflict which sets the boundaries of political activity in a democratic society. The point that needs to be underscored is that a
preference for cooperation over conflict, while reasonable and
understandable on the face of things, carries serious antidemocratic implications when it is extended to exclude the broad range
of conflict which is indispensable to individual freedom of choice.
Mayo's distrust of politics, parties, and most of the forms of
political action stems from his own crisis approach to the state of
the world, a feeling of pending disaster that can only be averted
by the positive leadership of his chosen elite of industrial managers. As we have seen before, those who constantly contend that
what is at issue is nothing less than survival itself must, by their

[4] Elton Mayo, *The Human Problems of an Industrial Civilization*
(New York: Macmillan; 1933), p. 185.
[5] Bendix and Fisher, op. cit., p. 316.

own definition of things, propose various emergency measures to meet the crisis. The small "d" democrat, of course, cannot help but be overwhelmed by both the diagnosis and the prescribed cure. But perhaps the dilemma of modern man is not as cataclysmic as many of the alarmists would have us believe. Perhaps there is still time to contain the conflicts of our restless social order within the limits of a broad pattern of common purposes. Unanimity of purpose, no; "spontaneous cooperation," not likely; the elimination of conflict, never. But those who would seek these ends, whether in the world of utopia or here on earth, will either have seen the medieval vision or dreamed the beautiful dream of an unreal future. For the difficult and complex realities of the present, however, their nostrums will have far less meaning and applicability.

What really confronts us here is the elitist position in one of its most modern garbs. The elitism of Plato's Philosopher King was not difficult to understand: those who by birth and training were qualified to lead were vested with power and authority. But something new has been added to the contemporary version of elitism: namely, the mass society. The masses, living in a chaotic world that is falling apart from hatred and bitterness, know not what they do or what they should do. Thus the function of today's elite is new and different. Their superiority, as Wolin says, rests on "its excellence in manipulation."

The *locus classicus* of this formulation was in the writing of Pareto, but it has become commonplace in a wide variety of twentieth-century theorists; in Lenin's theory of the Party elites; in Nazi and Fascist ideologies; in the various theorists of managerialism; and in Mannheim's conception of the role of social scientists in the planned society. Now the crucial theme in all of these writings, and the one which supplies the dialectical counterpart to the elitist strain, is the emergence of the "masses." [6]

[6] Wolin, op. cit., p. 420.

It was Orwell who reminded us earlier that one of the requirements of utopian rule was an inaccessible elite and an available
population. Much the same theme reappears here. The people,
having been transformed into a mass, are now set to confront an
elite whose responsibility to the whole of society is made manifest by the way it uses its considerable skills in communication
and persuasion. No one claims that the United States today is a
full-blown mass society. The crucial point that is made is that the
"democratic public" are being transformed into a "society of
masses."

The concept of mass has been put to many different uses, in
much the same way that the notion of elite has received wide
political currency. It is sufficient to say here that the general
focus and concern is the undifferentiated mass which emerges
when tradition and custom in society have lost their force and
the social structure itself no longer provides a sense of communal purpose and solidarity. It is this condition, as Wolin
points out, which sets the stage for the dramatic confrontation
between the elite and the mass:

> The elite is a sharply defined group, possessing clear qualifications
> and performing a vitally useful role in the social system. The concept
> of the elite fits naturally with the tradition of political and social
> theory in which hierarchy, order, and differentiation are fundamental
> ideas. . . . The mass, in contrast, is undifferentiated, amorphous,
> banal in its tastes, lacking in a defined role and conscious purpose,
> the unattractive deposit of an age of rapid social change, the last
> social battalion without ties of communication, affection, and loy-
> alty.[7]

It is the elite, by enlightened and purposeful use of its administrative skills in gaining cooperation and fostering consent, that is
increasingly responsible for the state of well-being in society.
And make no mistake about it: consent is important, not only to

[7] Wolin, loc. cit.

those who are its careful engineers but to the isolated, lonely individuals who are searching for personal meaning and identity in an impersonal age of organization. But consent does not mean self-government as it is understood in the traditional vocabulary of democratic politics. The needs of men are no longer political but psychological. They cannot be satisfied by political participation and activity. In fact, the political has been transcended. Or, to put it another way, the political aspects of the organizational society are now the social skills of intelligent leaders who, having learned the important lessons from the recent teachings of sociology and psychology, are prepared to oversee the process of leading us away from conflict and toward cooperation. An elite, now that it recognizes man's true interests to be his human instinct to belong, is prepared to sacrifice individual choice and participation for the more important goals of integration and cohesion. In the process both politics and political man have been cut up into little pieces, a result that is clearly in the manipulative tradition.

The major criticism of manipulation, however, goes beyond its anti-political implications. In a democratic society an individual in a position of leadership and authority, whether he be a corporation manager, social scientist, politician or psychiatrist, must weigh carefully the cost of using his understanding of the reasons people do things so as to get them to do things he wants them to do. In a totalitarian society, where people's lives are being manipulated all the time, there is no reason to expect that such matters will be given much attention. But in a democracy there is considerable uneasiness when a person's privacy and integrity have been violated to the point where a knowledge of his motives is used to direct his behavior. This is the core issue of individuality in a mass age. In the automated future the problem will be that of modern man surrendering himself to scientific and technological progress until he is more and more willing to look to others, either experts or machines, to solve his problems.

One of the unsolved questions of our time is how much of the individualism and autonomy of the past can be embodied in the various collective forms of the present. The rapidly growing interest of the Soviet Union in the possibilities of automation provides an important and disturbing dimension to the whole problem of the transition from what Bruno Bettleheim has characterized as the "useful but mindless machine to the manipulator if not the killer of man." The concern of the Russians for the deeper ramifications of the impact of automation is only further evidence that Soviet ideology is framed in response to the newest conditions of mass civilization. It is not surprising that many of the conditions which the Russians find are similar to those with which we have also become familiar. The modernization in techniques of production has produced similarity and standardization in the United States as well as in the U.S.S.R. Society itself is often regarded as a conglomeration of undifferentiated individuals in much the same way as E. H. Carr once said that science treats matter as a conglomeration of undifferentiated atoms. Individuals are more and more conditioned in uniform ways for uniform purposes. In both the United States and the Soviet Union the processes of industrialization have tended to depersonalize the individual and to make the machine and the organization more and more his masters. It is in this sense that one can say the contemporary problem of individualism has no precedent anywhere in history. The basic question is whether we or the Communists are more fully aware of the problems and potentialities as they relate to the individual. The impact of automation will result in raising anew the problem of the role of the individual in society and of the relationship of society to the individual.

One cannot talk about the Soviet Union for very long without confronting an inescapable fact: that all of their plans and programs, whether these be for automation, education, military policy, or space exploration, are grounded in the totalist ideology of Marxism-Leninism. In the Communist view automation is but the latest technological development in the further control of nature which ultimately will lead to what they call the liberation of man but what we have reason to believe will be the further control of man. To many Americans automation has a fairly simple connotation: it means replacing men with machines and thereby throwing a lot of people out of work. In the Soviet Union, however, automation means much more than this. Along with every other form of technological advancement it has become an important part of national philosophy and planning. Although the U.S.S.R. started late and is still behind the United States, everything in the Russian environment encourages the increased application of technology. The Kremlin is giving automation the same urgent priority it earlier gave missile development, and American experts predict that Russian achievements in this field within the next ten or twenty years will be equally startling. The program of the Soviet Communist party, presented to its 22nd Congress in Ocotber 1961, recommended a planned socialist system of economy which "combines the acceleration of technical progress with complete employment of the entire population able to work" and further noted that "automation and complex mechanization serve as a material foundation for a gradual development of socialist labor into communist labor."

It is worth dwelling for a moment on this theme because it goes to the heart of the fundamental conflict between the Communist world and our own. In a very profound way the differences which lie at the root of our present-day struggle reflect our competing outlooks for the future. The Communists tell us that, as society moves to communism, "the whole people will arrive at a single Marxist-Leninist world outlook." In the Soviet Union today some of their best scientists, philosophers, and theoreticians are hard at work combining Marxism-Leninism, Pavlovian psychology, techniques of small-group control developed under the Cheka, automation, cybernetics, and computers in a massive effort to bring about the "withering away" of the state and a new dawn of true communism.

Not too long ago I had occasion to read a number of articles by Soviet philosophers, mathematicians, physicists, engineers, psychologists, and physiologists on the philosophical problems of cybernetics.[8] These writings reflected a deep interest in the methodological propositions of cybernetics, but of far more importance they indicated a serious and intense dedication to the Marxist-Leninist development of modern science. In the writing on cybernetics and the area of its application it was made abundantly clear that this newest engineering science has great potential for solving problems of automatic control and self-adjustment. Then, in a statement which reappeared in one form or another in all of the Soviet papers, all of the scientific pursuits were covered in the warm and reassuring blanket of materialistic dialectics and Marxist philosophy, making clear that the more closely cybernetics is connected with dialectic materialism, the more fruitfully it will develop.[9]

This, of course, is nothing more than the Marxist sermon restated in its most modern form. But if it is a Marxist sermon, there is also a Marxist moral. The moral which the Soviet dialecticians draw is that automation, cybernetics, and every kind of computer mechanism will bring man closer to the day when he will fulfill his highest aspirations as a human being because

[8] The term "cybernetics" means the application of knowledge of machines to the study of the functioning of biological, psychological, and social systems.

[9] See, for example, E. Kolman, "What Is Cybernetics?" *Voprosy Filosofii,* No. 4, pp. 148–59. For an English translation, see Anatole Rapoport, "A Soviet View of Cybernetics," *Behavioral Science,* April 1959.

the Marxist-Leninist leadership possesses the true vision of how man should be related to his society. To appreciate the full meaning of automation and cybernated systems as they will emerge in the Soviet Union it is necessary to understand that Soviet psychologists and physiologists are devoting much of their time and energy to studying these modern instruments of change and control as powerful forces which can be used to explore not only the central nervous system but all patterns of human behavior. The automated future toward which the Communist theoreticians are pointing must be seen in its entirety. The engineers and technicians attend to their own special tasks, the physicists have their own laboratories, and the psychologists and propagandists work in theirs. But they are an integral part of a total system, and the binding cement is the all-embracing catechism of Marx and Lenin.

One example will point up the importance of seeing things whole when we want to understand the thinking and behavior of the Communists. It has long been the Soviet view that the theories of psychoanalysis are antiscientific and serve only to restrict human reason. They are rejected by Soviet scholars and physicians on the ground that they lack scientific substance. It is neither necessary nor possible here to examine this controversy at any length. We need only understand the reasons for the Soviet attitude toward psychoanalysis, for their position reveals once again the pervasiveness of their total ideological belief system. Soviet physicians and psychologists start from the premise that the psyche is a reflection in the brain of objectively existent reality. Simply stated, this means that in the Marxist view man is conditioned directly and wholly by the society in which he lives. Human consciousness reflects human existence and this insures what is repeatedly called the "oneness of man and his environment." The significance of this assumption—that is, the determinist belief that there is no gap between nature and human nature and, for that matter, that there is no such thing as human nature and its fantastic quality—this cannot be underestimated. I would further add that its real meaning has serious implications not only for the way in which the Soviets view science and medicine, but for their approach to all of the world's problems, from automation to zoology. The Soviet scientists and philosophers are all agreed that man cannot and must not be fenced off from his environment, from the reality of which he is a part and outside of which—to quote Dr. D. Dedotov, director of the Institute of Psychiatry of the Ministry of Health in the Soviet Union—"outside of which, indeed without his oneness with which, he is inconceivable." Man is not seen as an independent individual, changeable and complex. He is looked upon as a predictable automaton who, in the hands of those who have knowledge and power, can be pressed back into nature's mold. We have come full circle and are back in the world of utopia, Communist style.

In the Communist scheme of things prescription follows very closely upon description. Thus the United States, it is claimed, is a sick society because it is thoroughly diseased with the rotten cancer of capitalism. What the Communist doctor immediately prescribes is a heavy dose of Marxism-Leninism which will restore the nation to health. The prescription is clear to anyone who will follow it: control the environment and you can control man; or, in the more perfect self-regulating system which the Communists are intent upon reaching, condition man in such a way that he controls himself. It is hardly surprising then, that Pavlov's teachings, stemming from the control he exercised over his laboratory dogs, have assumed such widespread currency in Soviet science. The mastery and development of Pavlov's methods are not only being worked out for the "objective exploration" of the brain's functioning, but his investigations of the conditioned reflex are being extended to every form of human behavior and are currently providing a basis for new theories in

Soviet government and law. Only the man of absolute power in the Communist world can become excited over the prospect that man can be experimented with. Thus the real challenge to us from the Soviet development of all forms of modern technology is that the power they are determined to gain by the victory over nature may result in the ultimate enslavement of man. Eric Hoffer has made the observation somewhere that, despite the spectacular advance in science and technology, the twentieth century will probably be seen in retrospect as a century mainly preoccupied with the mastery and manipulation of man.

It is necessary to remember that in the Soviet Union the entire automative process of the future is looked upon as an important lever leading to the "withering away of the state." Professor Robert North has said that on the simplest, most mechanical level the machine can serve as a repository for storing and retrieving, at a moment's notice, the citizen's health, education, employment, and other records wherever he goes and whatever he does. Presumably when the state has "withered away" everybody's file, in all its detail, will be available to everybody else. In the ideological remolding program of the Chinese Communists in Yenan from 1942–4, each individual, to use their own term, was "struggled." What this means is that in this so-called "struggle phase" of training the psychological forces in the environment were so manipulated that they penetrated into the recruit's inner self until he could present an acceptable confession. This document, along with other personnel records, were then put into a folder which accompanied the individual thereafter in his career, from job to job and place to place.

It is the belief of all Communists that the individual, living in a kind of solar system of independent but interrelated self-regulating collectives, will discover his true creative personality in its fullest sense in his complete identity with the collective whole. Theoretically, he will live his family life in a family collective; his children will be raised in the more efficient self-functioning communal nurseries; he will go to work in still another self-regulating collective, the factory—only now, because of the onset of automation, he will leave his job at noon and make use of his added leisure time in another collective, say, his boating or swimming club. This is the communist theory of what the self-adjusting future holds for man, at least in its barest outline; and automation, computer systems and all the rest, incorporated into the grand design, will help put the theory into practice.

It is said that when the giant machine which has all the answers is finally completed, the first question to be programmed through the apparatus will be: "Is there a God?" And the answer will come back, "Yes, *now* there is." What this suggests is the sobering possibility that the exclusive use of computers may result in a situation where only one answer is possible. The danger would arise if and when, in our frantic quest for certainty, we began to manage our affairs in such a way that we "computed" ourselves into the future by eliminating the possibility of having meaningful alternatives to consider. Whatever may be the potential rewards of the newest technology of today and tomorrow, they cannot be allowed to remove from man the freedom to make choices, a freedom which remains an indispensable pillar of an open, democratic society. It is another way of saying that while man will very likely be forced increasingly to entrust large areas of his life to those who manage the machines of the automated age, he should be constantly on guard that the requirements of the machine do not render obsolete his personal freedom.

〰〰〰〰〰〰〰〰   4

The attacks on democratic politics are of many kinds and come from many directions. In this chapter we have seen that those who would do away with conflict in society in exchange for cooperation and harmony often have a vision of a millennium with a happy ending, where the final revolution has removed all the economic, social, and psychological causes of bitterness and struggle. Or perhaps their goal is the more mundane one of saving contemporary man and society from the afflictions of industrial conflict. In either case they have a vision of a society without politics because in the process of rooting out conflict they have destroyed the meaning of freedom, and where there is no freedom there is no reason for political activity.

The writings of Erich Fromm are particularly relevant in this connection.[1] Fromm is looking to the day when contemporary man would achieve the final realization of his true self, the totally integrated personality. But today, Fromm argues, man is bewildered, powerless, and alone. If he could become fully integrated, his asocial drives would vanish and only sick and abnormal persons would remain who are dangerous to themselves or society. It is important, however, to notice how Fromm would translate his humanistic ethic into social reality. It is not his ultimate goal but rather the means of its implementation that poses a serious problem for a democratic society. Throughout his works one finds a basic (and by now familiar) theme: harmony, integration, and adjustment are desirable; conflict is bad. There was a time, in the Middle Ages before the rise of modern society, when men were integrated and functionally related to the whole. But not so in our present-day impersonal, industrial social order. Thus Fromm claims the problem of man today is the problem of modern man. But the important point is this: once Fromm has formulated the problem in this way, his discussion of ethics and morals has a peculiar ring to it. Instead of maintaining that

[1] Specifically, I have in mind his *Escape From Freedom* (New York: Rinehart; 1941) and *Man for Himself: An Inquiry Into The Psychology of Ethics* (New York: Rinehart; 1947).

ethics are necessary because conflict exists, Fromm says no real
ethics can be found until conflict is rooted out. Yet how is it
possible to conceive of moral action without conflict? When
conflict in individuals is identified with neurosis, it becomes
extremely difficult to discuss ethics.

It is also difficult to conceive of political action in a society
without division and conflict. When conflict is identified with
"social disease," it becomes impossible to discuss politics. It was
said earlier that freedom is the key and that conflict is indispensable to a free society. It is a point that is often hard to put across
because the idea of a society without conflict is attractive and
inviting. Common sense alone tells us that no one wants to
struggle for all of the good things in life. Peace is much more
pleasant and desirable. The difficulty with this line of reasoning
is not that it is wrong, but that it does not go far enough. As we
have tried to show, the argument is not carried through to the
point where it must join issue with the long-run implications of
precisely *who* is to eliminate conflict, why—and how.

A number of years ago Stuart Chase, unaware of the anti-
political overtones of his own position, came up with a classic
presentation for doing away with the bitter conflicts of "selfish
interests" which he said were the bane of democracies. He had
little patience for American politics or politicians and even less
for the multiple-interest groups in the United States which he
felt were at variance with the "public welfare." Needless to say,
he favored the "public welfare" and was opposed to those whose
theme song was simply "My Country 'Tis of Me." Having reduced the problem of political conflict to this level of simplicity,
his solution was easy and eloquent. The picture he painted of his
"Mountain Conference" is worth reproducing here in some detail, and the reader is asked to watch how neatly Chase has
circumvented the very business of politics by imposing his own
set of ideas and values.

Sometimes I have a clear picture of the way the Agenda . . . could be presented to the people. I see perhaps a hundred leading Americans, men and women, meeting in some high, quiet place to prepare it. They are not the kind of people who are active in Me First groups. They are scientists, judges, teachers, university people, philosophers of business, lovers of the land, statesmen; and they think in terms of the whole community.

I picture them as people without ideologies or dogmatic principles, aware of their own shortcomings and the general inadequacy of mankind, as Wells put it. They are accustomed to approach a question with a scientific attitude, and to look at all the major characteristics of a situation before leaping to a conclusion. They are aware of the pitfalls of language. Supermen, if you like; but if there are not a hundred of them in the country today, America is in a bad way. We had more than that in 1787.

They ought, I think, to go up into the mountains somewhere. Perhaps the Navy would invite them to Sun Valley, whose beauty and remoteness would give them perspective. The young veterans recuperating there would remind them of the urgency of their tasks. They could look at the Sawtooth Mountains of Idaho, blocking the sky to the north, and remember the majesty and splendor of their country.

Chase then says that he can see the chairman getting to his feet in front of the big blue tapestry in the Lodge dining room to open the conference. He is a social scientist from somewhere on the coast, Chase tells us. His face is a little drawn, and he drums on the table with long fingers. "I shall not quote him directly, but paraphrase his address, as I imagine it."

America, he says, has reached a milestone. We have met here to consider what we can do to help our country pass it safely. It cannot be muddled past; deliberate action must be taken. If thoughtful citizens like ourselves have no practical suggestions, the action will be taken anyway by generals—or by demagogues. . . .

We who are meeting here, I take it, represent no economic interest except that of the consumer, which means everybody. We are not specifically for "labor," for "capital," for farmers, for organized medicine, for Wall Street, the West Coast, the export trade, the department stores, or for the manufacturers of Shocking Radiance perfume.

We are not in favor of "capitalism," "socialism," "fascism," "communism," "individualism," or saving the world by the introduction of planned parenthood. We have gone through these vague ideologies and come out on the other side. We are in favor of keeping our minds open and the machines running. We want the community to go on, not to stop dead in its tracks as in 1929.

We are not prejudiced in favor of private business, government business, cooperative business or non-profit business. We believe that each has its place, depending on circumstances; at one extreme stand the courts, which are certainly a function of government; at the other stands the aforesaid Shocking Radiance, which is certainly a function of private enterprise—with maybe just a dash of the Federal Trade Commission in the formula. In between, it all depends.

We have been called together to attempt a division of the "in between." A problem clearly stated is halfway solved. We want to run a line between the area where the public should be responsible, and the area where private interests should be responsible. . . .

We have come here, I take it, because we believe our democracy can find the brains. If anyone in this room does not believe that a managed economy is compatible with political democracy and civil liberties, some mistake has been made in the invitations. That is one assumption we were all supposed to make. We do not have to assume its eternal truth, but without it as a working hypothesis we can do little more but toss a dilapidated ball of argument around the same old dusty circle. We assume that our democracy *can* manage its affairs, and we have met to prepare a temporary plan of management. . . .[2]

One would like to be able to say amen. But in going all the way to beautiful Sun Valley, Chase has simply given us his own vision of the kind of world he would like to see and the men and women he would like to run it. That, indeed, is one way to

[2] Stuart Chase, *Democracy Under Pressure* (New York: The Twentieth Century Fund; 1945), pp. 133–9.

dispose of individual differences and group conflicts. However, it was pointed out a long time ago that if men were angels there would be no need for government. Since then we have learned that the function of democratic politics and politicians is to prevent deeply divisive social and economic antagonisms in a free society from disrupting its consensual basis by providing the institutionalization and tolerance of conflict.

At the beginning of our republic James Madison spoke of the "ills of factions," by which he meant the danger of unchecked conflict leading to the tyranny of one class or faction over the rest of the community. He said we had a choice: either to remove the causes of conflict and factions, or control their effects. Many, of course, have chosen the former, insisting that if property were diffused equally throughout society, factions would in turn be removed. The Communists have advanced the same argument, claiming that when the economic and social differences created by a class-dominated capitalist system are eliminated, conflict will be ended and men will become equal. But Madison felt that without factions there can be no real liberty because factions are the basis of freedom. The challenge to a free society was to keep the factions from getting out of hand, to control their effects not by removing them—this would destroy liberty—but by instituting a republican form of government that would act as a political broker among all the contending groups and interests in society. This is the Madisonian tradition that has become dominant in American political life. It has also provided to this day the most impressive argument and justification for the acceptance of conflict as a major factor in the safety of free politics.

CHAPTER SEVEN

The Commitment to Democratic Politics

Necessarily there will be compromise. But the difference between expediency and morality in politics is the difference between selling out a principle and making smaller concessions to win larger ones. The leader who shrinks from this task reveals not his purity but his lack of political sense.

BAYARD RUSTIN

Such a view of politics, rather than the dedication to some absolute . . . is possible, however, only when there is a basic consensus among contending groups to respect each other's rights to continue in the society. The foundation of a pluralist society rests, therefore, on this separation of ethics and politics and on the limiting of ethics to the formal rules of the game.

DANIEL BELL

1

In the preceding chapters I have drawn attention to the cluster of assumptions and propositions which, as they took their particular shapes, revealed an anti-political quality. In a real sense my concern has been with a state of mind, a way of feeling, a disposition. Given its special gods and passionate certainties, the temper of anti-politics is a pattern of intellectual, emotional, and behavioral elements which can best be compared to the set of attitudes engendered by a strong religion. Its effect is to treat politics as a poor relation, thereby obscuring its identity, distorting its meaning, and denying its value—in short, to depreciate the state of the political.

At no point have I meant to suggest that politics reigns supreme, solves everything, or is omnipresent. There are many levels of personal and collective behavior that are completely outside the sphere of politics. After all, it is still only the second oldest profession. Nor has my principal concern been with the right of the militant idealist, the ideologue, the utopian, or the man of conscience to espouse any point of view he wishes. Their voices are as indispensable to the continuing democratic dialogue as are the countless others that make up the clamorous chorus of a free society. My concern has been different, in both emphasis and purpose. Instead of adding still another voice to the familiar and sometimes weary debate over the substantive issues of public policy, I have wanted to shift attention to some of the procedural dimensions of decision-making and to reassert the importance of the commitment to democratic politics.

2

More than anything else, the major concern of this book has been to draw a distinction between different attitudes toward politics. I have tried to show that the values, preferences, and prejudices examined in the previous chapters point to a common bond, namely, the pursuit and attainment of an absolute purpose. For example, the political ideas of the left wing and the right wing are not a set of pragmatic precepts for the simple reason that politics is not perceived as a matter of trial and error. Based on their own angle of vision, the final and true purpose of politics can only be achieved when the right ideas, integrated in a comprehensive, closed system of knowledge, are applied to the organization of society. This is the doctrinaire spirit that proclaims an absolutism in politics, combining "prefabricated interpretations" of reality with a rationalism that becomes a passionate faith. Thus the function of politics is to impose the "truth." In other words, political activity is dictated by some goal or "ideal good" external to the immediate society. The standard for the conduct of politics is above and beyond and therefore excludes the interests of individuals, the force of public opinion, or the conventions of the community. Only reason, arbitrarily claimed by the self-appointed few who "know" what is best for the people and what needs to be done, yields insight into the meaning of reality. And only *their* reason can grasp the rules by which politics is to liberate the rest of society from their mistaken illusions. Other sources of political guidance characteristic of a political democracy are rejected. The wisdom of prudence or experience, the wisdom of convention and enduring institutions, intuition, consent, passion, interest—these are all treated with indifference or neutralized with hostility. For politics has been made into a rational science, or, more accurately, a manipulative art based on rational science.[1]

---

[1] In his *Knowledge, Opinion, and Politics: Public Opinion as an Ingredient in Political Theory* (unpublished doctoral dissertation, University of California, Berkeley, 1956), Professor David Minar examines nine political theories drawn from the history of ideas and analyzes them for their implications for public opinion. In considering theories which parallel Plato's, i.e., which define politics according to external standards and exclude the use of public opinion, he writes: "Consider, for instance, the theories of that political group which regards itself as the 'vanguard of the proletariat.' Marxists may regard themselves as fundamentally moved by the stream of history; they also will admit to a moral compulsion to bring about the apolitical classless society. Both these motivations stem from an external standard for political activity. The Marxists 'know' what should be done or will discover it through the interpretations of the initiate. Public opinion is certainly of no value

But there is an altogether different attitude toward politics. At its root is the basic premise that empiricism is the "ally of freedom." Policies and institutions are judged not as an extension of hardened preconceptions, but by their results. Principles are deduced not by abstract thinking, but from the observation of events. Someone once said that he loved arguments on principles because he never had to bother with any facts. But anyone in political life knows that only after the facts are in can the difficult decisions and choices between various courses of action be made in the light of principles. Furthermore, the task of politicians is to reconcile the many conflicts of interest in society, a reconciliation that cannot be accomplished from an unshakable commitment to dogma, but by dealing with the common problems they have to face and a willingness to make concessions. This, as it has been called, is the politics of compromisable interests. It has also been called the responsibility of political life which cannot be evaded except by those who shirk "the more difficult problem of living in the world, of seeking, as one must in politics, relative standards of social virtue and political justice instead of abstract absolutes." [2]

I am fully aware of the difficulty in distinguishing between these two attitudes towards politics—that is, it is overdrawn and its applicability tends to vary. In this connection, however, two comments are in order. First, I have intended to be suggestive,

---

to them. More often than not, it is a force to be transcended and quashed, usually through violence. The 'trade-union mentality' of the workers, for example, is a conventional hold-over from pre-existing ways of thought, irrational in terms of the 'real' goal of politics. The 'right' end of political action is independent of the opinions, attitudes, and desires of the people, however 'public' these may be. Marxist politics, then, would ignore public opinion as much as possible; where it could not be ignored, it would be overridden by force, or used, or changed. At any rate, it could not serve as a moving guide to correct action." P. 360.

[2] Daniel Bell, *The End of Ideology* (New York: Collier; 1960), p. 287.

ANTI-POLITICS IN AMERICA

not definitive. Secondly, the distinction I am making here is an analytical one, although I am convinced that in a large number of cases it is also a concrete distinction. I have focused on a wide assortment of purists whose general outlook and temper is anti-political because I have wanted to call attention to a trend, one which in some circles is already a pronounced tendency. The moralists, the idealists, the ideologues, however difficult they may be to define or portray (and they are), and whatever differences there may be in the ends they pursue (and there are many)—they are the ones who are most scornful of democratic politics. The moralists reject political activity because there are no ultimate values in the political world. The politician must compromise; the moralist cannot. The idealist is deeply troubled by the great gulf between democratic ideals and "democracy in action." It has often been observed that those who suffer the greatest disillusionment in politics are those who have been most dedicated to the normative order, to what *ought to be,* and are subsequently confronted with the factual, with what *is.* The ideologues have no use for democratic politics because their infallible guide is a closed system of knowledge which provides them with answers to all questions and solutions to all problems.

Let it be said again: these men, these groups, these voices are necessary to a free society. To paraphrase Richard Hofstadter, they are "the counterweight to sloth and indifference." But their function is not to make laws and they seldom determine policy. To a large extent their chief currency is talk. They petition, pray, exhort, decry, demand, denounce, and, above everything else, they protest. In some societies where revolutions are the rule and law and order are an interlude, their cries may even become weapons in the streets and they will seem to move mountains. But in this country they labor under severe restraints, not the least of which is an advanced and successful industrial order with a tangled mass of technical and administrative detail. There is no reason why those who live and thrive in a rarefied moral atmosphere and, in Lasswell's words, "harry the dragons," should not have their say, but a more urgent need is for men and women of creative imagination and practical vision who will turn their thoughts and talents to stubborn political realities.

There will always be those of outspoken zeal for whom nothing less than some large social transformation will occupy their thoughts, arouse their feelings, and unleash their energies. A student of mine once said to me, in discussing a paper he was writing, "I agree with the abolitionist Wendell Phillips. I am concerned with the heart of this country. My questions cannot be answered with politics-as-usual or by hard-headed politicians." I suggested that he might be asking the wrong questions, or perhaps the right questions but in the wrong way. His indignation was swift. "They are the only questions worth asking," he said. "We live in a society filled with ignorance, prejudice, selfishness. The country is riddled with crime. We have the highest incidence of mental sickness in the world, and the rate of suicide is climbing. I look around and I see corruption everywhere. The people are demoralized. I could go on for an hour."

"But what is the question?" I asked him.

"The question is why," he replied. He said it again: "Why."

"We're really talking past each other," I said. "Your concerns are filled with moral conceptions that look to far-reaching goals. I want to break them down to particulars so we can move in on them with concrete proposals. This takes money, muscle, time."

"You'll be too late with too little," he said grimly. "What this country needs is a socialist revolution." (I was reminded of the story of the wag who posted the following announcement: "The revolution will be held on Wednesday. If it rains on Wednesday, the revolution will be held indoors.")

There is an inevitable tension between those who demand too much and want it immediately and those who, as Walter Lippmann once put it somewhat cynically, must "placate, appease, bribe, seduce, bamboozle, or otherwise manage to manipulate" in order to get whatever the political and economic traffic will bear. One can take inspiration from those who oppose war and injustice and be stirred to great heights of emotion in their call for peace, freedom, and equality. But the politicians, including the greatest of this country's political leaders, must deal with more than principles and conscience. If a president cannot always satisfy a reformer by pointing farther and aspiring higher, it is because he knows that he lives in "an everlasting NOW." Thus Stephen Douglas could say of President Lincoln at the climax of the Civil War, "He is preeminently a man of the atmosphere that surrounds him"; and Lincoln could write in answer to Horace Greeley's cry for emancipation, "I would save the Union . . . If I could save the Union without freeing any slave, I would do it; and if I could do it by freeing all the slaves, I would do it." In the end, observes Professor Hofstadter, "freeing all the slaves seemed necessary." The point to be made, with respect and without apology, is that Lincoln was a political man. He was not a man of moral frenzy or moved by moral absolutes. His approach to slavery flowed from his conception that his role was to be "a moderator of extremes in public sentiment." Professor Hofstadter puts it this way:

. . . the Proclamation was what it was because the average sentiments of the American Unionist of 1862 were what they were. Had the political strategy of the moment called for a momentous human document of the stature of the Declaration of Independence, Lincoln could have risen to the occasion. . . . His conservatism arose in part from a sound sense for the pace of historical change. He knew that formal freedom for the Negro, coming suddenly and without preparation, would not be real freedom, and in this respect he understood the slavery question better than most of the Radicals. . . .[3]

[3] Richard Hofstadter, *The American Political Tradition* (New York: Knopf; 1948), pp. 128, 130, 131-2.

The distinction I am drawing here is more than one of style. It has to do with temper and outlook. On the one hand are those who think in terms of the ultimate potentialities of social conflicts, and, on the other, those who look for the concessions and compromises by which they can be softened. The former, caught up in the current of general principles and theories, turn their thoughts to abstract laws and morals; the latter see the world more in terms of concrete questions and specific persons and talk about material interests and personal needs. The first are impatient with the democratic political process because, holding a definite and rational opinion about every question, they want only to give effect to this opinion and see it translated at once into action. The second, aware that the process of coalition-building is the democratic method of peaceful adjustment, are committed to the institutional arrangements of politics through which political decisions are ultimately arrived at.

Inescapably, the fundamental problem, at least for those who give more than lip service to the democratic political process, is the untidy relationship of means to ends. One can afford the comfortable luxury of certitude if his only thoughts are about goals. It is the troublesome question of choosing effective and permissible methods by which to achieve them that separates the wish from the deed and fantasy from reality. But the plain truth is that there are many people who are seldom in touch with the obstinacies of the real world. Far removed from the dilemmas of choice, they discuss the issues of the day with like-minded supporters who provide intellectual and moral reinforcement for their own views—in a word, with ideological mirror images of themselves. These are the detractors of politics who, unable to accept the unwelcome realities of political life, seek refuge in a pleasing ideology or plausible theory, seldom suffering a fact getting in the way. Although they represent the full range of the political spectrum and are widely separated in beliefs and values, they are joined together by a common wish: they would like to make a whole society conform to the special pattern they would lay down for it. As escapists from politics, they would impose their own rationality on an irrational world. That politics thrives on the clash of interests and ideas in a free society is, to them, neither relevant nor important. Their sentiments lie elsewhere. They have no interest in the fact that politics is the process by which differences in society are sympathetically understood, intelligently discussed, and peacefully resolved. From their standpoint this is a politics of compromise, of mediocrity, of humbug. Their commitments are grounded in principles, of which the first and foremost is that no principle is to be traduced by the untidiness of politics. They are not concerned with "right conduct in a political situation," but with right conduct, *period.* Since they will not search for "right political action," they settle for substitutes. Traveling the reductionist route, they think of politics in non-political terms.

A case in point is the wildly emotional response of those who have excoriated the United States for its role in the war in Vietnam. I am not talking about the millions of Americans (I include myself) who oppose our military policy in that country or our general posture toward China. Specifically, I have in mind those whose declarations of censure have the tone and qualities of a sectarian ultimatum rather than a reasoned criticism and protest that might evoke public support and have some political impact. Their preachments, like their placards, deal in wholesale condemnation and categorical imperatives. Like the abolitionists who wanted nothing less than instant emancipation for the slaves, their cry is for the United States to leave immediately, if not sooner. This is the metaphysics of "immediatism" whose vague and unfocused prescriptions are more theological than political. There is no talk of alternatives, no discussion of methods and procedures, no concern about consequences. Just as the abolitionists went among the people of the North decrying slavery as an evil thing, so today's moral zealots pass out their leaflets denouncing the action of the United States as a breach of all the Commandments. Taking strength from their own fixed conceptions, they demand immediate withdrawal. They may even urge civil disobedience, not because they regard this act as a "legitimate, if ultimate, means of registering dissent" or as a "statement of conscience" in a political democracy, but because any tactic will do if it will demonstrate the sickness of American society. They could not care less that for many Americans civil disobedience is a last resort, an "exceptional measure" to be used only after every other channel of democratic pressure and persuasion has been exhausted.[4] They are perfectly willing to under-

---

[4] One of the most impressive statements on the subject of civil disobedience appeared in *The New York Review*, November 25, 1965, over the signatures of Irving Howe, Michael Harrington, Bayard Rustin, Lewis Coser, and Penn Kimble. Under the general title of "The Vietnam Protest" the authors spoke directly to the problem of when and how civil disobedience is to be justified in a democratic society. I have used some of their language above, but there is more that deserves to be quoted. There is a "crucial difference, which should not be blurred, between individual moral objection and a political protest movement. It is one thing to say, 'I cannot in conscience fight this war.' It is quite another thing to advocate resistance to the draft or efforts to use its provisions for conscientious objection as a tactic of the protest movement. The latter course, we believe, could lead only to disaster, the reduction of what is potentially an expression of popular outrage to an heroic martyrdom by a tiny band of intellectual guerillas." In another passage they write: the Vietnam protest movement "has by and large been able to express its dissent openly and publicly, through the usual channels open to members of a democratic society—and this fact would seriously call into question any effort to employ civil disobedience as a political tactic by an organized movement. We question the rightness, for example, of recent efforts to stop troop trains in California: they involve an action by a small minority to revoke through its own decision the policy of a democratically elected government—which is something very different indeed from public protest against that government's decision or efforts to pressure it into changes of policy. Tactically, it might be added, such attempts at 'symbolic' interference with the war effort are self-defeating. . . . A 'revolutionary' tactic in a decidedly non-revolutionary situation is likely to do little more than increase the isolation of those who undertake it."

mine faith in the democratic process if that is what it will take to serve their purposes and to expose the hypocrisy of American life. For them the problem is unambiguous and uncomplicated. The war in Vietnam, like slavery in its day, is a sin, and, as Professor Hofstadter reminds us, "one does not seek to purge oneself of sinfulness by slow degrees—one casts it out." Thus they cling to the "dogma of immediatism" even though they cannot provide any guidelines of action. They offer no proposals that might actually affect the course of events. In fact, their formula is the essence of moral simplicity: to put an end to sin, one must stop sinning. To call a halt to war, one need only stop warring.[5]

It is not surprising that in every major social crisis there are militants who are contemptuous of the democratic political process. Their natural posture is one of fiery protest, not searching inquiry. Their angry negations, like those of the prophets, are stronger than their affirmations. In the words of Roger Heyns, chancellor of the University of California at Berkeley, they are "surer of what is wrong with where we are as a society than of where we ought to go."[6] Unlike those in positions of power who must assume political responsibility for their actions, they can dissociate themselves from the uncertain chain of cause and

[5] Hofstadter, op. cit., pp. 143–4. Professor Hofstadter's analysis of the abolitionist movement is perceptive and instructive. " 'Duty is ours and events are God's!' blared Garrison. '. . . All you have to do is to set your slaves at liberty!' 'To be without a plan,' cried his followers, 'is the true genius and glory of the Anti-Slavery enterprise!' " Hofstadter goes on: "The abolitionists were even less clear on how the Negro was to become an independent human being after he was freed. . . . Lincoln, who struggled conscientiously to imagine what could be done about slavery, confessed sadly that even if he had power to dispose of it he would not know how. The abolitionists likewise did not know, but they did not know that they did not know. The result was that when formal freedom finally came to the Negro, many abolitionists failed entirely to realize how much more help he would need or what form it should take." Ibid., p. 144.

[6] Quoted in the San Francisco *Chronicle*, November 13, 1965, p. 7.

effect. Safely removed from the risks of political decision-making, they need never concern themselves with thoughts of strategy or plans of action.

In the absence of a commitment to democratic politics, it is easy to wash one's hands of it.

⁂ 3

In this country we take our politics for granted—I mean the *fact* of politics. More specifically, I refer to the fact that our political system, with all of its faults, operates and functions from one year to the next, one election after another, providing a measure of agreement and continuity which produces, if not always the right answers, at least responsible leadership, stable policies, and peaceful change. It is not every country in the world that can lay claim to such good fortune. I do not overlook all of the other achievements of the United States when I say that one of its most impressive accomplishments has been the successful shaping of a constitutional political system to the needs and aspirations of its people. I am talking now of politics in its broadest and most democratic sense, and at the same time of its most necessary constituent and attribute, the politician. I am aware that in speaking this way I can never make rational contact with those who treat everything as a matter of principle and for whom political action must inevitably be transformed into an occasion for a great moral crusade. But these are precisely the people who need to be reminded of the purposes of government and re-educated in the meaning and value of the political process.

"I am a conservative in my politics," says a supporter of Senator Goldwater. "My politics are liberal," says the old-time New Dealer and present-day advocate of The Great Society. "I believe that socialism is the political answer for this country," says a bright graduate student majoring in economics. These are legitimate positions which need to be forcefully expressed and given a responsible hearing in the political market place. But the point I am stressing is that the small-"d" democrat, if he is truly and deeply tinged with democratic beliefs, will recognize above everything else that politics is not any one political doctrine. Politics is conservative in that it builds into the fabric of society the important benefits of established order. Politics is liberal in its inculcation and reinforcement of democratic values such as civil liberties, institutionalized opposition and dissent, and political equality. Politics is socialist to the degree that "it provides conditions for deliberate social change by which groups can come to feel that they have an equitable stake in the prosperity and survival of the community." But as Professor Crick correctly notes, "The stress will vary with time, place, circumstance and even with the moods of men; but all of these elements must be present in some part. Out of their dialogue, progress is possible. Politics does not just hold the fort; it creates a thriving and polyglot community outside the castle walls." [7]

This, of course, is the real meaning of the commitment to democratic politics; these are among its basic tenets. But there is an additional thought, indeed a significant dimension, that needs to be underscored. Beginning with the assumption that there is no sole and exclusive truth in politics, there is the further rejection of any idea that claims a preordained, harmonious, and perfect scheme of things to which men are irresistibly drawn and to which they are bound to arrive. Democratic politics is not to be confused with political religion which, in many non-Western countries, is the powerful symbolic force that can "universalize values linked to the widespread desire for better material condi-

[7] Bernard Crick, *In Defense of Politics* (Chicago: Univ. Chicago Press; 1962) pp. 135–6.

tions." Widening the scope of politics to embrace the whole of human existence, political religion affects the most fundamental needs of individuals "by specifying through the state religion the permissible definitions of individual continuity, meaning, and identity." Democratic politics is not a doctrine, philosophy, or ideology that can be militantly organized for a moral purpose; it is not concerned with "transforming the social and spiritual life of a people by rapid and organized methods." [8]

Many of the nations in the world today whose present and future development will not follow in the Western patterns have never had the conditions, incentives, or time to discover the virtues of the democratic political process. This is all the more reason why we who have tasted its fruits and been the beneficiary of its advantages should proclaim its successes, value its qualities, understand its deficiencies, and defend its purposes. Our "reconciliation system," where secular ends never really become sacred, emerged from a heritage that included the eventual compromise between religious tolerance and political freedom which ultimately led to the social pluralism incorporated into the meaning of democratic politics. We have learned from the history of others that where there is messianic government, politics as such disappears. When government becomes the only source and sanction of morality, freedom is replaced by coercion in the total pursuit of an absolute collective purpose. Thus we understand, or should, why in a democracy it is not the extension

[8] David E. Apter, "Political Religions in the New Nations," in *Old Societies and New States,* ed. Clifford Geertz (Glencoe, Ill.: Free Press; 1963), pp. 61, 63. As Professor Apter indicates, his point of departure is J. L. Talmon, *The Origins of Totalitarian Democracy* (London: Secker and Warburg; 1955). But he has developed his own typology to analyze the new nations with which he is immediately concerned, including Guinea, Ghana, Mali, China, and Indonesia. I have drawn on this article, if only minimally—his purposes here are considerably different than my own—because his concepts were pertinent and appropriate.

of government that limits politics, but the political process that restricts the extension of government. It may be arguable whether totalitarianism or democracy has the more driving faith in its ultimate goals. What is beyond dispute, as Talmon makes clear, is that "the final aims of liberal democracy have not the same concrete character. They are conceived in rather negative terms, and the use of force for their realization is considered as an evil." This is the liberal democratic pattern, where it is assumed that politics is a matter of trial and error, and political systems as a whole are regarded as "pragmatic contrivances of ingenuity and spontaneity" offering a more piecemeal solution to the problems of social change.[9]

Not long after the United States sent its troops to the crisis-torn Dominican Republic in the spring of 1965, Richard Rovere, in a typically discerning "Letter From Washington" in *The New Yorker,* spoke of the difficulties of any Dominican government being able to survive without a prolonged military occupation. Then he touched upon a significant point. "Dr. Bosch lasted only seven months. It is said he would have lasted longer if he had not been such a poor politician." Rovere went on to say that the Trujillo regime, which lasted for thirty-two years, "provided limited opportunities for democratic politicians to develop and exercise their skills."[1] It was a penetrating observation because it went to the heart of one of the most troublesome questions facing every country throughout Latin America that is receiving American financial assistance: that is, do these governments have the political capacity to bring about the urgently necessary domestic reforms? This is not the place to examine the many ramifications of this whole subject. What I am talking about is the serious problem of a fundamental disability in Latin Ameri-

[9] Talmon, op. cit., pp. 2, 1.
[1] Richard Rovere, "Letter From Washington," *The New Yorker,* May 15, 1965, p. 207.

can politics, a disability that is related to the way leadership practices its role and demonstrates its political competence. Concretely, do the Latin American political leaders lack the required political skills? There is, of course, no single answer that applies to all countries. One thing, however, seems clear: apathy cannot be made the whipping boy, tempting as this may be. There is widespread apathy in the United States, and it is now something of a commonplace to point out that here in our own country "the figures on political participation are so low as to give support to the contention that the few act politically for the many." [2] The evidence is incontrovertible that only a small percentage of American citizens are "very active" politically, and probably one in fifty, or 2 per cent, can be said to have any real semblance of "political influence." The traditional argument, presented in every high school civics textbook, is that democratic theory requires a much higher rate of citizen participation, and usually concludes with a strong appeal for everyone to take an active interest in public affairs and to be sure to vote. I do not wish to become involved here in the many complexities which this simplified formula overlooks. The point I want to emphasize is one which I feel is too frequently missed: that the minority who are politically active, together with a sizable group of leaders committed to political careers, "saves the United States from the worst consequences of apathy." Thus, as Charles E. Lindblom has suggested, "If the outcome is different in Latin America, we should perhaps stop wringing our hands over apathy itself and look instead into the performance of the politically active and their leaders. How have they failed?" [3]

The basic issue is what might be called a potential crisis in

[2] Julian J. Woodward and Elmo Roper, "Political Activity of American Citizens," *American Political Science Review,* December 1950, p. 875.

[3] Charles E. Lindblom, "A New Look at Latin America," *The Atlantic,* October 1962.

political skills. We ridicule the American politican as a matter
of course; it is part of the national pastime. What we forget is
that democratic politics is more than simply a struggle between
political leaders to see who will be elected. The struggle is a
competition in the exercise of skills in adjusting and bringing
together the conflicting demands of the people, and then, if
successful at the polls, in negotiating alliances with other legislators and administrators. These are skills which are cultivated in
the give-and-take of the political arena, and if we in this country
tend to downgrade their importance and minimize their value, it
is plain that the great majority of countries in Latin America
cannot afford to do so.

Professor Lindblom's concern about the necessary requirements for skillful political leadership is not only instructive in its
application to Latin America but supportive of our own argument in defense and praise of the commitment to democratic
politics. Their deficiencies in this regard are our assets, and for
this reason serve as an important reminder of how and why we
have been able to build a political system which has reduced the
potential for civil war and therefore endured. Consider some of
Professor Lindblom's observations and comments:

(1) In many Latin American countries political leaders lack essential information about the conditions and terms on which peaceful
reform might be possible. Thus they are ill-informed about how the
various sections of the population might be satisfied and how conflicting demands could be reconciled without repression or revolution.

(2) The consequence of ignorance is that more or less democratic
political leadership is paralyzed. Ignorance shields the established
political leader from having to respond to growing signs of unrest,
permits him to assure himself that inaction is, after all, as sensible as
misguided reform, and leaves him without any capacity for leadership when reform is violently demanded.

(3) Many Latin American political leaders do not even conceive

of policy making as a task in mutual adjustment of citizens' demands, but see it instead as a technical process of applying correct solutions to well-defined problems.

(4) If leaders had the necessary information, skill, and appreciation of the need for politics of adjustment and accommodation, would they find that the time for mutual adjustment has already passed? Have positions been too firmly taken; are demands already intransigent? It seems clear that for the most part the masses in Latin America have not settled fixedly on specific demands. If leadership could play its role, there would be many possibilities for peaceful adjustment of demands. The masses are still uncommitted, and the dominant groups are now willing to explore politics as a task in conciliation; the situation is not yet beyond hope.

Professor Lindblom then has some specific suggestions to make as to how political leadership skilled in mutual adjustment can be developed. I mention two of them here because, again, they point up some of the positive features of our own democratic political system:

(1) One kind of leader that needs to be identified and encouraged and who can accomplish a harmonizing function is the demander, the leader of some group in the society whose shared interests are a source of strong—and in some societies, dangerous—demands on the political system, the counterparts to our labor leaders, lobbyists, and certain congressmen and senators who represent a sectional interest. In the United States, of course, we count on these leaders to express group interests that must be satisfied if we are to enjoy domestic political peace. But, more important, we count on them also to find ways of channeling group demands so that their satisfaction is not intolerably costly to other groups in the society.

(2) The other kind of leader is the communicator, the disseminator of information. He is often identified in the United States as a specialist: journalist, editor, researcher, professor, author, or lecturer. In fact, however, in the United States much of the information that is brought to bear on policy making is assembled and distributed by parties to disputes, not solely by the specialists. In public controversy, congressional hearings, and discussion among political leaders, the desire of the activist to make his view prevail motivates much of

the communication of information. Thus, some of the communicators are identical with politicians or demanders.[4]

I have quoted Professor Lindblom at length because his remarks are among the best I have seen for their insight into the craft of politics and the craftmanship of the politician. He puts into sharp relief an important and indispensable truth about a democratic society: that the politician is as much "the human embodiment of a bargaining society as any single role-player can be." There is a realistic understanding that it is not enough to be attracted to politics simply by principles, and that political issues cannot and should not be settled strictly on their merits. Above all, there is a sensitive awareness that the most successful politician is one who can grasp the motives of others by blending his feelings with theirs—in the words of George H. Mead, one who is able "to enter into the attitudes of the group and mediate between them by making his own experience universal, so that others can enter into this form of communication through him."[5] This is one reason why the language of democratic politics can never be the language of absolute ends.

꧁꧂ 4

The anti-political temper in the United States, as we have seen throughout these pages, is given expression in a variety of different forms. One of the ways it sometimes reveals itself is in its hos-

[4] Ibid. I have reproduced Professor Lindblom's own words, although I have pulled them together from different parts of his article. I thought so highly of his approach and analysis that I had this same piece reprinted in its entirety in a book of readings I edited for college undergraduates, *Issues of American Public Policy* (Englewood Cliffs, N.J.: Prentice-Hall; 1964).

[5] George Herbert Mead, *Mind, Self, and Society* (Chicago: Univ. Chicago Press; 1934), p. 257. However, I stumbled onto the reference in James Q. Wilson's fascinating book, *The Amateur Democrat* (Chicago: Univ. Chicago Press; 1962), p. 11.

tile approach and attitude toward the problem of power. In saying
that politics in a democracy is a process of discussion and conciliation, I have also been saying that politics cannot be divorced
from power. It is not necessary to contend that power *is* politics
or that power is the only concern of politics.[6] After all, politics
involves the struggle of ideas and values as well as of force. But
the function of a political system is to deal with its problems, and
one of the hallmarks of a democratic system is that there will be
disagreement over what should be done and how to do it.
Conflict, we have said, is at the heart of politics, and the phenomenon of power—its pursuit, its exercise, its distribution, its
control—is clearly part of its business.

It is not an accident that many of the severest critics of
American society today tend to separate the idea of politics from
the idea of power. Some of the leading spokesmen of the "new
left," convinced that American life is morally corrupt from top
to bottom, point to what they call the present political "awaken-
ing" as a strong protest against power and all those associated
with it. It would be a mistake to believe that the only reason
they are so disenchanted with this country is that they do not
have power themselves. Their indictment rests on different
grounds.

In a remarkable essay entitled "The Disease of Politics," Theodore Roszak puts the case with exceptional clarity. "Politics," he
says, "is the organization of power, and power is the enemy of
life." The measure of power "is its ability to make life what it
would not be; to break, bend, control, crush, direct and destroy

---

[6] Not surprisingly, there are many people who equate politics with
power politics, as if power were the sole category of political science.
Someone who has come close to this position on different occasions is
Harold D. Lasswell. See his *Politics: Who Gets What, When, How*
(New York: McGraw-Hill; 1936). For a critical examination of the
concept of power, see David Easton, *The Political System* (New York:
Knopf; 1953).

life. The end of power is the inhibition of growth, which is life. And whatever interferes with the growth of things and of men participates in death. Whatever its credentials, it is in alliance with death. That is what power is, and nothing else."

The important question, of course, is whether power is simply and only what Roszak says it is and "nothing else." The difficulty with unqualified attacks on "power" is that those who make them, while they may simplify for themselves the target on which they can vent their unrestrained anger, overlook an important fact—that power is essentially plural in nature and therefore is more appropriately viewed in terms of "powers." The power of the federal government to send troops to Birmingham, Alabama, in defense of civil rights for all Americans cannot be discussed in the context and language of an "alliance with death." The power of the Allies in the Second World War that crushed the fascist powers cannot be equated with "the inhibition of growth" or the "enemy of life." Power in itself is neither good nor bad. It depends on who exercises it, how it is used, and for what purposes. In short, power involves political considerations.

But Roszak is not much interested in such matters. In looking upon power, in Shelley's words, as a "desolating pestilence," he has no real awareness of the raw materials with which politicians and political leaders must work. Furthermore, he feels "politics has always been a neurotic business." Thus he turns elsewhere for the answer he seeks. He suggests that there is a new rebellion making its presence felt across the land, made up of

inscrutable poets and crackpot painters, of visionaries and folk singers and angry old philosophers, of marching mothers who want their babies' bones made of calcium not strontium, of kids from Yale scrambling aboard submarines in the New London Navy Yard, of kids from Fisk singing on their way to jail. . . . Here are the

[7] Theodore Roszak, "The Disease Called Politics," in *Seeds of Liberation,* ed. Paul Goodman (New York: Braziller; 1965), p. 450.

foolish things of this earth who confound the wise. For the essence of their politics is not power, but love: the sheer love of being alive. The future, if there is to be one, belongs to them.

Not politics, but love: this is his answer. "It is love that brings forth and nourishes life, that sustains it in its sufferings and mourns for its defeat. Love thrives on spontaneity . . . it is like a child at play, the gentle enemy of order, of efficiency, of organization." So it is not love, after all, that makes the world go around, Roszak tells us cryptically. "Love lets grow; but it is power that makes go . . . The world belongs to politics, which is to say, the world belongs to death." [8]

One can easily see why Roszak and many others who make up the "new radicalism" in America are apolitical and anti-political. Quoting from the *Journal for the Protection of All Beings,* Roszak enthusiastically endorses their refusal "to take politics on politics' own terms, abasing itself in fear and trembling before the blunt, brute fact that these are matters of life and death for the human race involved here. That may make politics terrifying, but it doesn't make it any less mad nor any more worthy of our respect." There is little question that in Roszak's mind he is dealing with pure madness. "A suicidal pathology is at the root of our politics," he writes. Speaking in tones that are sure to inspire his supporters, he says, "We must fight our way out of the moiling, suffocating arena of politics so that we can with distance recognize the essential sickness of the games that are played there." Given this assessment, one is not surprised to hear him say that ". . . our world is not beset by problems to be solved, but rather by a disease to be cured." [9]

However repugnant the interrelationship of politics and power may be to those among the "new radicals" who follow this line of reasoning, it can neither be replaced by love nor reduced to love. The genuine sense of outrage which they feel at the

[8] Ibid., pp. 451–4.   [9] Ibid., pp. 446, 450, 453.

injustices and brutalities which American society imposes on those who are without power, "people who lack the defenses of money, status or a white skin," does not alter this fact. There is much that is terribly right in their description of impersonality, manipulation, and fraudulent conformity in the United States. But the question is whether Paul Goodman, whose many writings have dealt with the sense of powerlessness which the "new radicals" insist pervade American society, is right in defining the human predicament today in such a way that he can state without hesitation that "we cannot look to politics" for any possible solutions. The point that cannot be overlooked is that like the extremists of the far right who, in their view of things, also see this country corrupted by its leaders and infested with moral decay, the "new left" has allowed its passion to extend far beyond politics. Their profound hostilities have long since soured them on the democratic political process. They affirm that nothing less than radical social change will do. The very presuppositions on which human relationships are based must be revolutionized. Conflict must be replaced with cooperation. The trend to centralization must be arrested. There must be a return to "community." How are these things to come about? By dispensing with the politics of power and turning instead to the power of love—in Goodman's words, by learning "to live communally and without authority, to work usefully and feel friendly." [1]

Goodman is speaking for a radicalism that is fundamentally at odds with our conventional political categories, an existentialist revolt that is *in* American politics, but not *of* it. "As so often happens in American radicalism," observes Christopher Lasch, "power and authority themselves are defined as the source of evil. Politics then becomes non-politics; for politics," he emphasizes, "is not 'feeling friendly' but that which has to do with

[1] Paul Goodman, "Getting Into Power," in *Seeds of Liberation*, p. 444.

power." [2] Power, whether it is used for good or evil, cannot be ignored. Goodman, however, is turned in another direction. "Pacifism," he says, "is revolutionary: we will not have peace unless there is a profound change in social structure, including getting rid of national sovereign power." Lasch is quite correct: "this is not politics, but daydreaming." Goodman believes that "nothing less will serve" than ringing down the flag. Again Lasch, who knows that a revolutionary change in this country has never been farther away, makes the critical point: "If we can't have peace without a revolution, then we are powerless indeed. We had better assume that we can have peace by changing our foreign policy; or to go a step further, that we can restore something like democracy without engineering a revolution." [3] It would be politically hopeless to believe otherwise, just as it is intellectually bankrupt to insist that a desire to know power or to serve it will automatically make a person "impure" and, what is worse, force him to betray his own values and standards.

[2] These comments by Christopher Lasch are from a review of a book by Paul Goodman, *People or Personnel: Decentralizing And The Mixed System* (New York: Random House; 1965), that appeared in *Commentary*, November 1965. Anticipating that Goodman might reply that the "psychology of power" is itself a "neurotic ideology," Professor Lasch observes: "So it is, when it becomes an ideology; but an understanding of the neurotic obsession with power should not be used to rule out power arbitrarily, as a subject of political analysis. Ruling out power simply means that Goodman's proposals become subjects not for political discussion at all, if politics is concerned with the institutional relationships among groups of people, but for psychology. Having analyzed the evils of centralization—a political question, because it involves the distribution of power—Goodman prescribes not political solutions but therapy. As Robert L. Heilbroner has pointed out, he does not call on anyone to give up power; he only asks them to give up the psychology of power—an appeal that is not so disturbing as Goodman likes to think." Lasch's point is very much the same as has been made here in an earlier chapter, namely, that for all of the significant contributions of psychology, it cannot provide a theory of politics.

[3] Ibid. The remarks by Mr. Goodman are quoted in Mr. Lasch's review. For a review by Professor Lasch of *Seeds of Liberation*, see *The New York Review*, September 30, 1965.

Whatever else may be said about the philosophy of Black Power, it is perfectly clear that its principal advocates in the civil rights movement reject the notion that power must inevitably corrupt. In fact, they are making the opposite claim. They are saying that the very absence of power also corrupts. They are not the first nor will they be the last to make a conscious bid for political power. In other words, it is not necessary to look upon power as an unmitigated evil. By the same token, however, one does not have to worship power to acknowledge its importance in modern society. It is too early to tell whether Black Power will come to mean black racism and "black death," as Roy Wilkins, executive director of the National Association for the Advancement of Colored People, has warned, or turn out to be self-defeating and dangerous, as Whitney M. Young, Jr., executive director of the National Urban League, believes. One thing is certain: the ultimate success of Black Power will not depend on the moral fervor or militancy of those who adopt it as their rallying cry. The more important test will be whether or not those in positions of responsibility and leadership, having accepted the need for political power, also recognize that its effective use requires a prudent political sense.[4]

[4] A case in point is Saul Alinsky, a professional organizer of the poor who is a radical because he thinks power, talks power, and seeks the use of organized power for those who do not have it. For many years his Industrial Areas Foundation has been in the business of helping slum leaders develop a disciplined, broad-based power organization that would be strong enough to get concrete concessions from those in positions of authority who, in turn, can help move a community to make necessary and important decisions. But Alinsky's radicalism is not directed to overthrowing the government, and he does not preach violence for the sake of violence. Nor has he any personal interest in leading a "movement" in the United States. He wants to organize slums, and he goes about it on a door-to-door, day-in-day-out basis. His goals are material and they have to do with the here and now: better jobs, better schools, better housing, better garbage collection. His fondness for the emotional and moral rhetoric of radicalism does not interfere with his acute sense of the political and practical when it comes time to

One of the central questions to which this book has been addressed can be simply put: is democratic politics superstructure or foundation? Those who say it is superstructure take the road of reductionism. They seek to reduce political problems to other components—social factors, economic causes, ethics, the influence of class structure, cultural conditioning, conscience, morality, or anything else which will serve their particular idiom, interest, or ideology. Some are modest in their claims. Perhaps all

---

use power and make demands. In a marginal sense he is in the tradition of American pressure politics, having learned his organizing techniques from the more militant segment of the labor movement in the thirties (Alinsky is the author of *John L. Lewis: An Unauthorized Biography*, New York: G. Putnam & Sons; 1949). He has often opposed the tactic of Negro demonstrations, as he did when Martin Luther King led his march into Cicero, Illinois, in the summer of 1966, because he feels the only likely result will be to set back the Negro cause and make the job of gaining concessions from the white community that much more difficult. His point is very simple: you cannot negotiate with a hate-filled, howling mob. His major contention and commitment is that one must have power to oppose power, which is essentially a restatement of Madison's view that the basic political struggle in society is the endless conflict between opposing groups and factions. The difference is that the group he cares about and is trying to organize has never been *in* the struggle because it has been propertyless and powerless.

There is no doubt that Alinsky is more interested in conflict than consensus. But he also knows that no democratic society could survive on conflict alone. His argument is that after there has been a rearrangement of power, *then* there can be consensus. Or, as he puts it, "How do you have consensus before you have conflict?"

There is, of course, an impatience and anger in Alinsky, as there is in all radicals, especially those who go after their goals with a fierce belief that the end justifies the means. But inasmuch as Alinsky is more interested in concrete results than moral indignation, he will always have one eye fixed on a very practical consideration: what methods will be the most effective in bringing about the immediate goal? As we have said throughout these pages, this is the inevitable question of the relationship of means to ends which is the central problem of politics and power in a democratic society.

For an excellent account of Alinsky's political philosophy and methods, see Patrick Anderson, "Making Trouble Is Alinsky's Business," *New York Times Magazine*, October 9, 1966.

they want to show is the close connection between politics and ethics, only to end up removing the former and concentrating on the latter. Others, promising a richer harvest, want to get "behind" institutions and processes in order to reveal the "underlying" forces which dictate the shape of political affairs. In either case politics is regarded as a derivative form of activity, one that is best understood in terms of more "fundamental" factors. As Professor Wolin has observed, this is the view of those who believe that politics possesses no distinctive significance and pertains to no unique function.[5]

Those who view politics as foundation believe it has a life and character of its own. They recognize that in a democracy it is both unavoidable and necessary because they know that politics is an indispensable requirement for self-government in a free society. Politics is not regarded as the pursuit of ultimate truth, which is why it cannot be mistaken for ethics or religion. Nor can it be reduced to economics or law or psychology or science or morality, although their interconnection is undeniable. Politics is an activity to be valued in itself, and as such cannot be trans-

---

[5] See Sheldon Wolin, *Politics and Vision* (Boston: Little, Brown; 1960), especially Ch. 9, "Liberalism and the Decline of Political Philosophy," where this point is developed historically and philosophically. It should also be noted that Professor Wolin devotes his final chapter to a discussion of the new turn to "society" which left no room "either for politics and the practice of the political art, or for a distinctively political theory." Thus Proudhon "looked forward to a time when politics would be reduced to an impersonal body of principles and men would be governed by scientific truths: 'Politics is a science, not a stratagem; demonstrated truth is man's true chief and his king.'" Wolin continues: "The century was nearly unanimous in its contempt for politics: the Utopian Socialists banished it from their ideal communities; Marx predicted the withering away of the state and its replacement by an administration of 'things' based on the necessary laws of society. Durkheim summed matters up: 'political questions have lost their interest'; they affect only 'a small part of society,' never its 'vital knot.' We must look 'under this superficial covering' to find 'how the great social interests exist and act.'" Ibid., pp. 360–1.

formed into an orderly arrangement of ideas and beliefs or a set of predetermined goals. Above all, politics is a way of resolving individual and group conflicts in a free and open society with the least amount of coercion. The democratic problem is not how to eliminate politics or to reduce it to something else or to subli- mate it in some other way. The problem is to discover how we can gain the necessary knowledge of politics to enable us to act wisely in a context of conflict, ambiguity, and change.

INDEX

Abolitionism, 25, 72, 266, 272, 274
Act of 1718, 157
Adams, Gordon M., x, 195
Adorno, T. W., 84–5, 214
Advisory Committee in Constitutional Democracy of the Rockefeller Foundation, xi
Affirmation Act of 1722, 154
Age of Analysis, 190
Age of Anxiety, 48
Age of Reason, 26
Age of Reform, The (Hofstadter), 55, 65
Agrarian Socialism (Lipset), 129
agriculture, 57
Agriculture, Department of, 123–4
Alien and Sedition Acts, 39–40
Alinsky, Saul, 288–9 n.
Almond, Gabriel, 216–17, 219, 221–2
Amana Community, 229
Amateur Democrat, The (Wilson), 282
America First Committee, 41
American Coalition, 42
American Communist Party, The (Howe and Coser), 113
American Dilemma (Myrdal), 100
American Dreams (Parrington), 230
American Federation of Labor, 116–17
American Friends Service Committee, 140–1
American Journal of Sociology, 208
American League Against War and Fascism, 123
American Legion, 39
American Liberty League, 41
American Opinion (Welch), 54, 67
American Political Science Review, 57, 106, 205, 211, 279
American Political Tradition, The (Hofstadter), 270
American Revolution, 39, 161
American Right Wing (Ellsworth and Harris), 42
American Sociological Review, 198
American Student Union, 123
American Unionist, 270
American Youth Congress, 123
Americans, The (Boorstin), 156

America's Future, Inc. (Gordon), 74
Anabaptists, 131
Analysis, Age of: *see* Age of Analysis
Analysis of Political Behavior, The (Lasswell), 209
Anglican Church, 155
Anglophobia, 56
Annals of the American Academy of Political and Social Science, 106
Anti-Intellectualism in American Life (Hofstadter), 23
anti-isms, 2, 40, 66–8, 83–4, 123, 130, 147, 214, 264, 274, 282
Anti-Masonic Party, 40, 45
Antioch Review, 13, 19
Anxiety, Age of: *see* Age of Anxiety
Apostolic Christianity, 87
Approach to Peace and Other Essays, An (Hughes), 169
Authoritarian Personality, The (Adorno), 85, 214–15, 217–19, 221
Authoritarianism and Leadership (Sanford), 85
authority: obedience to, 136–7; Freud on, 198; personality trait, 204, 208; and government, 205; concept of, 210; and Germans, 211, 213; and right-wing movement, 221
automation, 69, 252–4, 257

Baez, Joan, 23–4
Barnhart, John D., 57
Baruch Plan, 175
Bavarian Illuminati, 49 n.
Behavioral Science, 254
behaviorism: voting, viii; social, 190, 199; political, 200, 206–7, 214; human, 239
Bell, Daniel: cited, 37, 51, 53, 64, 67, 84, 117–19, 124, 128–9, 264, 267
Bell, Wendell, 205, 207
Bendix, Reinhard: cited, 106, 193–4, 208, 210–11, 247–8
Bennett, D. J., 190–2
"Better Red than Dead," 178, 185
Beyond Dilemmas (Woodward), 136

Index

About the Author

JOHN H. BUNZEL is associate professor of political
science at San Francisco State College. Born in
New York City in 1924, he did his undergraduate
work at Princeton University, graduating *magna
cum laude* in 1948. He received his master's degree from Columbia University in 1949 and his
Ph.D. from the University of California at Berkeley in 1954. Professor Bunzel has also taught at
Michigan State University and Stanford University. He is the author of *The American Small Businessman* (1962), co-author of *The California
Democratic Delegation of 1960* (1962), and
editor of *Issues of American Public Policy* (1964).
A frequent public lecturer, during the presidential
campaign of 1964 he conducted a weekly television program in San Francisco on *The American Voter* which received a national award. He
has two children and lives with his wife in Belmont, California.